TIME BOUND JUSTICE

Anand S. Mittal

Foreword by
Murlidhar Chandrakant Bhandare

ATLANTIC
PUBLISHERS & DISTRIBUTORS (P) LTD

Published by

ATLANTIC

PUBLISHERS & DISTRIBUTORS (P) LTD

7/22, Ansari Road, Darya Ganj,
New Delhi-110002
Phones : +91-11-23273880, 23275880, 23280451
Fax : +91-11-23285873
Web : www.atlanticbooks.com
E-mail : info@atlanticbooks.com

Branch Office
5, Nallathambi Street, Wallajah Road,
Chennai-600002
Phones : +91-44-64611085, 32413319
E-mail : chennai@atlanticbooks.com

ISBN 978-81-269-1027-4

Printed in India at Nice Printing Press, A-33/3A, Site-IV, Industrial Area, Sahibabad, Ghaziabad, U.P.

प्रेहि प्रेहि पथिमिः पूर्व्येमिर्यत्ता न पूर्व्ये पितर परेयूः *(Rigveda10/14/7)*

Keep moving on the tried pathways of your ancestors with conviction and determination to live and leave behind a better world for your successors, shall serve the purpose of your being here for a short period of your life.

No one can stay here for ever. Everyone has to go away. All big or small have already left.

This work is dedicated
to
All mature intellectuals

Shri M.C. Bhandare is a senior advocate on record of Apex Court and has been President of Supreme Court Bar Association between 1985-87. He also remained associated with several organisations of legal and social importance. He also has been MP in Rajya Sabha for three terms and is presently the Chairman of UNESCO Appeal Board. He is the Governor of Orissa at present.

Foreword

It is really interesting to read this book entitled *Time Bound Justice*. The book is a laudable contribution to the cause of fair, speedy and affordable justice and other social issues.

It reflects the sufferings of a common citizen in our country caused by the enormous delay in disposing of cases. Justice along with liberty, equality and fraternity are the four pillars of our Constitution. In every way, the first pillar of justice protects the remaining three pillars. Speedy and cheap justice is the core of justice delivery system; however, it is increasingly being negated. There may be many reasons for the delay but none of them is excusable. What is impressive about the book is that it is not interpreting or dissecting the law. It deals with practical solutions by closely examining day-to-day problems faced by a litigant. It covers a wide spectrum of legal justice in our society and gives an omnibus approach for curing the system afflicted with the cancer of delay.

Divided into 15 chapters, the book covers the entire malice prevalent in justice delivery system in our country. It contains well thought out practical and pragmatic solutions and suggests reforms to improve our judicial system. The author has rendered a valuable service to the noble cause of justice.

The work is deeply thought, well-knit and worth reading.

Murlidhar Bhandare

Murlidhar Chandrakant Bhandare
Former Member of Parliament
Chairman, Legal & Human Rights Department, AICC

Preface

The word 'democracy' sounds very sweet to every ear. It generates a feeling of freedom and security beyond a sense of liability and commitment. The preservers of democracy often apprehend that if absolute power can be blamed to make absolutely corrupt, then absolute freedom can also make one unlawful. In the foremost relationship between a citizen and his nation, it cannot survive for long, if it remains one sided. Expecting too much from political set up of the country and ignoring our duties, we cannot go much far. Those who consider democracy a system of absolute freedom are misunderstanding the real doctrine of democracy.

Of all systems of governance, the parameters of democracy are so flexible that it can have different shapes in different countries. Broadly identifying these variations in undeveloped poor African countries, where power is confined only in few hands, common citizens lead horrible deprivation of due rights; while in the developing Third World nations, the power is grabbed strategically by a few more white collars. The face of democracy in developed nations has also been deviated towards capitalism. So, democracy in today's world still suffers few setbacks even if being the best of all systems of governance. Actually, varied limitations of democracy need a thorough and sincere anatomy, today. Such precincts of democracy need to be eliminated at all levels, in order to carry on basic values of life to which democracy is always committed.

Coming out of the times of swords and arrows when the governing strategy was at the mercy of most powerful monarch, we are still at the outset of strengthening today's democracy in all those countries where it is in practice for some years. Debate on upholding human values was initiated in earlier times in Athens in 400 BC. Aristotle for the first time talked about such political philosophy. Preceding monarchy was shared by Catholics in the entire Europe annihilating ancient philosophers and thinker to defend Biblical concepts. Getting desperate finally the Age of Renaissance arrived in Europe, which led to French Revolution in 1589 that ended with public execution of Louis XIV, replacing the rule of tyranny and terror by 'rule of law'.

The contribution of Roman Emperor Augustus was remarkable as he vigorously established the rule of law over the family interests. Starting from direct democracy the concept of rule of law progressed to constitutional democracy for a bigger country where the powers are concentrated in elected and selected individuals as per their quality and capability. It is a famous saying that "Rome is not built in a day". It is a true remark as democracy has its own historic background that changed the face of the world.

After the era of Greek philosophers and Roman emperors, thinkers remained busy in grooming the shape of democracy. Edmund Hobbes (1588-1679) discussed repercussions of French Revolution in his book *Reflection of Revolution in France*. The Aristotelian political philosophy was put forward in changed perspectives by Rene Descartes (1595-1650), through his book titled *Meditation of the First Philosophy* in 1641. This work proved another remarkable milestone in the progress of democracy as it justified the approach of French revolutionists who were fighting for democracy to become the ultimate way of governance. French philosopher, writer and revolutionist Jean Jacques Rousseau (1712-78) through his book *Social Contract* contributed to the French Revolution and firmed footing of democracy in other courtiers of Europe. Contemporary architect of democracy like Voltaire upheld the 'importance of transparency in democracy'. And for that he had to sacrifice his own life. He fearlessly advocated a transparent democracy where people can rule by their own convictions and constitution and formulate the way they wanted to live.

German citizen Karl Marx's work was much ahead of democracy for its idealistic approach. He pressed upon the place of a nation to be the highest. Karl Marx condemned having any right to personal property as he was confident that everything belonged to the nation. Thus, the 'philosophy of communism' was idealistic. Russian Revolution ended into communism in the year 1917 bringing up USSR. Soon within a short period of 50 years USSR became another world power *at par* with United States of America that had achieved freedom in the year 1776. Experts claim that this leap of over 200 years over United States became possible due to the sense of high discipline, commitment and determination inculcated through communism in the countrymen. Joseph Stalin was so harsh that he was sometimes termed as a 'dictator of communism' as people often faced denial of human rights in the name of patriotism until the era of Nikita Khrushchev arrived. Lack of accountability of government to the citizens, finally converted communism becoming dry, harsh and one sided system of governance.

The citizens cooperated but the promulgators made the entire system a personal property failing Communism to be a one side track due factors like lack of freedom of expression and no periodical rejuvenation of political system, absence of a fair and independent judiciary and ignoring people's reaction to new policies. Finally, citizens started disliking it and one day they fully negated it. Mikhail Gorbachev who dared proposing liberalization through *Glasnost* and *Perestroika* brought a ray of hope to the people of USSR to get liberated from the monotony. Yeltsin took advantage of this fluid situation and became the hero of break up and freedom of USSR faction nations plunging once big power into begging.

The message is clear. It is that positive thinking and a balance between people and the Government is essential in any system. And this opportunity is very much available only in democracy. If Russian communists could be positive to democracy and amalgamate stake of democracy to make communism a two way system, it might have worked well. Modern China is the evidence that teased off the iron curtain by honestly conducting periodic change in leadership. However, even being the best system of governance, democracy is failing for its own loop hole and is not advancing the way it is claimed for.

The number of developing countries is the highest in the world today. But the democracy failed here to take a footing for many past decades. Democracy in these countries is restricted formally to adult franchise only enabling these nations to boast themselves being the biggest democracy. The inside story of such developing nations is against the basics of democracy. Law and order is suffering from gross corruption and highhandedness of bureaucrats on one side while autocratically delayed delivery of justice on the other. The police are shooting to kill the demonstrators with an intention to teach them a lesson on one side and media is busy in covering fashion shows, on the other. More painful is that the elected representatives are busier to save their own existence in politics.

Despite of being rich in natural resources as well as in human resources, most of these countries are failing to utilise these assets to their maximum advantage. The problems of unemployment, limited means of earning in rural areas, day-to-day inflation, communal unrests, scanty water supply, poor quality of life, delayed legal justice, unreliable police and persisting trauma of insecurity have become plight of citizen.

Recently, International Information Programme of United Sates Department of Information (IIPUS) declared the following eleven pillars of democracy which are as follows.

1. Sovereignty of the people,
2. Government based upon consent of the governed,
3. Majority rule,
4. Minority rights,
5. Guarantee of basic human rights,
6. Free and fair elections,

7. Equality before the law,
8. Due process of law,
9. Constitutional limits on government,
10. Social, economic, and political pluralism,
11. Values of tolerance, pragmatism, cooperation, and compromise.

Adding more to this, intensified and exhaustive debate on democracy by political scientists of the world through their numerous research papers still goes on to make it flawless. They believe that basic features of democracy must include the following:

12. Government by People's true representatives,
13. Defined Constitution, providing Fundamental Rights, *viz.* Right to profession, free movement, Expression, social justice, legal justice, religious faith, security, livelihood and Right to equality,
14. Perseverance of Law of the Land,
15. Establishing Rule of Law through legal justice and effective, executive agencies,
16. Transparency and accountability of all organs of the system of governance,
17. Perseverance of Human Rights,
18. Majority Rule and minority Rights.

Marty Gallanter, an American political analyst says: "All the ills of democracy can be cured by more democracy. When the controversy gets going, the wisdom of Al Smith will speak pretty loud that 'One does not cure democracy's problems by limiting democracy."

In an article titled 'Alternative Future' Robert Jensen in Texas Observer magazine, dated 21 June 2002 writes: "There is no alternative to democracy. Capitalism is the only future. Free markets are the essence of democracy." while reviewing another write up on 'Defying Corporations, Defining Democracy'.

Thus, different scholars have different views as to how democracy can be made a flawless system and what can be the possible future of democracy. But such views given by experts on democracy see it in localsied purview while by others, the global perspective is different. Attaching democracy to economy is not a hard and fast rule.

Capitalism had already failed to impose democracy in Iraq on gunpoint. Therefore, democracy is more an institution that people accept and maintain on their own. It cannot be imposed by using force. If people want to lead their lives with any other system than democracy, no one can force them. It is a basic and ultimate system of gentle convictions by experience of many centuries that this system cannot be painted beyond its basic features of absolute acceptance, openness and transparency. The basic features of democracy are universal and cannot be diverted from the benefit to all, to the benefit of a few capitalists. Democracy is a self-sustaining universally acceptable institution of specific and unchangeable philosophy.

There may be many debates on changing the face of democracy but 'law of definite proportion' of chemical compounds shall apply here too. A little change in its fabric will alter its structure to be a different system if we change even one element from its composition. For example, if water molecule is attached to one more atom of hydrogen, it becomes hydrogen-per-oxide, an absolutely different compound than water. But this logic does not convey the sense that there is no scope for improvement of democracy. Democracy always needs to be perfect in every country and people in control have to give a deep thought to it.

It is undisputed that out of all the systems of governance, democracy is superior being the most balanced and flexible system but using force to accept it is undemocratic. People who attach democracy with economy have to have a rational approach than to be rash to describe a different face of democracy as the real face. Recently, people of Bhutan and Nepal adopted democracy not because they are rich. In fact, they are poor nations. People here accepted democracy because it is a government by the people, of the people and for the people. Constitutional democracy scores over all other systems of governance as it can be moulded to the requirement of the citizens of a nation legitimately.

It is better if the modern thinkers attach democracy to literacy than to economy. Arab countries are an example where rich and illiterate people are comfortable with monarchy. Do you think that there is anarchy and no rule of law exists there? Not the least. Being illiterate they are comfortable with monarchy where thieves are beheaded till date ignoring Human Rights Charter of United Nations. Their richness too does not generate any urge to go for democracy. But when a nation acquires 100 per cent literacy shall choose democracy for its unparallel benefits. Whether rich or not, it is the question of ethics and understanding values of life and protection of human rights which can be guaranteed only through Constitutional democracy. Imposing democracy in illiterate countries is nothing but giving them a bundle of corruption and all the ills of democracy. If democracy is the most flexible system to make people enjoy freedom, they may also have to be trained what freedom means. Uneducated and untrained masses cannot uphold democratic values as is happening in most of the developing countries.

The working of all five most effective organs of government in a Third World democracy has become so damaging the interests of citizens that democracy here, has become anti-people to deplore the basic interest of unpatronised common citizens. Innocent citizens are suffering at the hands of 1. Police, 2. Bureaucrats, 3. Judiciary, 4. Media, 5. Politicians. In these countries masses are in no comfortable conditions and even middle class, who is the largest in number, is suffering at the hands of all these five organs of the system in juvenile form of democracy even after sixty years of achieving freedom. So, what is the outcome to defer the forth coming collapse of such a shattered form of democracy before it is too late? It is an issue of deep pondering and making a way through the jungle of oddities that have cropped up due to our absurd fear to change the British Law or the comfortable life, the policy maker acquired after coming to power.

We have no alternative to democracy even though it has been misused and deshaped by the people in power. These five organs have developed nexus together and have led to the emergence of a typical culture to go hand in hand to ignore the interest of common citizens. The irony is that if we change any of the elements of democracy, its face will be changed. So, how to handle this situation and what should be the way out to fight out such gigantic ills of Third World democracy? We have to carefully study where the weak points lie in their composition and functioning. There may be a need to bring certain nodal changes in all the five organs and it shall be a timely effort. Such measures have been proposed by the author as a new system of governance named **'Peoplism'**.

There is big debate in United Sates to limitise democracy. The incoming theories proposed are conflicting. But it does not mean that the debate should stop. We have to find out ways to amend laws and formulate new policies and take harsh measures to amend lax laws to overcome ills of democracy one by one in a coordinate manner. Advocates of democracy may not feel attacked directly if changes are brought by practicing Peoplism for some years in order to achieve true democracy. How democracy shall be different from Peoplism has been given in Chapter 19th in brief of the book taken from a different book titled as *Alternative to democracy: Peoplism* by the author. Different measures suggested therein have been justified by citing cases, some of which are as under:

Peoplist philosophy of governance is very close to democracy. This system has been conceived to be more effective and judicious than the ills of democracy. It is a meticulous effort not to overlook the achievements and merits of creative and peaceful citizens to push forward those who cherish of being law-abiding good citizens. It is not a system for those who believe in exempting merits to issue gate-passes to contemptible aspirants for any other reason than quality.

Peoplism is a strict and straight system that is reverse to the flexible, discriminatory and inconsistent democracy. It advocates human rights, human dignity and natural justice to all deserving and dependable citizens. If on one side Peoplism is the other name of discipline, it is very considerate to those who are suffering from demerits of democracy that are not amendable and have invaded deep inside the system of governance.

To revolutionise the working of government some white elephant conventional ministries have to be replaced by new ministries as under, in Peoplism.

1. Ministry of Internal Security: The Ministry of Home will look after remaining departments of national museums, archives, museums, UPSC, NHRC, disputes in religion, and so on and shall continue with them except matters and all such bodies that maintain law and order in the society. But this new ministry will especially deal with all types of internal forces including police, security services in public and private sector, para-military forces.

2. Ministry of Vigilance: This new Ministry will take over all supervision of the working of all other ministries and shall be empowered to hear grievances from public against any complaint from any other ministry. It will formulate Code of Conduct for every portfolio as well as define duties, privileges and liabilities of all the employees. This ministry will hold and maintain Direct Action Cell system.

3. Ministry of Executive Services: All the bureaucracy will come under this ministry. Appointments will be affected by the relevant ministry but the record of employees shall be maintained by this ministry parallelly. This ministry shall be a part of disciplinary proceedings, promotion and transfer of employees and will have every right to alter the decision of any other ministry in the above matters. This ministry will have no business to interfere the departmental decisions by the ministry and the specific and defined function of different ministries.

4. Ministry of Academic and Defense Research: Shall take care of research work in different Universities and Institutions. It shall work independently of University Grant Commission and shall have its own funding to encourage research work of many types in the country.

5. Ministry of Domestic Industries: Shall look after only cottage industry which runs from home for the people living below line of poverty and shall be liberal to give them loan to start means of earning from their home and shall assign consignments to buy the product back.

6. Ministry of Water Management: Shall see disbursement of natural resources of water among states by evolving a formula for proper distribution of water resources of the different States. Shall encourage water harvesting and improvised recycling of used water or run off rain water and so on. Shall also hear complaints of water mismanagement by Jal Corporations in different States and make policies on it.

7. Ministry of Community Health: Reconstitution of present hospitals in private sector only and formulate policy for their services to the masses by starting many new departments for the treatment of many community diseases on behalf of government and cease to work independently away from government as a private shop. At least fifty per cent involvement shall be for serving masses free of charge.

8. Ministry of Synthetic Chemicals: Needs a separate ministry to look into every day coming in new materials and their applications and manage the vast world of synthetic materials for different industries.

9. Ministry of Man made Energy Resources: Funding for research and installation of projects.

10. Ministry of Internal Business: It pertains to all kinds of trading business inside the country.

11. Ministry of Public Grievances and Think Tank: Gathering public opinions, conducting seminars, workshops and debates on various issues of different ministries and subjects in news. Shall work in coordination of ministry of planning.

12. Ministry of Religion and Secular Harmony: Coordination among followers of different religions and arranging joint functions to bring them closer.

I extend my sincere thanks to the Chairman, Atlantic Publishers & Distributors (P) Ltd. for his immense cooperation in bringing out this marvellous piece of work.

Anand S. Mittal

Contents

Introduction

Today, it appears that being in litigation is a big punishment. Increasingly, people are approaching courts more out of compulsion than out of confidence in the judicial system. Corruption has raised its ugly head, where it could not be seen a few years earlier. The five 'Cs' of a Judge, *viz.* character, calibre, compassion, courtesy and common sense are to be seen rarely. In the temple of justice, money has become God.

The Judicial Commission is yet to see the light of day. It is frightening to know that the workload of 40,000 vacancies of judges in the country is forcibly being thrust upon the shoulders of existing judges. Are we really so poor that we cannot afford to have an up-to-date judicial system? Is judiciary more expensive for the government than having air travels and big newspaper insertions to highlight personal biodata of politicians from public funds or wasting public money in a number of absurd activities of elected politicians of this country? The pretension seems to be 'Yes'!

We have proved our mettle several times whenever we really felt committed to anything. But alas! awakening sparked more in common citizens than politicians. Vast human and natural resources fail to bring about a change in the mindset of those who have capability and responsibility as well, to change things to better. During the last six decades, people who dominated Parliament remained comfortable with the ugly shape of administration and judicial system in many ways and for many reasons. The citizens of India elect such parliamentarians who have an urge and attitude to bring positive change in the prevalent system and who are sincere, honest and justice-loving towards their fellow countrymen; who can improve the functioning of police and the judicial system to be prompt and just. In this largest democracy of the world, we must use our right every time to bring right people to the Parliament, who can fill more than 40,000 vacancies of judges to help the judicial machinery avoid delays and deliver justice in time. In the present book, six 'Schedules' have been designed to simplify the legal processing for quick disposal of cases. Having a vast field experience of all levels of courts, I have pointed out certain feeble areas in the working of courts and suggested workable remedies as to how the anomalies prevailing in the existing working of courts can be rectified. All these suggestions have been stipulated with a vast scope of adoptability within the present conditions. The suggestions need to be modulated as per requirements to have maximum results to make justice delivery system faster and more accurate within the given framework of time.

In this book, the ills of Third World democracies, to which our country also belongs, have been dealt with on comparative ground and some measures have been suggested to improve the functioning of system of governance. The proposals for various circumstances, where no written guidelines are available, shall prove to be of great use to enhance capabilities in shortest possible time, in a better way. As a precaution, no specific country has been referred to quote incidents or experiences of individuals. Precaution has also been taken for not attacking the sovereignty and dignity of any specific country and whatever has been exemplified, may be taken as a sheer narration in support of the points raised in the text. Even any criticism of the present system directly, may not be taken as disturbing as many proposals have been suggested for a new system of governance called 'Peoplism'. The term 'Peoplism' has been explained in this book with the help of a comparative table discussing various policies of democracy and it has been studied in detail in chapter 19. In this system, the claim to reorganise the true democracy in the first stage of Peoplism, will be like a system that gives a 'limited democracy' or in other words 'an alternative to democracy'. Tabular comparison of working difference between democracy and Peoplism will again start a fresh debate. All the concerned are invited to participate in the open debate on this new concept of limited democracy which will train the citizens for practicing Peoplism to finally embark on true democracy.

The book also proposes techniques like 'Direct Action Cell System' by replacing mobile courts, which claims to create a fear in the minds of the corrupt for being watched by competent authorities. The concept of setting up 'Civitals' on the line of a civil hospital may also help people to have their grievances registered quickly and ensure immediate minimum relief to the aggrieved party, in almost the same way as an injured person is given first aid in the 'Casualty' of a hospital.

For Peoplism, the book also suggests extensive use of computer in filing complaints before a competent authority that is working in wider public interest using e-mail, fax-transmission, etc. Officially launched by the President, in the apex court in the year 2005, 'e-Judiciary' is entertaining writs/complaints from distant places. Having received documents and text through internet, the case file is created the same day. Its processing is done by the court staff till a date is fixed for appearance of the litigant. It has proved to be of great use and is accepted by the litigants throughout the country. Chapter 14 gives a brief account of Constitutions of many countries, to apprise the readers of what other people think of legal justice, humanity, social security and dignity of life for its people, preserving human values and human rights.

While conceptualizing the philosophy of Peoplism, Indian democracy has been tagged as a failed democracy, due to specific sad experiences in courts, at different levels. Out of many, one is that the benefits of liberty failed to percolate to the poor slipping out of the strong grip of those influential people who are part of the system of governance. Those, who are in position and power, are capable of obtaining the benefits of democracy but the have-nots are still deprived of what people call 'Fundamental Rights or Human Rights'.

Is it not a surprise that we have got a code of conduct for teachers but we have not thought of drafting and implementing a code of conduct for police, lawyers, judicial officers and other effective officialdom who rule the society? Besides, provision of Article 50 of our Constitution which restrains judicial officers from being treated as government employees, does not include lawyers and cops and still these two classes are free from having any code of conduct for them. Therefore, to some extent, they feel guarded with constitutional immunity.

Developed nations like USA, UK, France, etc. which are the patrons of democracy, have taken precaution to make democracy a balanced venture. American democracy is equipped with a code of conduct for judicial officers in the form of '7 Canons'. The code of conduct for lawyers and judicial officers given in this draft basically covers sensitive zones that can provide opportunity to go corrupt. Keeping the malpractices and the various loopholes in day-to-day working of courts using corrupt practices of authoritarian negligence by staff and others, separate codes of conduct for both lawyers and the judicial officers have been drafted under the title of Peoplism. But there is certainly no bar on having it modulated and adopted as such by any state, union territory or a country where people are suffering from delayed justice by defective and incompatible judiciary for more than one reasons.

Now, there is a dire need of such codes which are strongly reasoned with substantial grounds in order to rectify the professional anomalies and to upgrade the quality of justice. It has been discussed in chapter 18 of this book.

As soon as a case starts in the court of law, the judicial officer comes to know where the substance lies and he/she also makes up his/her mind what type of orders may be possible. But he prefers to go through procedural stages which waste a lot of time. At this stage the court must be prompt in passing over the stages of giving few dates and must try to move towards the final hearing. Normally, what is happening now is that the slow pace of progress of the case gives a message that the judge is not in a position or a mood to take responsibility to pass orders and so adjournments are given and the liability is thus shifted to the next incumbent judge. The judge must also discourage lies by penalising the doer while deciding the case so that people are deterred from claiming unlawful gains from the court.

There are lawyers who only take up legally strong cases but there are others who prefer to plead in favour of illegality. Though the profession of advocacy does not permit any lawyer to differentiate between the clients or reject the client who is on the wrong side of law, and his job is to help whosoever comes to seek help, yet, the judge is supposed to take a notice of those lawyers who are habitual of standing on the illegal side of the law. This knowledge must be taken into consideration while delivering justice to the affected party.

Courts are the last doors to be knocked at for legal justice. But surprisingly, nobody has ever made serious efforts to bring a code of conduct for judicial personnel in last 60 years. If proper law is drafted in this direction, it will certainly save innocent suffering people from the ills of the present legal system. I hope that the present book will create a nationwide debate on a number of issues raised herein and the suggestions given may be adopted by any state or central government in and outside the country to make justice delivery system effective, time bound and just in the interest of suffering litigants at large.

Anand Prakash Sharma

Former Spl. Correspondent

Hindustan Dainik

The Classes of Disputes

1

Lawyers need to specialise in a particular branch of law and groom their work to perfection by counseling, consulting and studying the decided cases during their practice.

It is a general perception that a lawyer can handle all types of cases. But it is always better, if lawyers specialize in one discipline and become expert in that discipline.

Big reason, as to why a senior lawyer gets a proper hearing with greater attention and care by the court, is that the court knows that he will not waste court's time as well as he shall place his contention to the point, within a shortest available time. However, to overcome jumbling of many data and their nature of working, legal cases may be classified into different following categories:

1. Constitutional Matters: Constitution of every country contains certain unexplained zones. These areas need to be elaborated, explained and authenticated citing examples of international conventions in certain cases by the dependable agency most likely by the apex court. However, there has not to be any clash on explanation of various Constitutional provisions, yet stakes propel many issues for public debate. Such matters are of great interest, as these issues mostly pertain to the Fundamental Rights of common citizens.

Such issues must be dealt with as urgent as it should not linger on years together, in order to minimise hatred among people of two states or two religions. Peoplism shall evolve methods to carry out 'National Consensus' on such issues.

Invitation to join 'Think Tank' shall be kept open for accepting practicable and workable ideas and solutions for serious consideration from registered organisations and identifiable individuals to resolve the issues of national importance, in the Ministry of Planning.

Such litigations are mostly argued in the final court, as such matters are not confined to certain section of society but these cover general masses as a whole. The maximum time for such cases shall not accede by thirty days. This class will cover issues like dissolution of Assembly; religious disputes; amending already existing laws and Master Plans; quashing *ultra-vires* rules and illegal circulars; validity of an election and so on. Maximum time limit will be 30 days.

2. Political Disputes: Criminal cases on politicians need to be dealt by separate and independent courts in separate premises as these are full of drama and working of regular courts is entirely disturbed affecting entire day's work. Special arrangements in general courts are to be made by administration to remove hurdles hampering work of other courts. The question of security of VVIP makes the entire premises inaccessible for everyone.

Swindles, Frauds, misuse of authority, nepotism, bungling and misappropriation of public funds, favouritism, sex-offences, bribery, criminal conduct, and other offences covered by Indian Penal Code by politicians, in power, need to be handled by independent separate courts to make the process of justice fast, transparent and free from media pressure. New punishments have to be designed for such persons who use their authority under the grab of statue they have been entrusted for. In such cases, the violators have to be charged for Breach of Public Trust also. Citizens, who have deputed an elected representative certain job and entrusting them to carry that out, need extraordinary public punishments. Those, who misuse their

---

Think Tank: *It s a pool of suggestions and ideas from everyone. E-mail address can be used as Think Tank. For example, for our think tank is: people.anand@gmail.com. You can send your response about this book to us and your experiences with working of courts to us.*

position deliberately to offend innocent citizens shall be charged, for more than one offence. This new provision of law can also cover all officials in different organs of governance under the stature of the Hon'ble President. Maximum time limit is 120 days.

3. Disputes between States: In a federal nation, there may be certain disputes on sharing natural resources, especially, water. For such disputes, in fact, the Planning Commission must have power to impose its national policies without demanding any sacrifice from the people in question. The citizens must also allow projects of national importance to go through without much fuss. Recently, land dispute in West Bengal and other protests against construction of dams raised a vital question of uprooting people from their ancestral land. Such human problem has to be tackled with great care. Yet, not all such disputes should be handled by the apex court. Rather, the affected people must be negotiated substantially and be involved in the progress of the project. After the project is complete it must also involve the locals in running the project. The first advantage of the project must go to the repatriated people and to this respect a national policy be formulated. Any efforts to politicise such national programme be dealt with severity, otherwise, it will be impossible for any government to construct mega structures in the country which are becoming need of the hour as essential assets of every nation. Beyond human angle these are to be strictly implemented in the wider and long-term interest of the nation. Disputed States to share their resources must decide things in the national interest and should respect the verdict of especially appointed Commissions from time to time. Awarding affected people with judicious compensation in cash or kind can be one of many solutions.

However, such issues must be dealt as urgent as possible and it should not linger on for years together, in order to reduce hatred among the affected people of two States. Peoplism shall evolve methods to carry out 'National Consensus' on such issues. Invitation to join 'Think Tanks' must be kept open for unprivileged citizens, from registered organizations and identifiable individuals asking them to give practicable solutions to various national or regional problems for the consideration of Ministry of Planning. Time bound justice shall make it possible to dispose of such matters to include affected people in **'Jury'** during the hearing when it comes before the court. The maximum time for such cases shall not accede by 30 days.

4. Public Interest Litigation: Through such litigation no one specific, can be a personal beneficiary. Such litigations are aimed at wider public good. All litigations pleading for a common interest need to be handled with great care and respect by the courts. It is condemnable that in a country, where nearly 2.4 million people are herded into jails as undertrials in sub-human, unmanageable conditions, without providing basic human needs like healthcare and proper food, etc. a Public Interest Litigation (PIL) is dismissed not on merits of the issue but on alleged procedural flaws. Contravening with the merits of the case, dismissal of such important PIL is nothing but a judicial wrong. PILs are to be treated on merits without a personal passion and personal consideration of the individual judge. Dismissal of such PILs is deplorable as it pleaded restoration of human rights of detainees and interest of a large number of under-trials which are not being managed properly by the Government. In a developing country, where judiciary has become less effective due to a number of short-comings of government, it is not appreciable to dismiss such PILs for no valid reason. Perhaps, it was done because there is no accountability of judiciary to the masses. If a court is attached to the finality, it has to be very careful for the merits of issues raised therein PILs than to dismiss them on premature grounds. In this case, the court could have passed directions on the petitioner to present the PIL again after redrafting and rearranging the contents. But dismissing such a PIL of wider public importance outwardly is really a serious matter on the part of the court.

Jury: *A group of respected and acclaimed citizens of substance numbering from 12 to 20, that hears court arguments and give their opinion before the court announces final verdict.*

Procedures and technicalities are framed to make the work systematic and convenient. Any how, if the purpose of a PIL is understandable, before a Peoplist court, it would be attended by the court with first consideration. A PIL if reaches the stage of appearing before the Court's Bench, it is bound to get a proper hearing and must not be dismissed on technical grounds by ignoring merits and gross approach of the petition.

Recently, dismissal of a PIL in the highest court praying unconditional immediate release of overstaying under-trials is unfortunate. This PIL raised many other issues like amending law by highlighting various flaws in the working of police system due to certain flaws in Criminal Procedure Code. In this PIL, several court cases were cited to expose a number of flaws in court proceedings and prayed the court to do something about them. But unfortunately the court failed to appreciate it. It is unthinkable that the text and material from this PIL was used by a specific judicial officer to write letter to the Prime Minister to make certain changes in the judicial system. The question of 'Mass Legal Education' was raised in this PIL for the first time, was also mentioned in this letter. Thereafter, a **'Mass Legal Education Programme'** was launched with a bang.

But ultimately it was lost in obscurity due to lack of commitment to the cause. Such concept-snatching by the persons of first level, is really shocking. Public debate on such wrong decisions of court has to be encouraged in Peoplism so that the court remains conscious about public anguish or public opinion about them as these days the courts become conscious about those cases which are high lighted by the media in comparison to the daily routine cases of ordinary citizens.

In Peoplism, mandatory provision to entertain PILs of wider importance had been provided. PILs having technical flaws of processing, etc. will still qualify for admission and hearing. Despite of dismissing such important PILs outwardly,

---

Mass Legal Education Programme: *This is a big programme by the government to educate masses about common laws on day-to-day incidences like basic knowledge of Constitution, Citizen's rights and duties, human rights, Fundamental rights, rent Act, accident, fire, etc.*

the court shall manage to redraft or redesign the writ through Legal aid Department of the court.

There are instances, when PILs have been put in cold bags leaving people's cause to uncertainty by ignoring the seriousness of continued feuds. Disputes between two States for water (Kavery water dispute), disbursement of electricity produced in a State and sparing it to the neighbouring State, territorial dominance, etc. need to be disposed off by the competent court in shortest possible time. Religious issues are far more urgent to be disposed of. Keeping such cases pending for a long generates hatred and bloodshed only.

Peoplist shall prefer to set-up exclusive and independent courts to hear PILs of wider public interest at all levels of courts. PILs in Peoplism shall be encouraged when presented by petitioners-in-person. Presently, sincere litigants, who are not lawyers and act as petitioner-in-person, face hardship in the courts and within the premises of courts for everything at all stages because the courts or its staff think that they are not backed by any 'Association'. Litigant in person in Peoplism shall be entertained equal to the lawyers by virtue of a defined law. Complaints against any maltreatment to PIPs (Petitioners-in-Person) shall be entertained by 'Judicial Commission'. The maximum time limit for such Public Interest Litigations shall not accede 6 months in any case.

5. Criminal Cases: To make the process of filing a Challan faster in criminal cases, Peoplists have proposed to take few measures. Since these cases involve police and other investigatory agencies to provide evidences, these are the most time-consuming litigations. Nevertheless, to bring out facts in stipulated time period; multiple level investigations will be a solution. In Peoplism, the Investigation Officer (IO) at the police station will prepare primary documents. But a second investigation officer shall be appointed parallelly by 'Special Cell for Investigation' (at the Police Head Quarters), where the IOs will be trained specifically for investigating a case, as per latest and defined methods and techniques. These officers at **'Special Cells for Investigation'** at the police HQ, shall be trained to study Forensic Science methodology and crime-psychology of criminals and suspects and also be well-versed with latest scientific tools and techniques being used in western countries. In Peoplism, the maximum limit for completing the investigation is not to accede by six months. Speedy performance at all levels shall go to the CR of the investigating officers. The proceedings in a filed case shall be settled by the end of 9 months by the respective court. However, the IO can frame his own strategy to investigate a case but within the 'define parameters of investigation'. The accused shall not be totally at the mercy of the IO and he/she shall have some of his/her rights till the investigation is completed. In case of calling the accused to the police station for interrogation in all conditions, the summoned person will have the right to accompany, at least, one of his/her acquaintances, who will not be stopped to watch question session through the glass-window in a specially designed 'interrogation room'. The questions will always be relevant and connected to the crime and shall be on record in writing. The interrogation room shall be fitted with recording devices and these must, by all means, be in working condition, will be a mandatory duty of the SHO. The accused cannot be interrogated at any other place than his own house or the interrogation-room where he/she can be watched by his acquaintances during interrogation. The entire interrogation can be recorded by the side of the accused on either of the electronic medium, if the accused desires so. For convenience, the police can be asked for a copy of the recording, by the accused and that it shall be provided by the police, on demand. The accused will have the right to get his own recording prepared for his own record for the purpose of the court. The recording along with available evidences shall be submitted to the court along with the challan in one go. However, at present, there are no guidelines for the IOs as to what has to be asked. The IO is at full liberty to question the accused the way he wants. But now everything

Special Cells for Investigation: *Such a Cell shall be constituted at the Police Head Quarters to have a parallel investigation to cross check the facts and maintain a fair and just investigation. Licensed Private detectives can carry out their investigation independently in favour of accused.*

shall be observed by family members through a transparent glass from a distance during question session.

The interrogation method and parameters shall be entirely different in civil matters than in criminal cases. Different types of offences have to be investigated in time bound manner differently by different defined strategies by the IOs.

The police shall be discouraged to have custody of the accused and for that courts shall be liberal to grant bails in case of bailable offences. Inevitable change in Cr.P.C. will delete a number of cases from non-bailable to bailable offences to minimise rush in jails. Accused in custody shall be open to make calls to their family through a demand phone call from the staff on payment basis on a fixed day of the week. The accused cannot be deprived of many liberties until his crime is proved and he is convicted. For the purpose of investigation and interrogation, the accused can be available during his/her bail also. This working shall certainly reduce pressure of under-trials in over-packed jails.

No accused shall be left on the complete mercy of police and give police a liberty to extract confession from the person in its custody. The opportunity of using third degree method is against law through out the world and no law allows the cops to use force to extract confession in their place under a threat to life or any kind of black mailing. The police must be trained to use psychological tactics and scientific methods to round up a criminal by his own admittance by giving the accused full opportunity to defend himself properly. Extracting confession by the police virtually also did not work in the past as the accused always enjoys his right to change his statement in the court of Law. Therefore, if the police are really serious to fight out crime, it will have to evolve reasonable and really wonderful methods to un-arm the criminal and reach the root of the crime. In Peoplism, such exhaustive training and practice shall be imparted to the investigating police personnel that no interrogation shall be vague without a real success.

Frivolous and fake cases by police are numerous. These are filed by connivance of police with the criminal minded superiors or influential persons in society. The author has an experience of his gratification by police to force to withdraw a complaint against certain rich and influential person. A criminal case was filed 320 km away from his home to create hardship to give up. In a case registered on him u/s 406, Breach of Trust, the IO asked many irrelevant and objectionable questions to harass him and withdraw his complaint. For example, what is the age of your mother? The reply was 84 years. Where does she live? Reply was 'at the old age home'. The next question was 'how does she live alone without a husband? The answer was 'she was a widow'.

Practically, there have to be defined subjects, of which the IO can frame his questionnaire. He will place these questions in any form. Parameter to ask questions shall be defined. IO cannot be allowed to do any excess on the accused illegally and criminally, in the name of investigation. There have to be certain rules as to how an enquiry is to be conducted and how the case has to be investigated. The sufferer need not look at the face of the IO to do justice with him. To make things easy, the Police Acts have to be approved by a Central Committee in the Ministry of Vigilance at center level, with special provisions of law to the requirement of a particular State. The Right of amending Criminal Procedure Code will be to the Central Government only and the State can do so, only after the due approval of the Parliament. States will not amend their Police Acts and Cr.P.C. without the permission and knowledge of the Central Ministry of vigilance, no matter if the question of law and order remains with the State. Rules to investigate a particular type of crime shall be the same in all the States, although certain part of it may be individualistic as per the requirement of the case the State and the investigating officer.

Fake FIRs, fake encounters and fake arrests automatically become punishable in Peoplism through imposition of 'Consequential Punishments'. In case of failure of a case in the court of Law, the erring cop shall be punished for filing a fake case. The code of conduct for the cops shall impose restrictions on misbehaviour, immoral conduct, objectionable language and misconduct.

Code of conduct for bureaucrats, police persons, judicial officers and lawyers and even for every employee of the government shall be necessary. For a better and democratic functioning of any institution, such codes are to be formulated. The Private sector already has such conduct unwritten by having a specific work culture there. Such codes are essential so that no one can feel unchallenged and can function with a sense of accountability.

Peoplism is bound to provide latest designed forensic laboratories in all the capital cities of all the States. Selected qualified officers shall be trained in advance countries to learn the latest tools and techniques and know about working of latest equipments. They will further train their subordinate technicians accordingly. The judicial officers in criminal courts shall also be trained before shifting to these courts, about available scientific tools and techniques to appreciate the evidences during argument. The defense Lawyers and public prosecutors too shall have a right to learn these new techniques and visit these labs to verify the authenticity of findings to cross-examine the parties. Tomorrow, the findings will not be based merely on perceptions, pre-notions, suppositions and whims that misguide a judge to use its unlimited discretion to dispose of a case but now it will be based on facts and figures. The laws in Peoplism are so direct and transparent that these will replace extremely coarse and whimsical ways of police to handle a criminal case and to save innocents from prosecution.

Timely finishing the investigation will enable to minimise the possibility of manipulation by the investigation officer, as he knows that he cannot waste time to ripe a situation for extortion by giving sufficient fears to the party to be investigated. There has to be, by all means, a fixed schedule to define the maximum time limit in different categories of offences for investigation (Ref. to 3rd schedule 13th Chapter). It will not only improve the efficiency of the police but also will make it more reliable. Reason being to this is that there are crosschecked investigations of two colleagues parallelly from different agencies and the final report for the court shall be prepared by the third senior officer who has the authority to question the quality of investigation. No single officer shall have free hand to temper the evidences, extort comforts and trap an innocent, as it is opened to a single IO at present. Also, the final liability will come on the shoulders of the third senior officer.

It stands to be ridiculous for police to be a real petty pawn to politicians, much less to their own superiors. To such reasons, their performance is not always taken as the real cause of their promotion in their department. The promotion department in police must own responsibility to have records of all the cops for their overall performance to appreciate and honour or impose penalties in case of a negative report. **'Police Grievance Cell'** shall be set up in all the police districts to register and redress work related problems of cop. Such Cells shall be constituted by the personnel from representatives of Public (not politicians) and the retired IPS officers. The number of the members of this Grievance Cell shall not exceed by five with quorum of three. It will be a welfare authority beyond the exclusive control of Police on it. This department shall nullify victimization of good cops at the hands of politicians and biased senior police officers. Any cop can approach this department for his/her protection against uncalled for harassment. Maximum time limit for deciding criminal cases is 200 days.

6. Civil Disputes (property/rent and others): It is an irony that judiciary in developing countries believe that a civil suits is not urgent and can be kept pending for a long. But, this is untrue. Such misconception shall be discarded by deciding civil cases within a prescribed period. It is a hard-fact that the matters, which are not covered under criminal offence, are covered under civil matters. Civil disputes shall be dealt in civil courts which will be sub-classified into many sub-categories according to departments to which they belong. Matters on ancestral property shall not prolong more than two years.

Police Grievance Cell: *A special cell in Police Head Quarters to entertain complaints, work related problems and harassment of cops by her/his seniors and threats of any kind from out side.*

7. Service Matters: In service matters, the service years are limited but handling of service matters by judiciary is taken with normal pace. The cases proceed like a civil case completely ignoring that a full family is waiting for the decision to come to restore the job of their guardian. Apathy and humility becomes the fate of the litigant. Adjournments in long pending cases are repeatedly not to be granted, lapsing the service period month after months. For unconvincing petty reasons, adjournments are granted in service matters, where everyday is paid to a person holding his/her job. Throwing admitted cases in cold bags is injustice practiced by even in High Courts. The matters affecting the bread and butter of the entire family must be treated as urgent with the aforesaid logic, even without making any law on it. Beyond the provisions of Article-50 of the Constitution, the judicial officers too have to wait for their salary in the first week of every month which is spared from public exchequer. So, it is needless to set the value of salary for a salaried person. The courts must understand that their family also waits for the salary they as a parent bring home.

The judiciary is an essential part of our lives. Qualified people have been assigned a specific work to be carried out as a part of their duty against what is being paid to them. There can be no judicial officer who can take up his job without his/her salary as a social work only. To exempt them from government job title, is aimed at providing them immunity from political and bureaucratic interference i.e. making them independence to work without fear or favour from any powerful section of the system while making decisions. From bureaucrats to police; from politicians to business tycoons, all fall under the jurisdiction of judiciary. At present, there is no thought to make a hurry to decide service matters on priority basis. Lingering on service matters like any other property matter or civil matter has to be stopped. In Peoplism, therefore, service matters of all nature shall be decided within months and be taken up, out of turn on priority basis, if dealt in a civil court. However, it is suggestive that service matters will be dealt by separate courts and not in the courts like today's Teacher' Tribunal which has lost its credibility for its careless way of working. The Central Administrative Tribunal (CAT) and Delhi School Tribunal (DST) and other such Tribunals failed to establish credibility for their own faulty working in the past. Government always took Tribunals very lightly to keep their posts vacant for years and many such instances are on record where the government did not bother to fill vacancies in this Tribunal for more than ten years, in some cases. Those who are trapped in these Tribunals are suffering beyond imagination. Virtually these small judicial bodies were used politically or bureaucratically as a launch-pad to promote certain favourite judicial officers to high court through this back-door. There are cases filed in 1979 and the contesting teacher has died in waiting for justice. The case was decided in 2007 only, i.e. after 28 years only. In these 28 years not less than 13 presiding officers came and left on promotion. The most interesting part of this case is that in these painful years, the Tribunal kept adjourning the case and hearing the case 'partly' till date. Delhi School Tribunal dealing with termination cases only. It failed to decide another case number 34/91 in last seventeen years and remained pending while the litigant was retiring in June 2008.

There have to be independent and separate full-fledged courts to deal with service matters. In these cases, lone suffering employee is put to repeated harassment by organised, rich Management which is followed by the civil court. The court in such a situation, must not forget that the petitioner is alone before an army of supporters of wrong doers, who want to prove themselves unchallenged for their illegal act being a power. There is a need to provide with provisions in law where wrong by executives are to be brought on record and consequential punishments has to be imposed on such executives, who are found guilty of manipulating prescribed Acts, Rule and Regulation to injure a particular individual for personal vendetta. The court will be bound to give priority to such serious and deliberate violation of set law. In such case the court has to have a positive attitude towards the sufferer. Classification of such cases of criminal manipulation of law (departmental rules and regulations), shall be taken as attack on Government and the dignity of Parliament who framed these laws. It may be dealt with the charge of conspiracy against the State. Priority of placing cases before the court, after reading the writs (Appeals) applications, etc. with the permission of sub-registrar, can be classified in the priority list. Cases of termination shall have first priority.

If we analyse the entire proceedings of the court in a case, we can calculate easily that the courts give its maximum time period in the entire processing and hearing a case to be maximum 2-3 hours. But adjournments of three to eight months consume year after years. Out of many, there have been instances, where a wrongful termination of services, was decided after thirty years after the litigant was retired by a High Court. In another case, the litigant remained without job and without any alternate income for nearly twenty years depending on the verdict of the court but the court dismissed the case after keeping it pending for two decades and without owning any responsibility for exhausting the entire service period of the litigant. For such reasons of absurd and callous and irresponsible and procedure-based attitude, service matters shall be decided within maximum period 3 months in case of termination and 6 months in case of other administrative disputes.

8. Financial Disputes: Matters pertaining to money matters will be dealt by separate courts. Such court will cover all kind of suits of recovery tax evasion, refund and other such matters will have specifically qualified judges. Judges will be chosen (selected) from revenue departments and be placed in Double-Bench to complete the quorum. It is not fair that a judicial person is asked to sit in any court and make decisions. Judges also will be trained for technicalities of the discipline on which he/she has to pass orders. Maximum period is 3 months to resolve revenue dispute.

9. Consumer Disputes: Consumer Forums were started to keep consumer disputes away from regular courts to give justice in a faster manner and reduce load of regular courts. The working was planned much simpler. But these days, lawyers have pounced upon these Forums converting them into full fledged courts. The presiding officers also enjoy adjourning case years after year. In a case number 1834/99 a district consumer forum dismissed the case on maintainability after a period of three years and adjourning the case at least 20 times. In Peoplism, few specific measures are taken to make these forums consumer savvy. These will be ramified and specified to household sales, after-sale-services, water disputes, electricity disputes, repayment of dues to banks, cases of recovery, installment default, allotments, etc. in it. The proceedings in the consumer court will be heard directly from the aggrieved party and no lawyer will be allowed to plead for either party. Maximum time limit is 50 days.

10. Matrimonial, Dowry and Harassment Disputes: Disputes in marriage are other frequent litigations. It becomes more serious, especially where the couple has kids. Keeping the trauma of two families in consideration, a positive approach will be the first priority to bring both the contestants to the common point of compromise, if the forum sees a single possibility to resolve the crisis by counseling and persuasion.

Psychological and physical needs of innocent children shall be a serious concern the forum along with other issues of dispute. The earning parents in dispute shall bear the expenses of children as per their source of income. The 'Spouse Cell' in each police station will also hear the teasing and torture stories of troubled husband/wife and shall file complaints from both the sides. Such disputes shall be finished within 6 months.

11. Petty Tribal Issues: Such issues will be resolved by Registered ***Resident Welfare Associations*** in cities and by Gram Panchayats in villages. The law enforcing agencies, primarily will not resolve these issues. Therefore, RWAs will be equipped with specially prepared code of conduct for the residents. This code of conduct will empower the RWAs to enforce certain bindings on all the residents who share the

---

Resident Welfare Associations: *Registered Resident Welfares are going to occupy a significant place in public administration in Peoplism. These bodies are legal; elected, educated, committed to social cause of unquestionable identity clear identity, mostly comprise with experienced senior and respectable citizens.*

public conveniences arranged and brought by the efforts of RWA in the area. These courts shall solve petty disputes of hooliganism in residential areas without taking help of police and shall take help from private security services. RWAs are to be regionalized as legal entities like Pvt. Ltd. companies and must work within a defined framework of Society Registration Act 1860. The police must take the version of RWAs as the first truth, as RWAs are accountable for any wrong and manipulation under IPC. Maximum time limit of such litigation will be 100 days to conclude the case.

The local police have to be bound by the decision of RWAs by virtue of newly drafted law on this issue by the Peoplists. The registered RWAs also shall pass such bindings as per provisions of Memorandum of Association as a mandatory part of it as per prescribed law. The management of RWA can enforce its decision through a resolution, passed by the managing Committee as a legal binding on the defaulting members to cooperate the RWA for carrying out directions passed on him/her in the general interest of the RWA. Since RWAs are a registered body these organisations are legal entities as per Section-6 of Society Registration Act 1860. The RWAs are to be empowered more for the welfare of its members and the law abiding citizens as a whole. The membership has to be a mandatory requirement of all dwellings in the new Law. All Gram Panchayats shall be covered by this law and in large village; it may be bifurcated in unit level RWAs of minimum fifty families residing in vicinity. From a bigger dwelling, RWA shall take a shape of consortium or a Federation. The Concept of Third House in Parliament has been drawn from these organisations in Peoplism.

12. Miscellaneous Issues: Many disputes that has not been covered by the above classes shall fall in this category and their way of working and the time parameter shall be decided on the basis of above mentioned cases by the court set-up to deal with such unclassified matters.

Nipping Crime in the Bud

2

Making Offence and crime short-lived.

For the last sixty years, no survey has been done on how effective the existing Law is. Authorities take it granted that the working of existing system of law is flawless. No one bothered to see, whether the provisions have remained timely effective or not. Authorities believed that Law framed by Britishers during slavery, would work after freedom also.

This misconception exists in the minds of those who claim to govern. They have no intention to look into the ills of Rules and Regulations framed about 250 years back. Since Britishers ruled a large part of globe in the past, they established their own laws in the slave lands and left its roots intact deep there, before they pulled out. Had the existing system of governance been the best, the Britishers would have had the same in their own country. Laws framed by British Rulers in their colonies are almost the same in large number of countries. In their own country, they have a different way of working and different laws.

Truly speaking, different law Codes like Indian Penal Code, Criminal Procedure Code and the Civil Procedure Code (IPC, CrPC and CPC) had been designed to handle slaves. These are basically devoid of Human Rights, Natural Justice and true representation of people in their governments. All these three documents are the basic elements of Democratic system of governance. If these codes are lacking few essential provisions, these are working against citizens and still consistently being overlooked by our politicians.

Constitution of newly freed countries in late fifty's was framed by many significant personalities of these nations. But it remained a misfortune of people that no one had ever seen these documents from the angle of updating them in last 60 years. Supremacy of authorities and brutality of police on slaves were the basic trait of British Raj. So, many absurd clauses still exist in today's law to keep the innocent citizens feared and remain in absolute terror of arrest by the police. Arrest of an innocent person on apprehension of a crime and framing a criminal case by a very junior police officer of the rank of ASI are basically planned to bring the accused all possible humiliation, is still hounding. Artificial encounters on the pretext of apprehension of a crime by the so-called gangster are a concrete example of police criminality. Framing people in false criminal cases, arresting innocent people in the name of alleged suspicion of a crime, have been grossly misused by police in these six decades. Till today, terrorising innocent citizens of their powers, to take any one to police station and detaining him/her overnight, using third degree tortures in the police station in the name of interrogation, filing fake cases without accountability, not filing FIR even in genuine cases, allowing illegal construction, land grabbing and encroachment on government land, illegal water connection, keeping a mum on open power theft; is a daily routine for the police and does not alarm even the Commissioner of Police. Though, it is against the ethics of oath every policeman takes but it has become a daily routine of police all over the country to ignore people's plight. To graft innocent people for records and rewards has become the culture of police department in last 15 years. The police that are empowered to arrest any one for 24 hours remain a mute spectator when such gross illegal activities are carried out by their colleagues before its eyes. They allow each other for all illegal activities in the police stations under the grab of a price for every illegal favour you need. Can any cop at any level deny that he is not aware of these facts? But no one tries to resist it. There are no rules for many things. So, these have been taken granted as their right. No one can question the police for not filing a case; detaining any person on apprehension, trapping innocents in criminal cases, using force illegally against any one are in practice. Murdering people under the cover of encounter is done fearlessly. In this system, the cops grab every right to evade its duty and let the crime happen to wait for a situation for extortion, has also become culture of today's police.

The picture of the society is painted to make it lucrative by media especially English newspapers. For them poverty is the last issue. The press is so immature in third world countries that it ignores the cause and concern of maximum number of unprivileged citizens than to print nude/seminude women on the front page for few readers. They ignore horrifying stories on poverty and helplessness of people of remote areas. Boasting politicians have joined hands with the pent clad gals in the media who cherish to ignore the fact that fruits of democracy are reaching to a particular class of elites and poor are made mute spectators. These hardly 5 per cent urban elites today boast of economic growth of the country, exhibiting Forex reserves and other sporadic achievements at the cost of lost Fundamental Rights of 95 per cent population. Unpatronised citizens in the country are left to be illiterate, ill informed, deprived of, blindly faithful to one of the political masters, superstitious and ignorant of country's basic laws. No villager living in a remote area does know what his Fundamental Rights are and what do the Human Rights mean. Government officials are enjoying power in all form. They have made their lives unquestionably comfortable at the cost of poor people who are the victims of economic disparity. Manipulation of public funds and working with unreasonable policies put forward by certain white collars in high places; who never bother to see whether citizens born in this land are protected with their basic civil rights much less Constitutional guarantees. It does not disturb them who are ruling the country. Their ways are so lucid that suit to all MPs, MLAs, bureaucrats, judicial officers, police officers and all those who are in power. In connivance together, they have grabbed the best of the nation and have become the masters of lives of deprived of citizens, have-nots and sufferers through ills of the governing system. To aspire for human rights seems to be a mock dream when even rural population failed to get proper electric supply, drinking water, medical facilities, sufficient means of livelihood, proper education, protected life from the clutches of goons and police on one side and basic requirements to survive for a dignified life, on the other. The condition of law is so bad and absurd at numerous places that not only offending women but innocent men too become subject to police degradation and inhilation in the name of maintaining law and order.

Beyond many concrete reasons, terrorism is one of the outcomes of government's failure on all fronts. If the power mongers mentioned above as sucking country's best resources and modulating Laws converting every good into their privilege, the sufferer citizens are looking at their faces just for a judicious hearing only. Deprived of due-human-rights, in order to survive with dignity, he is not even heard, by the effective authority. If we overlook courts for a moment, authorities that come before the courts have all their business to look into the plight of suffering citizens than to create a situation of total frustration. Many such power positions, do not own any moral responsibility for the creation of such dead end for citizens. One can imagine the chaos in the life of an innocent person, who has been implicated falsely by the police or who has been removed from his job illegally or whose the only bread earning family member is thrown into jail on false charges as an unattended under-trial. If on one side the citizens are facing apathy of the authorities, the most scaring fact is that the courts are not prepared to give justice quickly. The cases are not handled in a dignified manner. Rather, these are handled more bureaucratically. The sensitivity to a thin line between being personal and being judgmental must depend on facts and figures of the cases. Still in these six decades no government, from different political parties, could improve judiciary and police to the changing circumstances. The phobia of courts and police is so high that even the Human Right Commission refuses to lodge a complaint against a case which is being heard by a ACP-SEM run court. The police are so highly powered that it can judicially prove an innocent person a criminal when an Assistant Police Commissioner slides into the arena of judiciary being a Special Executive Magistrate. In this illogical court the police justify all its FIRs whether it is genuine or mischievously lodged. The court of SEM is absolutely against the basic principle of Natural justice and the verdict of the Apex Court as held in case titled ***Arjun Chowbe Vs Union of India AIR 1984 SC 1356*** that "No one can be judge for his own cause". Since the police habitually enjoy taking law into its own hands the intelligent Parliament passed a bill to empower the police to do so through the office of SEM. Peoplism is bound to stop this practice.

Most of the peaceful citizens are traditional and do not dare to change their ways, even wrong practices. Recently, the Apex Court has issued directions to the Government at Center to fill vacant post of judicial officers but even after two years lapse; there is no progress in this direction. To implement police reforms suggested by 'Justice Maliamat Commission' recommendation by the apex court few years back, still remains unattended. Out of many, the Governments of MP, Karnataka, Bihar and others showed inability to implement these reforms on the pretext of shortage of funds. In such a bad situation, the Center should have come forward to allocate financial assistance to these States on the grounds of certain Barter programmes with these States. But the priority list of the Center unfortunately misses police and court improvements. Practically, the Center should have understood the importance of improving these to organs as its first priority to give people proper legal justice timely than to water public money in "Asiads". In Peoplism, the Center shall allocate funds to internal security that includes police and judiciary, equivalent to the amount spent on Defense of the country.

Reforms in Peoplism include 1. Set up of State Security Commission, 2. DGPs will get two years term, 3. Police officers will get minimum two years tenure in the field, 4. Separation of police working of maintaining law and order from criminal investigation, 5. Setting-up an independent 'Police Establishment Board' to look into transfer, and promotions, 6. Setting-up an **'Independent Police Complaint Authorities'** (IPCA) for disciplinary action against erring cops on one side and entertaining grievances from the cops on the other.

Stubborn attitude of police or a judicial officer is always unjust as they feel themselves to be a superior class, which they feel is virtually bound to rule. For them, everything is fine and there is no need to make any changes. They feel that suffrage of people is attached to their own fate. All the politicians, bureaucrats and other officials are at ease and perhaps they personally feel themselves to be a different and superior class of other unprivileged citizens.

It is an established fact that disputes on religious claims often take ugly shape. A secular State has multifarious religious beliefs. The first two big factions of Hindus and Muslims may confront for their historical bias. Both these factions have their own roots with staunch following by millions of people. Babri Maszid demolition is the result of prolonged frustration of Hindus. The court had overlooked the issue for years and in repeated manner. It did not create a situation of negotiation and reconciliation in time for a mutual compromise. Ultimately, people took law into their hands and decided the case of their own leaving behind a deep wound forever on one side and a bundle of hidden fear on the other. Had there been certain clear verdicts by the court for favour to a particular side, such orders could have been reserved for a particular to go to the cold bag. It could also direct the government to call a 'consensus vote' through general elections or could have taken out via media to make the place a national monument preserving the Constitutional approach to repose people's faith in judiciary once again.

In another important incident of the Capital in which a vast land was notified in early sixties, by the Land and Acquisition Department under Master Plan 2001. The owners moved to the court and succeeded in fetching a stay order from the Higher

---

Independent Police Complaint Authority (IPCA): *An independent body located away from the Police Head Quarters. It shall comprise with the members of Citizen's Forum, retired and sitting judges of the State Courts and top bureaucrats from police and outside.*

Court in 1973. The owner started selling this vast, vacant and notified land to unscrupulous people at a desired price. The government agencies did not report the matter to the court and no contempt was filed under the influence of sharing booty by illegal sale. These plots were allotted in the name of 'for agriculture purposes' making the allottees licensees. As a strategy, these unscrupulous factory owners finally built factories on it and started manufacturing fake components of different machines. By the year 1982, there emerged a full-fledged Industrial slum having more than 3000 illegal factories on this notified government land. The vacant land was in use now. Factory owners made a Union and get this registered with the registrar societies. Politicians got this illegal industrial slum allowed by passing a resolution in house of representatives, putting a stamp of confirmed 'light Industrial area'. No government agency stopped this happen. Some of the industries were given registration and bank loans. On the other hand, the vast vacant land, which the contesting litigants were unable to protect, was grabbed by continuously migrating people from nearby States and built unauthorised houses on it. At least, five new colonies were built in a span of twenty years and civic authorities kept helping these illegal occupants on behalf of area politicians by diverting water supply of legal occupants to illegal colonies here, got their new ration cards to create a solid and bigger vote-bank.

These vote-banks were encouraged to take illegal connection from the pipeline, which was supplying water to lawful residents of the area causing acute shortage of water which forced exudation of many families living here for the last 60 years to other colonies. The matter does not end here. The politicians never bothered to look at lawful resident's plight of acute shortage of water and overheard their written and oral complaints, even on moral grounds. District XEN of Delhi Jal Board replied quarries of registered resident's welfare association misguiding them. After that, the area politician instructed DJB to tighten the main gate valve to divert maximum water to these illegal residents at greater pressure and reducing the water supply of lawful consumers to almost nil. Old, ailing, senior citizens living here lawfully since 1949 were also not spared. Now, the status of this land is totally changed and appeal of the erstwhile owner in court claims this not to be a vacant land but a built-up area. The apex court has tuned down all such appeals. The erstwhile owner has filed a mercy appeal with LG once again to keep development work here suspended for more years until government fails to use this land and give up. For government, there are only two options of either removing all grabbers and encroachers from this notified land who used force against court stay order or retain this vast slum on this government land in the name of political-mercy. Had the case been decided in time, i.e. in the year 1954 and 1960, this vast public land would have not slipped from the hands of the government for M.P. 2001. But due to fifty years of litigation, the politicians could have an opportunity to create a vote-bank at the cost of lawful residents putting them to great misery. The situation is totally out of control of the government today as the equation is entirely changed. The litigation continued for about 50 years and the land remained under heavy grabbing, slipping out from the grip of authorities. Delay in justice is the main reason for this disaster. Therefore, justice in time shall preserve law and order in the society and unlawfulness shall not be allowed to encroach upon law of the land. The rule of law shall be easier for authorities to enforce which shall be a biding on defaulter to accept. If the process of not allowing residential accommodation changing into commercial was stopped well in time by civic authorities as per already existing laws, the torture of sealing and demolition would have not been affected citizens of Delhi so painfully. If the courts act fast to decide cases in time, the face of the society will change to our expectation and goons shall not dare raise their heads. But the hooligans are prevailing all around us as the courts have proved themselves to be ineffective due to routine delayed in delivering their decisions. Situation will keep swelling from mole to mountain and such mountain may not be an ordinary one. It may be a volcano. Pending cases of wider importance, especially of public interest, must be disposed of as early as possible and to dispose of them in time the 'PIL Courts' should be separate courts by a full bench at all levels of courts. Local issue PIL may be handled at district level court and so on. Pending cases that pertain to public property by Municipal Corporation, development corporations, NGOs, individual or group of social activists that involve the interest of masses at large, must not be kept on hold for any reason, whatsoever, they may be, to avoid growing hatred and frustration among the members of a vast population. Because the above example may be taken as a living example that if such disputes are not decided in time, all government land shall be grabbed and encroached upon and the fabric of society shall be torn off completely to the extent of total chaos. Let the juvenile bud not grow into huge cactus. So, nip such bureaucratic, political and judicial lapse in the bud by deciding issues in safest range of time.

Goodbye to Fake Cases 3

Framing and grafting by the Police and other government agencies shall not be a common practice of those in power.

Civil police is expected to be multifariously powerful and most potential force among all types of forces in a democratic set-up. But in third world countries, this force has transformed into the weakest armed force. Reason being is that the police are run by many masters and authorities. Rich can use it; senior officers can pressurize it and politicians can exploit it. As an independent force their existence is always threatened. Therefore, out of this frustration, it often goes beyond its limits leaving behind its morality and prescribed official duties, in an effort to establish their existence.

Police are supposed to be citizen's saviors. Police is called when no other workable help is available. It is really a powerful force to fight crime and help innocent law-abiding citizens by using their official authority as well as their technically enriched expertise. If on one side police is meant for fighting crime in the society, it is expected to always keep a balanced approach for both poor and rich. Before law, the police see every citizen with one eye. But the higher cadres in police, who can use their own mind to run the show, use undue liberty to use their own personal whims de-shaping police image by making a difference between and influential and an ordinary citizen. This attitude flows down to the last cadre of a constable taking a dangerous shape. This is one of the reasons that the police force is biased towards poor and under privileges ordinary citizens from the beginning.

If this principle comes to judiciary where the judges have started discriminating between rich powerful companies and a single individual employee and give undue favour to the powerful management will certainly be very dangerous in terms of social fabric and existence of democracy in any country. It is a general principle that those who are given authority have been expected to treat every citizen at par and feel more responsible to have a just approach.

Those who acquire authority for specific purpose by honest means, are always less dangerous than those who get it without much efforts. Judiciary is very effective instrument of our system. It preserves the rule of law. It has to be tough, nondiscriminatory, harsh with dreaded criminals; and gentle to law-abiding citizens. Filing fake case on innocent people is a practice by the seniors; otherwise, a junior person on the post of ASI cannot dare move to the court of law with a fake case. Higher ups through the concerned SHO remain to be a party in such cases. By the time, the accused is acquitted for his innocence; the erring police is to be left undone without a suit for damages by the acquitted innocent accused. Though such a suit for damages is possible but it is usually not filed separately to avoid more inconvenience. In case of losing a case by police, the risk is always lies with juniors. The senior officers are the secondary party but the entire music has to be faced by the juniors, who risked their reputation by following orders from seniors. Now, they have to be safer in future as consequential punishment will make such filing very dangerous for such obedient cops.

The First Information Report: FIR has become a 'Great Tamasha' in countries where the Parliament has not taken care to do any thing to make police accountable for not registering the offence. What to talk of reviewing and making rules against police inaction for leaving suffering citizens unattended and unprotected having acquired the sole discretion of police in many developing countries. Though such sole rights have been acquired by the police against Constitutional guarantee of Right to Justice, yet there is a need to do something in this direction. Peoplism supports sufferers to file a FIR through electronic media via fax, email and even through a registered A.D. post. In this system a complaint may be lodged at any police station as per convenience of the sufferer. The complaint lodging procedure will be simplified and liberal for the complainants. Reporting the crime by the police may be done by some identified social activists, registered NGOs or a third unconcerned party also, on behalf of the aggrieved party.

The attending process for a lodged complaint and converting that into a FIR, shall be made classified, involving more officers as a set procedure. It will not be the sole discretion of today's SHO. Senior officers will decide which complaint deserves filing a court case or which one can be sent to mediation Cell. All the complaints shall finally reach the II ACP or addl. ACP who is heading 'Information receiving system' (IRS) in his office. Information shall also be collected through e-mail also. The complaining party is at liberty to send the information to other effective agencies like the DCP, CP and Civitals parallelly for creating a witness.

The concerned police station, to which it should be taken up, the received information, shall be assessed according to its merits. There will be a list of categorical classification of types of complaints to decide which is a qualified case for a. 'Mediation Cell', b. small cause court or c. ad-hoc courts or c. court dealing in criminal cases or d. Regular civil court. Arrests will be made in the offences under which immediate arrest is mandatory.

Novel way to file a complaint is as under. Complaints may be filed through internet. E-mail addresses of all the police stations in a district and State will be available to the citizens in the form of a 'Information Booklet' issued by Ministry of Internal Security and Vigilance, available at a subsidized price in every police station. Website of all the State Police head quarters shall be made available to the citizens with complete hierarchy of police officers in this information-booklet. Specially designed Formats for filing a complaint shall be available on internet and in the booklet also. Sufferer in remote places can also send a SMS to the concerned and authorised NGO attached to the area police station. Details of registered NGOs with the police station fall under a police station shall also be available in this information booklet. It will be a mandatory duty of these NGOs to lodge a police complaint through their resources, i.e. mobile phones or email system or by a personal visit. Office bearers of registered NGOs may use e-mail service as an alternative to their personal visit to the concerned police station for the complainant, who is poor and without any resources.

Police stations in village areas shall be connected to District Police Station, where electronic system shall be essentially present to connect the police station with higher offices of the Commissionaire as a mandatory duty to maintain these devices. All the complaints shall go to the concerned officers in additional ACP's office. Parallel complaints, received to the police head quarters, shall also be directed to the concerned ACP's office for information. If the concerned officer finds merits in the case at the ACP Office, it will be sent back to the concerned police station to file a FIR or direct both the parties to 'Mediation Cell' at the ACP office or in the court premise.

Every District shall have 'Additional ACP', who will act as 'Mediation Officer' as well as Special Executive Magistrate. During mediation, law officer attached to the SEM office shall be accompanied by one mediation officer. On the contrary, the second regular ACP shall look after only administrative work of all the police stations under him and has nothing to do with the work of Additional ACP cum SEM.

It has been provided in Peoplism that no judicial officer (Judge) shall be having charge of more than one department and the cases of one kind only. The government shall allocate special exchequer for the competent and saturated capacity of judicial officers, number of courts, and fill all vacancies in all police stations providing enough of police infrastructure in the same way, it invests for the Defense forces, to achieve internal security and dignity of citizens preserved. Peoplism wants to provide shield to the citizens from outside invasion by strengthening its Defense system as well as protect citizens from the anti-forces inside our society by strengthening our police system and the Judiciary. Both Defense and internal Security shall be taken *at par* by Peoplists.

The Additional ACP/SEM/Mediating officer preferably, shall not be from police cadre. He shall be preferably a senior law expert having thorough knowledge of Law to act as the proposed law officer attached to the police to give his expert opinion before filing a case in the court of law. Such officers if have to be IPS there will be special class of recruits by the government to select law experts for such post is subject to Constitutional amendment.

In the present law, the police are empowered to arrest and put any person behind bars. If the police want, it can file a fake case on an innocent person to harass him to the extent of kneeling down to the demand of police itself or a demand of its paymasters and harass a person to the extent of committing suicide in the lock-up to settle some undisclosed score with the prey. The police often register criminal cases on a targeted person anticipating him to roam around courts for no less than ten years to come out of such fake case. It becomes more torturous when such cases are filed in a far-flung place in other State. It is unfortunate that for such case, the cop primarily does not have substantial evidences against the fabricated person. But the court procedures are so one-sided that for years together, he is forced to face hardship being an accused, even being innocent. He will be asked to stand up in the court at a distance in the category of criminals; he will have to be present in the court on all the dates in all circumstances. In case of his absence on one date, he may be arrested and produced before the magistrate through a warrant. If the court wants to favour the big tycoon on whose behalf the fake case is filed, it can harass a person to an un-imaginable extent. Suicide by such harassment is often in news. The court is empowered to cancel his bail and give him in police custody to face torture in police lock up and so on. It may be that he will come out of it, due to no evidence against him, but it may take ten or more years, is more than sufficient to pressurize him to give up before any demand of police or its paymasters.

Certain Sections in Indian Penal Code are so one sided that the trapped accused may not get bail in certain cases, especially if he is fabricated under a non-bailable offence. It depends on police how much revengeful it can afford to be, against a grafted person. Such absurd situation of law is not only outside the law but also illogical and ultimately pertaining to British Legacy. It is unfortunate that in a free nation where the police have become very unreliable still the courts take it granted to behave at the instance of police challan in ditto. Rather, there is a need to change the attitude and approach of courts to carefully look into the matter brought before it, in criminal cases. If there is no *prima facie* in the case and there are no substantial evidence filed with challan, the grafted person need to be acquitted on the first or second date, in spite of calling him to the court for few years to the stage of argument before charges are framed, which is in practice now. The fabricated person deserves to be acquitted as early as possible curtailing many stages of court proceedings and minimizing undesirable work load of the court by discouraging such frivolous filing and saving good citizens from protracted harassment.

The misfortune of the fabricated innocent may multiply making the situation serious, if the court is over-enthusiastic. He will have to face statement, cross examination of witness, etc. for years. So, there has to be some new parameters to decide the case at the time of framing charges and this stage must be treated as one of the most important stage in a criminal case. The police powers to bring any person in the dock need to be made more accountable if it comes to the court without mandatory material like substantial evidence and grounds of *prima facie*. During detention, the police are free to get any paper signed by the arrested person by putting him to unbearable torture. Custodial deaths are the evidence. The arrested person remains totally at the mercy of police and he may put to any humiliation like parading him/her even stripped off him/her as happened in famous Maya Tyagi case in eighty's in western UP at Meerut. If the prey is a woman, there is no question that her modesty will not be raged by the police in many ways. It is happening everyday in the police stations. FIR under certain non-bailable offences is so serious that on receiving a complaint, the arrest becomes mandatory. The suspected person is bound to be arrested. For example in Indian Penal Code, there are more than 35 per cent offences where the arrest is non-bailable. It needs a fresh look so shall be amended in Peoplism.

After taking a person in police custody for preliminary investigation, the police go to sleep after settling the accused in the lock-up. Police become busy in other affairs letting the detained person rot in jails for years, until the charges are framed. An innocent person, who had been put into lock-up or in a regular jail along with convicts, is forced to serve a term of punishment without being even tried and convicted by the court. For a progressive and civilized society, it is really a shame.

The atmosphere in the jail is so inaccessible that the under-trials are treated as at par with convicted criminals and are kept with convicts. Since the under trials are in transition, they become prone to everyone's wrath. It includes old convicts, security police and jail staff. All these parties treat under-trials to maximum humiliation and extorting all kinds of comforts from them. There is no system in the jail to discriminate and protect them from staunch convicts and all other convicts, who are in command inside the jail. No system had been evolved to give protection to the under-trials and so many a times they are seen committing suicide or found dead in mysterious circumstances. Thus, they are forced to serve a term without any court verdict on them.

If the cases are decided within shortest period, police atrocity at all stages and all places shall be minimised. The entire process of investigation shall be changed as mentioned above. The crowd of under-trials shall also be reducing considerably inside the jails. Time bound justice is one of the solutions to eradicate crime by authorities in jails and in lock-ups and protect citizens from cruel clutches of police.

Is it not horrifying to look at figures of under-trials? These are more than 2.4 millions. These accused have been practically throttled into congested-stinky jails, in the name of justice. If we take family members of these unfortunate under-trials by average five in each family, the figures comes to crores, who are parallelly made to suffer. However, there are provisions to sue the erring police, by the so acquitted innocent accused but no one does it as police can easily go more criminal, if it feels attacked. This is a common practice. Police, throughout world prefer to please rich business tycoons or sometimes to satisfy their own ego or to satisfy his superior to graft innocent people and torture them, wasting country's resources to fulfill their own interest. Time bound justice will put a bar on such misappropriation by police when such cases will be punished consequentially on manipulative cops against not ensuring innocent citizens a dignified and progressive life.

To our past experience, the police proved to be the best and easiest friends of criminal's plans of corrupt politicians. Out of numerous such cases, Jessica Lal's case is one concrete example of police connivance with criminals. Otherwise, police tolerates every disorder in society by going with habitual offenders exhibiting that to be a routine way of police working. Government-land grabbing, encroachment, illegal construction, illegal water connections, letting pet cattle and animals stray and loose on roads, capturing pavements to extend shop and vend the way one desires, etc. give good example of working of the area SHOs through their subordinates throughout the country. Despite of having knowledge of existing laws over such mal-practices; the police rather kept charging their fee, item wise to allow them to exist under their very nose. In spite of reporting the matter to the civic authorities the police allowed illegal construction on payment basis. No one dare punish such erring police in an immature democracy. It is verifiable of police records that despite of mushrooming illegal constructions and encroachment by residents even in authorised colonies, the police have ever made a complaint to the civic authorities to report such illegal construction and take action to clear the roads and foot paths for pedestrians. Rather, police prefer to be a party with offenders by charging their fee for every unlawful craving. Could there be any remedy to overcome such menace before the issue was taken up by the highest court? All those coming 'between the highest court and the encroacher' are punishable as other courts also could take action *suo motto* for such illegality in society. Peoplist shall bring everyone guilty on record and punish them accordingly. Illegal colonies on government land, encroachment of legal property, change of property-use, etc. are evidences of guilt of authorities in power that includes police also. Complaints to higher authorities against such manipulative negligence of erring cops by alert citizens normally fall on deaf ears. A police officer protecting its subordinate for a wrong done by him is a British legacy that is still continuing in his slave mind even today. Defending its own erring staff for its wrong on one side and snubbing the genuine complainant on the other also includes his harassment for making a complaint against a misconduct of a cop by filing a case of 'breach of peace' u/s 107-150 is nothing but persistence of British slavery in the minds of public servants.

Public Interest Litigation by RWAs shall be decided in a time bound manner. It is the foremost duty of the government to nip the lawlessness in the bud stage. Who else can be more genuine if a report is filed by a RWA? Peoplism will use all measures to nip the bud of crime to grow into a huge cactus by taking different measures other than 'Time Bound Justice'. The qualified and competent police officer shall know it well to prepare a sure-hit case for the court. From the time immemorial, since shrewd men in power, tried to cover up their own inefficiency and incompetence or tried to hide their own criminal conduct or act secretly at the back of their seniors, often do illegal things such as using force against innocent or against his own subordinates taking it granted that they will not retaliate. During dictatorship such unquestionable tendency is found to be at climax. For such people, their own interests are supreme and they never oblige the administration by doing criminal suppression of the real offenders. This suppression may have another face of a threat or a damage of the innocent citizens in order to terrorise them by unchallenged wielded powers to keep quiet. This terrorism from the authority may start from paper-war to the extent of murder or snatching a person's job or even killing him in the name of encounter.

There is another way to impose authority and create terror in the minds of subordinates by government officers including the police. Filing fake cases is a very successful technique. The police are using this technique since British times. Case once failing in the court of law has no accountability. A study reveals that such fake cases constitute more than 65 per cent cases of all the cases filed by the police. The judicial officer also knows that the case is bogus and the implanted person shall come out of it. But they prefer to go step by step as per provisions of criminal procedure code. It suits the police most. Passing through different stages of the procedure code is no less than a conviction. Therefore, it is against the basics of human rights. Out of police, courts and the accused, it is only the accused that has to fall a prey to prolonged harassments for these procedures. The manipulating erring cop who has filed a fake case remains comfortable throughout the years of litigation.

There is a great deal pending since long to amend the working of police. In practical, the police throughout these third world nations are not helping people. Rather, letting the situation go out of their control first by ignoring the sufferer's plight and encouraging the offenders and criminals, at their instance and take advantage of out-of-control situation from the sufferer. In a genuine crime incident, the police wait for a situation for extortion and exploitation of both the sides one by one. There is no need to quote any incident of such wonderful police; we have daily pasteboard of media full of bravery of police on innocent citizens. For establishing their credibility, they are killing innocent people in the name of terrorism and gangsters and issuing a press release painting that to encounter in self-defense was exposed in ACP, S.S. Rathee's case. It is a general observation that people for the first time come to know so-called terrorists and gangsters from police sources only, when citizens see few people dead of police bullets. They are normally unknown people. Had they been well known area terrorists or criminal gangsters, as the police claim, their photos and other identity must have been available with television and in the press beforehand. The question remains unsolved as to why people see them for the first time when they were killed by the police? Can it not be a fact that the police are killing innocent people for creating a good police record or to get out of turn promotion or departmental recognition? They are not killing Abu Salem, Daud Abraham, Charles Sobaraj and many other such dreaded people but such murdered persons are always small and unprotected people.

Today's police are stopping us to trust them as they are working for those who give them more than their salary. Personal gain inspires them more than the cause of society and protection of law. IPS officers are working under high pressures from their rankers and rarely dare go independent with their own convictions. So, this force has become almost an anti-force for the society and they are really good for nothing.

Death of Official Hooliganism

4

Stubborn officers will meet their fate within shortest time.

Another big problem before employed citizens is the high handedness of superiors in the name of rules, regulations, discipline, quorum and specific culture of the institution. Considering their position and actions unchallenged, they feel that subordinates are their slaves. They feel that all the rules are for subordinates and no law rules them. They are the law in themselves. Self-respecting subordinates easily become victim of their torment to the extent of losing their confirmed jobs or get attacked physically at their instance.

For example, the CEO of a leading newspaper warned the Union leader to go back to his folds who was pleading of taking a dismissed correspondent back to work. The CEO told that they have removed her. She may go to the court. They might see the matter, if she was reinstated by the court after fighting the case for ten or fifteen years. Though the option to seek court's intervention in such matters is always available before the sufferer but the party in command, uses courts delay as their weapon against an employee. The employers have started taking undue advantage of court procedures and court culture in delaying justice to the employees whom they do not want to continue in job, any more. There is no sunrise for the dismissed employee even if he/she wins the case in a legal fight. It shall be very relevant to quote a remark of a court here. The employee lost his job nearly 18 years back. He prayed the court to decide his case early. The court said "You are in the lowest court here, so, do not make a hurry because after this court gives its decision in favour of either of the two contesting parties, they will go into appeal and there after the case also may go to the Supreme Court. So, the matter does not finish here only". By saying so, the court itself proved to be an ineffective measure to seek justice through them. In such a situation then, what is the choice? There seem to be few options to deal with injustice. One is either to submit to the unethical desires of the management or change the employer or go away from the place of atrocity and start a fresh. Then where does the judiciary exist? Where is the independence we achieved in 1947 and where is the Constitution of this country?

Courts may thus, be badly failing to protect the various provisions of the Constitution to provide citizens a dignified life after 1951. The irony of the entire gamut is that during slavery there was no possibility to fight for citizen's rights and we were pre-decided what type of life is to be led. But now, the roses which were shown through the presence of Constitution proved artificial and citizens are strayed to waste their lives in court corridors. Otherwise, we are still slave of police, government officers and judiciary. Freedom is still a dream for have-nots and unprivileged citizens. Do we have to make a compromise like cowards with this situation or we can fight it out. Yes! We can fight it out to our advantage if we opt for limited democracy or limited liberty by adopting Peoplism. In Peoplism no one shall have just freehand to do anything or manipulate anyone.

In another good example, a dismissed employee was heard after 30 years when his case came on its turn after his retirement. Though he was reinstated paying him all his dues, but no one could pay him for the gross humiliation of the entire innocent family faced for these 30 years, due to the wrong decision of stubborn boss or a junior court. Perhaps, judiciary was aware of its helplessness, to return the lost 30 precious years to the children of this unfortunate person for the loss of their academic growth and a deserving career and still did not try to give anything to compensate his showdown without slapping the errant officers who was behind the cause of action. Ignoring the guilty is like pardoning the vindictive officer who generated cause of action or the lower court who kept the case pending for such a long period.

Bringing 'Right to Information' in force is really a remarkable work. Still, officers are boldly misguiding people provoking another fight to set the things right. Things against ills of politicians, erring police, unsatisfied judges, blockheaded bureaucrat are so confidently done that one has to exert hard to budge them by informing various effective agencies side by side. It is a journey to really an uncertain destination. One may be lost in the ocean of papers. But to unearth the truth, one has to sustain a long battle until success is achieved on the other hand, and consistently chasing the track to success on the other until success is achieved. Once you file a case against a corrupt official, you need to get justice in schedule time to become secured in your job or in your lifetime. But there is no point to go into such a litigation whose decisions become time-liberated for an unknown future.

In case of any excess, people now prefer to avoid police and also evade moving to the courts because they feel that both these agencies have gone far beyond their reach for delay and corruption within them. People's faith in courts will be reestablished only when the entire structure is reorganised afresh in changing circumstances. It is really advantageous that even in case of failure in one court you may go into appeal in the next court but it is not easy as another court case needs another life. The time consumed in repeated events of adjournments is tiresome and frustrating. Therefore, so many times people prefer to forgo their right to justice and accept what they get in the first stroke from the court. But 'Time Bound Justice' shall repose their confidence once again in judicial system by deciding case in shortest possible time giving enough space for appeal. Going into appeal, shall not be a serious matter any more. In present circumstances, in fighting a court case means putting the entire family to systematic harassment for many years. This is one reason that, the crime goes on rearing to its height. An illegal move or a crime by offenders takes no time to grow because it has nexus with official authorities and long rope from the judiciary, when a law abiding citizen is mostly alone and an instant victim. The trench between crime and punishment has been widened by criminals and offenders which the criminal may still cross by using the entire system as their tools but the victim remains rotting in the pit of justice may be, till he dies. Entire exercise becomes purely a paper exercise and life goes on steadily leaving behind everything good with the aftermath of injustice one faced few decades back.

In absence of any provision of consequential punishment, the officer who damaged you due to his fancy, remains unpunished and unchallenged even if he was proved a wrong doer in a court case. It is the rarest courage of a particular judge to pass orders of compensation to such victim and consequently impose penalty on the guilty officer. But no such provisions are available there in the present law.

Offenders are dare-devils as they are aligned and organized. On the contrary, individuals are easy bait for them. You cannot expect a life with self-respect as your lawful right. Everything is at the mercy of offenders and lastly that of police and the courts. Civil liberties and civil rights have yet to take a way in the lives of people in third world countries. People in power are uncrowned monarchs and autocracy is their way. Judiciary is far behind them. These high powered bureaucrats or business tycoons or mafias are over-busy and have no time to hear you, until you are a special person. You will have to suffer and bear, until you approach the last resort and wait for your turn to be heard which may be available only after ten to twenty years. It shall be again the mercy of 'My Lord' to give you relief or not. The court is helpless to return your lost years of humiliation as each of such loss cannot be compensated in terms of money only. But can any court return lost health, lost or dead body parts or killed family members due to insufficient means for proper treatment during these unfortunate years when the victim was waiting for justice. So, the courts are not giving justice, it only can give relief. Rests of the losses are yours that you can count as the cost of fighting for justice. That justice in third world democracies has really become a nightmare. It is possible only in developed countries where democracy is mature enough and justice is done in time.

In a country of hope, anti-forces prevail all around. Dominance of shallow and hollow way of life; lawlessness by few powerful people who have captured the society, violence by habitual criminals is being served to the law abiding citizens by the governments of these incompetent governing system in third world countries. Out of many fusty-musty reasons, one foremost reason is, letting the errant party Scot-free. Authorities taking advantage of statue entrusted upon them, needs to be caught by neck in a consequent manner. Defining of misconduct of statutory authorities is a must in this reference.

Each and every official position, big or small, shall be attached to defined duties, liabilities and a Code of Conduct. Such listing shall be done in all the departments for every position. Such demarcation and definitions do not exist now. Today, Head of the department works in a very conventional way; he repeats the same what had been practiced by his seniors. He works with his personal notions and hunches without minding some wrong attempts in the midway. There is no demarked and defined line of official working and official duties to minimise exploitation by seniors. Allegations like disobedience always remain in the pocket of the boss which he can use against any subordinate to teach him/her a lesson for not getting exploited by him/her. Escapist juniors always take such a situation to their advantage as they know how to remain in good books of the boss. So, the boss always becomes right and nothing is brought on record to define to limitise the authority of the boss. Such unfortunate situation has to go because it is very essential to make things transparent. Acquiring transparency in working is the first motto of Peoplism.

No More Court Crafts

5

White collared offenders will not be able to use court crafts to harass innocents any more.

Like open dreaded criminals, there is another category of criminals; the white collared criminals. They are educated, moneyed, well-connected and occupy a high place in society. Such influential persons can manage to use the various organs of system of governance, for their advantage. They themselves may be a part of some of the organs of the system or have clique with someone in commanding position. Politicians use these officers merely as their pawns in materializing their specified malicious desires. Officers in command see benefit in going with such influential people and solve their problems on priority for no valid reason. On the contrary, they never hesitate to pass orders on a layman that may fall into the category of 'technically wrong orders'.

Though, remedy to such orders is available in the form of 'appeal' in the next court but it all is procedural and time consuming. For such orders, obsessive attitude of courts is not reminiscent. So, one has to see the intention of the court to see such orders as inadvertent attempt or a deliberate exercise. However, there is yet no provision available in the law to treat such orders 'against the ethics of profession' and there is no thought to take the particular court into notice by the senior court for such conduct. The next court, even the highest last court is also incompetent to take action against such judicial officer who is passing technically wrong orders except transferring him. Peoplist has looked into such deliberate attempt to misuse of authority by certain judicial officer and will provide remedial measures to this effect by appointing a high powered Judicial Commission.

However, accountability of judicial officers shall be subject to this Commission to hear the complaints against the following misconduct of judicial officers working at different levels:

(i) misbehaviour/unexpected gesture or insulting attitude;

(ii) unpleasant language used inside court;

(iii) extra ordinary favour to either party apparent in passed orders or otherwise if it could be established;

(iv) extra ordinary delay by giving frequent adjournments on the plea of other party than the aggrieved party;

(v) not issuing certified copies within prescribed time limit;

(vi) not allowing inspection of file without delay;

(vii) not maintaining case-files as per prescribed rules;

(viii) not passing natural orders;

(ix) passing orders by ignoring facts and figures of the case based on presumptions and suppositions;

(x) not observing and maintaining given time framework;

(xi) not allowing proceedings stage-wise as prescribed;

(xii) irrelevant and poor quality of orders;

(xiii) technically wrong orders to benefit one party;

(xiv) forcing the litigant to argue in presence of 'written arguments' already submitted;

(xv) passing orders by ignoring existing law which the officer is supposed to know and

(xvi) over-looking citations from higher courts and not mentioning their contents in the order under Article-141 of the Constitution by ill intentions to illegally favour a particular party.

***Judicial Commission:** Country's highest administrative Commission to keep a check on judiciary creating accountability on judicial officers and lawyers for the wrong by them.*

The Commission will keep away from any complaints against the merits of the order passed by a court. For that, the provision of appeal shall remain intact. Penalties on the erring judges should not fall under any provision of Penal Code of the nation because the position and prestige of judicial officers has to be protected beyond immunity provided under Article-50 of the Constitution. Yet the nature of penalties may include only departmental action, to the extent of removal/dismissal and forced exit, subject to a Press-note as a mandatory part of penalty.

It has to be kept into serious consideration that until Quorum and dignity of the court is maintained and is upheld their status high, we cannot allow judiciary to work by using its authority fully and by free will to give just decision in the court room. Penalties imposed on guilty judicial officers have been prescribed in Judicial Code in Chapter 18th of Code of Conduct. A parallel code of conduct has also to be in existence in Peoplism for lawyers, against unethical professional conduct towards their clients and others. The severest penalty, to a practicing lawyer has been proposed as the cancellation of lawyer's right to practice. Such penalty will suffice to cripple him/her to continue as a lawyer. For this purpose the law degree may be stamped for as serious penalty to disable the same for further use in the same city or throughout the State barring him/her to practice as a free lawyer. He/she will, however, continue to be a member of Bar Association. All such penalties shall be open to provide sufficient opportunity to bring back the penalised lawyer to the mainstream once again by the Bar Association under the instruction of Judicial Commission. During enquiry, the delinquent officers shall be under direct control and protection of judicial Commission in place of the Bar Association. Depending upon the nature an offence committed under the Penal Code, the subjected judicial officer or practicing lawyers shall not be interfered by the Judicial Commission.

Judicial Promotion: Promoting a junior officer to senior post of Judges of higher court shall be affected through a specially constituted 'Promotion Committee' at the Directorate of High Court. The track record of each judicial officer shall be maintained by the Judicial Commission. At the first stance 'trial posting' shall be offered.

Country's highest Administrative Commission to keep a check on judiciary creating accountability on judicial officers and lawyers for the wrong by them. The Commission shall hear the complaints from aggrieved litigants and shall look after appointment of judges and their promotion through their track records before a regular promotion. Such posting can be affected on deputation posting in administrative position or Human Right courts.

The Judicial Commission shall recommend promotion of the judicial officer on 85 per cent on the basis of assessment of track record of the aspirant officer along with only 15 per cent recommendation from the Bar Association. The judges shall also prepare their own confidential report parallelly, on the basis of directions set by the Commission. Track record of all the judges by keeping all their decisions shall be maintained by the judge himself along with the fate of the challenged orders in the higher court of law. In case of vacating the orders of the lower court, the senior court shall send copy of orders passed by it in triplicate to (i) the judge whose orders are quashed, (ii) the promotion department, and (iii) the relevant Bar Association that has to impart 15 per cent of the total recommendation for promotion or demotion. The aspiring judicial officers writing their own CRs will submit their summary report of the track record of their performances along with supporting documents, to the promotion department when asked for.

The chief justice of high court shall head the Promotion Department along with any seven senior judges colleagues. The specially constituted DPC, once in a year, shall also have at least 5 members outside judiciary from eminent intellectual members of society including social activists from registered NGOs and journalists from national dailies only, without any politician.

Special exchequer shall be allocated for judicial system by appointing judges in all courts. No post shall remain unfilled by more than one month. The Promotion Department shall always be readily be available to submit the list of seniority and qualified judicial officers and the process of preparing promotion documents without any political interference which will be readily available to the promotion department. The confirm list shall be no secret and shall be open to Press two days before the announcement, to presume who is a better performer, who can be the next judge to the next court. The entire recommendation process shall be free from any political interference keeping them out of this activity by virtue of a new law in the Peoplists Constitution. The working of Departmental Promotion Committee (DPC) shall be highly confidential as the tenure of this Committee is short lived but everything will be transparent in the Promotion Department to public through Right to Information Act after an appointment or promotion is affected.

Ad hoc judges shall be appointed for small cause courts through a defined process. Senior lawyers, who are appointed as ad-hoc judges, shall be given priority for regular appointments as sitting judges in a parallel feedback to the promotion department and any lawyer, who had worked as a judge for small cause court for consequent two years, shall be recommendable by the DPC for promotion for the first appointment as a regular judicial officer. A Peoplist government shall take care of judicial system of the country as it constitutes the moral force of the society and ensures internal security and dignity of individual by getting justice in time. Strong and honest judiciary being the backbone of society is one of the most important components of a strong country. On the contrary, a failed or corrupt judiciary cannot give a peaceful and respectful life to its citizens. Since, judiciary is the last door to be knocked at for justice; it has to be more responsible and accountable for any wrong by it. Courts are bound to give justice and protection to the civil rights of citizens and defend their own dignity by taking contempt cases more expeditiously and carefully.

After facing a sequence of discouraging treatment by employer, administrative authorities, the police and judiciary cannot remain apathetic to the plight of the sufferer. The background of the sufferer has to be taken into consideration. Therefore, judiciary has to be quick and just to save society from humiliation and demoralisation. Courts must take every matter and every hearing as urgent because the litigant has approached it as a last resort after suffering the agony continuously for many years. Already harassed petitioner needs immediate relief like first-aid by passing interim orders to the deserving party, which is not happening now. Peoplism is committed to make interim relief to the sufferer an essential feature before starting a detailed trial and shall protect the dignity of both the parties equally. Petitioner-in-person shall be treated *at par* with the lawyers in Peoplism. He shall deserve every privilege *at par* with the lawyers in the entire court premise. Certified copies shall be made available to the PIP on priority basis and inspection of case-file shall become easier to the contesting petitioners-in-person.

There is much to do with various stages of legal proceedings in a criminal case. Lengthy and time consuming stages in court proceedings shall be clubbed to reduce lesser number of stages to make the entire proceedings simpler and quicker. The accused shall have every opportunity to place his version in written form, before the trial starts. Such statement of the accused shall be presented with challan by the police or directly by the accused in order to conclude the case within a scheduled period as proposed in Chapter 13th of the book.

In case, a person finds evidence of judge's connivance with the either of the parties or any other such act of unexpected conduct, it will be attended by Judicial Commission. For such an attempt, where a particular judicial officer acts feeling unchallenged, creating a situation before a suffering litigant to bear the torture of appeal a 'Code of Conducts' becomes necessary. On the more, till today no one knows the place where such reprehensive conduct of a judicial officer can be reported. So, there has to be a defined place for such a situation to be reported in a classified manner. Therefore, the demand for setting-up a 'Judicial Commission' is the need of the hour. The truth of supremacy of Constitution is undisputed and no one is above it. Judicial officers at all levels directly or indirectly come under the jurisdiction of Constitution. Any one who misuses constitutional authority, he/she is entrusted for, shall fall under special provision of Law along with the charge of showing disrespect to it.

For instance, in a high court case, a writ was admitted without passing any orders on either side and without giving interim relief. Admitting a writ means 'we saw merits in the case and with this interim relief the matter will be finally disposed of later.' In such case, interim relief becomes mandatory but it was done while admitting the writ. Otherwise, if there were no merits in the case, why it was admitted? The reasons are obvious. The court was not deciding the case while admitting it. The case, the court might have seen some merits in it. If there were no merits then why the case was kept pending for such a long period of few decades?

If the court hears such admitted case after a gap of 20 years and dismisses it without giving any relief to the litigant, it seems to be a deliberate attempt by the court to ruin the career of the litigant to appease rich respondents by taking heavy bribe at every stage in last 20 years. Otherwise, nothing else seems to be so logic than this explanation. In one case, the court was so determined to dismiss the writ after two decades that it refused to take submitted 52 paged 'written argument' into account. Not only this, the court had ignored to take five decided cases into consideration and did not mention them in dismissal order without caring for violation of Article-141 of the Constitution which imposes binding on lower court to honour the decisions of the apex court. This case remained full of technical flaws since beginning as the litigant-in-person was alone against a very rich NGO in Delhi. In court proceedings the petitioner was forced to wait for hearing losing his entire service period of 20 years and lastly he was refused any relief. So where is the justice?

The biggest question in this case is who is responsible for the wastage of 20 years of the litigant and what purpose has been served by admitting the case in 1989 except lapsing 20 years of the petitioner's service period by keeping him waiting to get his writ dismissed. Had the case been decided against the petitioner in 20 years back, he would have exercised his right to appeal in the apex court to decide the matter in the year 1989 itself. But now, near his retirement, any appeal would automatically be meaningless as the case of transfer will become infructuous due to his retirement in April 2008.

Since there are no rules about adjournments, the ruined petitioner fears to be lost in judicial obscurity. Time bound justice shall remove the provision of long-listing the cases by admitting them. It shall discourage to admit cases for future which is in practice now. If 'writ' had followed by its 'said reply' by the respondents followed by a rejoinder by the litigant, the case will be bound to be decided in continuation. This case too would have been decided on merits on the basis of mandatory documents were available with the court in the year 1989 itself. Such autocracy of courts has to be seen different from so-called judicial activism which is punishable in Peoplism.

The condition of smaller courts especially the Tribunals, are more erratic and autocratic. Till date, Tribunals have no rules of their own and these are not available on record. Though the tribunals are empowered to frame their own Rules as per the Acts under which the Tribunal works. It is on the line of as high court Rule or Supreme Court Rules. But it is painful that most of such small courts, do not frame any rules only in order to escape responsibility to do this extra job. In these tribunals, no receipt is given against a submitted document. The Tribunal has no convention to mention the events/statements and even the crux of arguments in the order-sheet, that takes place in the court room. If a document is filed on the desk or submitted in the court itself, it is not mentioned in the order sheet. The papers of the case-file are not stamped and properly numbered and there is always fear of pilferage of stake documents by the court staff which can be done without notice. Any complaint regarding such apprehension falls on deaf ears of administrative authorities. Then, the presiding officer of this tribunal takes it personal and ill. In addition, the presiding officers of these tribunals are free to adjourn all the cases listed for a particular day, if he/she is sitting in a meeting with her/his acquaintance or his/her boss or need to leave for home early. There are absolutely no rules and no one is hearing the complaints if these are filed with higher authorities like the Principal Secretary of Delhi Administration. Due to such ungovernable working, the rate of deciding the cases in Delhi school tribunal is only one per year. In two year's deputation, the acting judge (presiding officer), decided only two or three cases and moves to a higher position on promotion. Such tribunals are not serving any purpose to the dismissed teachers and this is used as a launch pad for judicial officers from lower courts to get promoted into a higher court from this back door.

It is unfortunate that presently, justice is not taken as the right of the litigants. Right to Justice is a trick. It is the sweet will of the judge only, if he/she can pass orders in time and give justice in a fair manner. Justice is not left as the right of the citizens but it has become the right of the judicial officers to impart it or dodge it. Time bound justice promises to remove all such disorders from the judicial system as it is already in the store of sad experiences with judiciary.

The court staff and the lawyers are aware of the fact that the cases will run for few years, so they become slow in their functioning and seek adjournments adding more time to the case. They are not bothered for early disposal of the cases and help to add any thing in the process of timely disposal of the cases from their own side. Everything is so routed to the convenience of office bearers. According to them, the litigants are visitors only but the relationship of staff of the court, lawyers and judicial officers occupies the minds of all these three factions in the court premises. They show least respect to the suffering litigants and try to take full advantage of his approaching them for justice. The lawyers always keep asking clients to pay tips and bribe to the court staff for every official work they are supposed to do officially to develop a rapport with them for a secured dealing in future. By lingering on litigation, they make themselves qualified to ask another round of fee from the suffering client. Time bound justice shall scrap such possibility by timely disposal of the cases. If the court staff and the lawyers are in the know that the case is going to conclude in next two months, they will all work with best of their ability, efforts and technical expertise to win the case in spite of inventing new ways to extort comforts from the existing clients.

Asking adjournments on one or the other pretext by the respondent lawyer is a usual practice in the courts because he wants to harass the justice seeker. Though, there is a provision of fine/compensation to the other party, in case one party seeks adjournment but courts take it easy and for petty things grant adjournment without imposing any fine/compensation to be paid by the requesting party. In Time bound justice there are strict defined rules for adjournments whose number is already decided as per nature of the case given in II schedule in 13th Chapter.

It is aspired that by following these schedules, the working will become more transparent and faster. The judicial officers will be strictly asking people to go according to the plans to avoid dismissal of cases or *ex parte* decisions. Lawyers cannot afford to use delaying tactics and court clerks will be only busy in their clerical work and shall not have time to manipulate in any way. Internet based availability of details of the case (downloading documents from a case on net, that includes, application, reply, adjournment (NDH-next date of hearing), annexures, copy of order and other such required documents), will minimise corruption in courts by the ministerial staff. This all is not difficult to acquire. If we commit to create a better nation, we can do it. Such a gift of a safe, secured, merit-respecting, accountable system of governance shall be the best gift to our kids if we can come out of our shells to create a country of pride by taking up issues of importance publicly, than to give them unaccounted money, buildings or other materialistic perishable gifts. Getting patronised by such influences, in prevailing conditions that develop due to imperfect and mal-functioning of different organs of the administration, few judicial officers also take it granted to use their unlimited discretion the way they can. Since there are no guidelines on the question of using discretion, lower courts seldom do not hesitate to act autocratically and of course illegally. It is unfortunate that in absence of accountability for passing technically wrong orders, the question of unlimited discretion become more damaging to the litigants. In on case, a civil judge in a trial court of north district, vacated stay without justifying, why it is being done. While logical grounds were on record to grant that stay. It should be a mandatory requirement of an order passed by a court to justify the verdict and decisions taken. Order passed without justification stand to be autocratic and unconstitutional and against the basic guideline of passing orders by a judicial officer.

If on one side, the politicians are busy in drafting and passing resolution for increasing their salaries and perks like the government employees, they do not even think of such lapses in the working of judiciary on the other side. It is condemnable because in a poor country, the social commitments are being converted into paid services on the pocket of the common citizen to which the politicians promised to serve. Making social work payable in terms of salary is corrupting the social work itself. Getting a cut from the limited public resources of a poor country for the social service has no convincing and acceptable logic at all. In a country, where more than 60 per cent people are living below poverty line (the standard of life below which basic needs like food, cloth and secured shelter are not available) such siphoning of public funds by the elected politicians is really betrayal to people's faith. Yester year's unpaid politicians who fought for freedom without asking a salary from public funds were far better and committed to the cause of nation than the politicians we have today. Gone are those days when politicians used to take one rupee as a token money and used to work more honestly with minimum paraphernalia in order to help the poor masses of a poor nation. Morality was valuable asset for then population. In those times also, the political families of those politicians used to grow to touch heights in their own fields. Leaders used to be honest to their dependents and the country as well. That is why they used to be better citizens than the present politicians are now. These politicians have left their names registered in our minds for ever and they were the real creators. On the other hand, most of today's politicians have made politics a profession, career and hesitate to take social work as a passion for the cause of society. So, by sharing public money form the treasury which is in their control now, today's politicians preferred to transfer public money in the name along with exorbitant perks against we trusted them to take care of it.

By the worst efforts to dismantle political system of the country, today's politics fails to shape society against media hazards. Rather, they encourage fashion shows and depend on film actors to fetch votes. Since they lack merits in themselves, they use cheap tactics to attract crowd. Politics is a larger shape of social commitment to localsied-society which has always to reach people as unpaid voluntary service. Commercialising the social commitments is nasty and not recommendable in any manner. Politics without ethics, issues, commitment and ideology has not to be the way of political existence today. If we erode basic ethics from our character or our way of working, it will change the entire complexion of the political scene in the political arena leading to the final collapse. Such a political pandemonium shall forfeit the basic purpose of being in politics. This is a big reason that politicians always remain threatened and feel unsecured even within their own party. Commitment and patriotism have been replaced by imbalance in political uncertainty that has now become a part of political character, due total loss of ethics and issues. Politicians even by acquiring prime position in the hierarchy are more worried for their retention than to think of bringing effective laws and drastic changes in the rotten British designed system. Maximum time and energy is lost in sustaining a party position and no time is left to do true service to the nation. The concept of being purity in public life in Peoplism is very potential where no representative shall take any salary from the public exchequer. However, the office bearer who gives full hours to their social work or political activities for the government as minister and active member of a party at the cost of their means of earning shall be compensated accordingly and no blanket payment shall be available to those who do not need it at all. Such honorarium shall vary from person to person after scrutinising the justification.

It seems that perhaps the process of updating judicial systems even has not drawn the attention of our politicians, who can play a vital role to do some thing about it, yet. Politicians have never been sincere to ask for simplification of court procedures and to make processing faster. Those who are effective to frame rules have no such preferences on their agenda. One of the big reasons to such apathy is the terror of courts. Word 'terror' is being used here because even the press wants to leave things untouched if they hear the name of court involvement in anything. This is true that no one has to interfere the proceedings of law and there is no need to touch it also, for the reason of getting it influenced by outer agency. But the issues raised here is not to interfere the court proceedings in any way but to make the entire working of judicial system more purposeful and it does not pertains to any kind of contempt or interfering the work of the courts.

Debating over the ills of our system is a national service and it is never aimed at the contempt of the prestige of judiciary. Anything untrue, playful, manipulative, alleging, aggressive, disparaging may be contemptuous but bringing facts from records before countrymen for asking suggestion from them to improve the system of governing the society, is never aimed at any kind of contempt. The media should get mature enough to own its responsibility and must come forward to work not only for remunerations but for a positive attitude to improve the working of our present judiciary which is the concern of every citizen. Through this book, we have ever been most respectful to the judiciary and repeatedly have pleaded to treat courts to be the highest institution among all other institutions of human resources. Nothing had been expressed to demean judiciary and its status in our society. Asking for a quicker and judicious system in the country is to awake the conscious of politicians who are competent to amend law on it. If people are suffering due the delay in courts, it is a serious matter and it has to be redressed with all humility and respect to the courts. While doing so, untrue and superfluous statements have not been put forward to replicate a situation always in the right perspective.

To escape responsibility to fill all the vacancies of judicial officers throughout the country is no way to maintain respect to the courts. We have to allocate special exchequer to meet out all necessary requirements of courts and its infrastructure, and for this, a public opinion has to be created. This book is a sincere effort in this direction and all must join this noble mass movement.

Coming back to judicial reforms, dire need to improve justice delivery system, has to be taken up on first priority, because courts are the icons of society and its conduct has direct impact on the society. If people do not get justice in time by the courts, where else the can ask for justice? Ran down of police support and half hearted bureaucratic cooperation against crime and lawlessness, people cannot be left to suffer for ever to their fate. Justice not in time, becomes obsolete and outdated by loosing its meaning in the changed circumstances. If the last door of courts is sealed with unnecessary complicated procedures, people shall be forced to make their own way to sustain their survival and this will be the real threat to the continuation of judiciary in such a frustrated nation.

Rules and procedures are framed to make working systematic and scientific to give quick justice to people. Procedures cannot be more important than justice. People need justice and do not want to be caught up by unnecessary and cumbersome procedures that usually hinder the journey for justice to make it more difficult and long awaited.

Directions from the apex court to up date judiciary was not attended to by the government. Evading issues is no solution. We all the judicial officers and common citizens need solution now and we have to take up issues raised here in the very interest of justice. The negative and distracted attitude of politician is so apparent from their lukewarm response to many good suggestions from Center needs to be changed now.

Appeal Needs Another Birth

6

By getting the case decided within a scheduled period, one can avail right to appeal than to die by not having time left for an appeal.

In such a situation when imparting justice becomes the last priority, the litigant is lucky if he gets justice in his lifetime. Lifetime means time in life when one has an active life. It is a common scene in the court premises to see octagerians roving from pillar to post. You might have seen very old people managing with a walking stick with great efforts in court corridors in search of justice. Those whose cases are dismissed for none of their fault but the fault of their lawyer, their plight is pitiable. Provision to fight against high handedness of appointed lawyer has been introduced in Consumer Act recently. But how many can afford such ramification of fight from an already going on fight to get justice? It would have been better if the penalty on a defaulting lawyer would have been slapped by the same court where the errant lawyer filed the first power of attorney and did not attend the court on successive dates. Justice not reaching in time and after its purpose is forfeited, has no sense and meaning.

There was a time when cases related with property disputes used to linger on for fifty or hundred years. But that time also when the judiciary was not so packed with workload, no body has ever thought that such a delay was due to the negative judicial attitude that time also. Today too, no one yet bothers to look into such exceptional feature of justice delivery system. However, no classification was yet done to prepare a priority list by Parliamentarians or Ministry of Law in last 60 years to speed up certain nature of court cases. Out of all PILs, service matters, detention in criminal cases have to be arranged in succession to dispose off them in a faster manner. Such a situation where everything is badly jumbled seems to be highly muddled to our liberty, dignity and right to justice. It is really a surprise that no effective person has ever come forward to affect quicker justice. In such circumstances, judges are also of view to ever-take long admitted cases more attentively. They still do not think that it is necessary to decide the cases in shortest time period to save the entire society from humiliation.

In a high court case, in a service matter, a double bench passed orders defining the main issue of the writ as 'academic' means 'only paperwork'. The petitioner waited for many years to get a particular issue decided through this admitted writ. But the court declared that the main issue of the writ has become time barred bygone issue due to long pendency of the case. It is interesting that the issue declared as academic was made academic for long pendency of twenty years by the same court. The court did not own any responsibility to spoil the case completely by keeping it pending and thereafter has no hesitation to declare the case academic losing all morality for the ruin of the career of an innocent litigant. Such ruling was held in circumstances when the petitioner is about to retire. In this case, the services of the petitioner were terminated during pendency of the case but the court held that the case of termination was to be decided first while the case of transfer was filed three years before. The court ignored the truth that if the transfer was held wrong, the termination would have automatically become out of context. But it was not done in this case. The judges dismissed the writ saying it academic, closing the chapters at their end, doing a vulgar injustice to the waiting litigant.

Time bound justice will increase efficiency of courts as well as encourage healthy litigation for common cause as these will be decided in a scheduled time period. Appeals shall be disposed off within a scheduled period and litigants shall have space to fight out atrocities within his life time. Thus, rule of law will be better established in society. Lawful citizens can live with their heads up as they can spare time to raise issue of common interest in other courts.

It is really appreciable that we have been provided opportunities to seek information from any government officer under RTI (Right to Information). Citizens can file PIL for common interest in the same context taking the 'received reply' as the first evidence. To tread such a venture is possible only when his own life is free from any other litigation and he has no pending case on his head. Fake cases on innocent citizens shall be disposed of carefully, before framing charges stage, within a stipulated period as per schedules given in 13th Chapter.

Time bound justice shall provide people dignified lives as law abiding citizens can afford to lead a constrain-free life. Also, finding crime, lawlessness and highhandedness failing in the court of law within shortest time, the law and truth will prevail in the society. On the other hand, crime will have a short life and all the civil rights of creative citizens can breathe a respectable life.

White collared offenders within the machinery shall be discouraged as they will meet their true end within no time and their dreams to drag their subordinate in a fake case will be shattered. These days, high handedness of seniors, ultimately take a shape of legal harassment of subordinates if he does not submit. Illegal orders by the boss are passed against him or he is trapped in certain court case in connivance with police. All such manipulations shall meet their true end and innocent accused shall have many opportunities and ample time to teach a lesson to the erring cops and erring seniors. This will also rectify domineering attitude of police on the innocent citizens bringing more humane consideration in their working. Time bound justice, thus, shall help to bring positive change in the attitude of police and senior officers due to early decisions. Consequential punishment for a deliberate wrong will improve standard of services by the government agencies. Time bound justice, in fact, will act as a double-edged sword that will always be out of its cover-case to acquit the innocent and impose consequential punishment on the erroneous achiever.

There is always a set psychology of every profession. A teacher shall behave like a teacher in England or in Congo; a cop shall behave like a cop in America or in Jamaica; a taxi driver will behave in the same manner in India and in Russia; a Lawyer will behave like a lawyer in Ukraine and in Japan and so on so forth. There may be a little difference of language, priority, attitude and hospitality, hostility, etc. but the psychology of profession shall always be almost the same. So, it may be reasonably presumed that conduct of judicial officers shall be almost the same throughout the world. For such reason, Time bound justice will not be the demand of third world developing nations only but the need of all the nations. If it has certain reasons to come to use, it will change the world establishing human rights and natural justice into the lives of victims of justice delivery system. Moreover, negative attitude of politicians, cops, government officials and even that of judicial officers at all levels, in any country shall get discouraged after 'Time Bound Justice' comes into force.

Affecting Quick Redressal 7

The pleasure of relief in due time is beyond description.

For bringing positive changes in any place, we need to have positive thinking. It needs time. In Third World democracy, most of the politicians waste most of their time in self maintenance and utilize most of their time and energy in saving their alliance government or destabilize the opposition. There is no Constitutional provision for periodical up-dating of national policies, programme and archaic laws. Neither, it has ever been a subject for a comfortable political debate. Many projects and programmes approved by the government are left in the mid, due to political instability. With huge investment of public money, the on-going projects often do not meet their dead-line and left hanging in lurch of political discord. Therefore, the need of the hour is that the opposition parties, beyond government, have to work as watch-dog insisting upon the ruling party to take initiative to completing already ongoing development programmes and projects of national importance than to abandon them when come to power.

The process of bringing out reports of several appointed commissions with a view to get it implemented in a time bound manner remains hidden. All the stages of completing the enquiry and investigation; placing the report in the Parliament within a defined period; debate and final acceptance must be attached to time bound implementation of recommendations. There is no point to keep these reports in a cold bag. All these stages must be formulated as a part of national policy beyond political turmoil in the country.

In Peoplism, no judicial officer will wait for his powers to act as judge after appointment. Any person appointed as a judicial officer/presiding officer of some tribunal shall possess powers as inherent. It usually happens in case where a bureaucrat is sent on deputation to certain legal department (or *vice versa*) where he/she is asked to preside over as a judge. Such a problem shall be over when one to one formula is implemented and additional charge to any judicial officer can be given only in rare cases that too by taking his/her consent only. Approval of reports of certain appointed Commission by the State head or by the Parliament shall go to bureaucratic blocks in relevant Ministries for giving it a shape of a Bill to develop its contents. The bill will be passed and be added to the existing Law.

There shall be no attempt by the legislation to pass any kind of Bill on themselves as "no one can be judge for his own cause". It is like wearing a mask of judge by the police to decide its doings to be right. Any advantage to the members of Legislation at State level or at the Centre level shall be passed by a specially constituted Commission that will decide the liabilities, salaries, perks, privileges, duties and even penalties for the members of such houses of representatives. Such Commission shall comprise of retired top bureaucrats, judges and senior members of all political parties inside and outside the government. All the members of such Commission will have equal status in a manner as the members of 'Jury' have. Such Commission shall be presided over by a person of first level such as former President, former Prime Minister, former General of Army, former Chief Election Commissioner, former speaker of Lok Sabha, former Chief Justice plus ten sitting members from Parliament representing different parties.

The legislatives shall be persuaded to pass a Bill to fill all the 40,000 vacancies of judicial officers in existing courts. Up-to-date judiciary will be aimed at imparting quick justice to the people. Expenditure from luxury of bureaucrats and politicians shall be curtailed enormously and the saved money shall be spent to improve judiciary, shall be the very first priority of Peoplists.

Today, the number of courts is not rational to the increasing population and increasing number of filed cases. No one in political arena has bothered yet to do evolve such a formula so that up-gradation of judicial ratio from time to time could be done. Peoplism shall prepare a comprehensive programme to evolve a formula of ratio among court-population and cases being filed. The situation shall be maintained updated by investing required amount of funds on first priority. If our judiciary is improved up-to-date reasonably, corruption from police, bureaucracy and even politics will go by itself. So, up-dating judiciary has to be the foremost agenda for Peoplists. These days our thrust on economic growth to come at par with developed nations is our first agenda. But to our consideration making few people rich and counting them world's richest persons cannot give basic needs of life to poor villager who is in horrifying shape now. If for instance, we start belonging to a rich nation tomorrow, this richness will be proved futile, if we fail to give freedom to our people from police terror and judicial negligence. No one can have dignified and respected life without justice in courts in time. Life without dignity is not only slavery but a curse. We have already experienced such life for many hundred years. So, to have a purposeful, effective and direct law we need to have a caring judiciary first. Then only citizens can claim to have secured, safe, creative and ordered life. And it is possible because it is only judiciary that is capable enough to take care of terror police and corrupt bureaucracy.

There are number of departments and portfolios in government, which work for more than one discipline. For example, Law secretary of Delhi Administration holds at least three portfolios together. He/she has to work as presiding officer in Delhi School Tribunal; as a judge in Motor Vehicle accident claim court and as the Law Secretary of Delhi Administration side by side. Such a situation prevails in other trial courts also. Some of the judicial officers are bound to act as master of all and jack of none. He/she cannot make justice to the work of any of these three departments, especially when he/she is appointed on deputation for a short period of two years only. This practice does not only over-load a single person but makes him/her half-hearted to take up any of these departments seriously. In any case, Peoplism shall not afford to over-load any judicial officer by more than one portfolio. It is very important and decided.

The work of a judicial officer is of intellectual nature. He/she is expected to read the files before coming to the court at 10.30 am. Is it practical for a person to go through 100 case files in the morning and keep their contents in mind which are every time altogether different from each other? So what comes to practice? The judge prefers adjournments even for small reasons. He has no time to go through the law books in library and study the citation quoted in different cases. But he/she has to totally depend on what situation arises in the court. He even does not bother to go back in the file to see previous orders and depends on the last orders on the order sheet and proceeds.

Everyone might have seen such behaviour of the judicial officers in everyday courts. Beyond this genuine situation before the judicial officer, there are personal constrains also. These include family problems, social obligations, departmental instructions and sometimes pressure from seniors. It is really side-splitting that out of such watertight situation certain judicial officers make money by using unfair means taking advantage of confusing chaos in the court proceedings. Otherwise, for a sincere judge, there is no space left to go that way due to over-packed schedule. Therefore, it is the foremost duty of countrymen to give space to judicial officers by reducing their work load by systemizing their working capability. They also need to be treated with respect and all dignity with many privileges. It needs deep thought and consideration from the politicians, at first. Those who speak against today's courts and blameworthy conduct of certain judicial officers, must think with cool mind whether we are doing justice with this specific rank of experts, if we expect them to do justice?

Anomaly and mismanagement is a feature of government departments due to undefined norms and unlimited discretion to use available resources. Despite of certain official guidelines and cross-checks by monitoring agencies, mishandling of finances is rampant in government making them either penniless in the mid of financial year or loaded with unutilised funds after the full financial year is over. A large number of politicians fail to streamline their schedules to use public funds at their disposal. What can be more ridiculous bankruptcy of common-sense be there than not to know the needs of their own constituency for which the funds are put at their disposal. Ministry of Planning once releasing the funds has no provision to keep a check on how the money is being used. There have to be specially constituted monitoring committees in collaboration of 'People's Forums' and relevant RWAs to keep a vigil on the utilisation of these funds in right direction or not. In case of improper use of funds, there have to be clear cut policy to release funds to a particular politician will depend on his conduct of the previous year, in the matter. Specially designed **'Coordination Committees'** shall extend their support to prepare programme in such a manner to make judicious use of available funds.

Proper management of money at the central pool needs to be done to spare money for important works such as updating judiciary.

The cases will be allocated to the officers not by their number only but by counting the number of issues in the cases to rationally distribute the work among all colleague officers, through a set policy. Peoplism shall also take care of the convenience and dignity of the judges to give them enough space according to their status and cadre and all shall not be treated with the same yardstick while giving work to them. It has not to be the sweet will of the allocation officer to distribute the work among judicial officers under a define policy open to all.

In Peoplism, honest Judges having clean record of their accomplishments (landmark decisions), shall have extra ordinary

---

Coordination Committees: *A body to look into allocation, disbursement and utilisation of public fund to various projects for general good of people. Its composition shall be decided as per requirement. Comprising with scheduled non-political members from the actual users of a policy in the society, taken from 'People's Forum'.*

privileges and honour from the government in public for their good service to the nation. May be highest civilian awards conferred on really good judges. Some of the special privileges will be attached to these awards. On the contrary, the judicial commission shall be very administrative in handling the complaints against misconduct of really not good guys.

The first priority of new system will be given to dispose of pending criminal cases on 2.4 million under-trials languishing in different jails. Special commission shall be set up to deal with these cases in stages to bring judicial system on track. Special Courts will be set up to speedy disposal of long pending cases of criminal nature as well as all the pending service matters for more than 18 months.

If on one hand, clear-cut policies shall be set up for 2.4 million under-trials speedy disposal of their cases will be affected by conducting courts inside the jail premises itself. Over staying under-trials who have already served more term than their 'would be sentence', shall be released immediately without any trial. Those under-trials who are in jail because they failed to furnish any guarantor for their bail shall be considered sympathetically and their trial shall proceed in fast track courts. Till their cases are decided, they will never be kept with convicts and shall not be mal-treated in jail. There has to be different manual for under-trials, making them more secured and attended, as they may not be proved guilty tomorrow. Under-trial has to be different from convicts by the attitude of jail authorities. If on one hand, rate of filing will be brought down by discouraging fake litigation, by using measures like consequential punishments; the judicial system shall be better equipped to dispose of cases speedily.

Non-Chaotic Cup-board

8

Cases will not pile up in the courts if a zero transaction rate is worked out and maintained.

In last five years (2002 to 2007), the gap of adjournment dates has increased from two months to five months. Reason being is the increased rate of filing and slow rate of disposal. In demographic language, increased birth rate and fall in death rate. Such a trend is bound to create congestion. The ultimate result is collapse. In between congestion and collapse, the concept of Darwinism comes into being. It teaches us of struggle for existence, survival of the fittest, natural selection, adaptation and emergence of new species. But in this case, the judiciary has adapted a novel method against natural justice (selection) to dismiss a number of cases unheard amass, which has been done in the month of January 2005 by High Court in Delhi.

The court has done justice to itself by doing injustice to the waiting litigants, whose cases were admitted many years back in 80s. One of such cases bearing CWP No. 2447/88 is a living example of this unlawful and unethical act. Such a conduct by a senior court is unexpected and is no less than an offence on innocent litigant who were fighting their cases without a lawyer in-person and was waiting for his case to be heard for two decades.

Beyond the truth of judicial officers to be special human beings, they have been chosen to accomplish specific work to deliver justice to the litigants. Against this service, these selected people are paid remuneration along with many privileges and facilities and gracefully placed in the highest place in society. So, they are most respected people in society. They have been put out of the arena of government servants not because they are not, but for the reason, to give them independence from any bureaucratic or political pressure and make decisions freely and independently. Though the Constitution had been improvised them not to be treated as government servants, still the salary and perks they are offered every month are from public funds and there are no discriminate funds in the treasury for them to pay them their monthly salary. They are a part and parcel of our society. But we love to give them a godly place and want to see them in the guise of almighty God. We too expect the judicial officers to see themselves as almighty person wielded with superpower of God, while sitting on the dais to deicide disputes among us. Courts are essential proud part of our society. We feel very bad when we are told that there is strike in the courts by lawyers and the lawyers have attacked judges or broke their chambers and hit the closed doors of courtrooms with shoes which was shut for a while seeing rowdy crowd of lawyers shouting slogans in rage coming towards the chamber, flooding towards courtrooms; or we read in newspaper that two high court judges manhandled each other like bad school boys. We really get hurt by the news that certain judge has been arrested on corruption charges. Our faith in judiciary shakes up by such information and we start feeling the necessity of a code of conduct for judicial officers inside and outside the court. We feel so hurt by such information as if our guardians are lost. Therefore, there seems to be a need to have a code of conduct for judicial officers and the lawyers to preserve their reputation from their own misconduct. It is unthinkable of such unfortunate and painful situation, when these highest placed people are bound to get instructions from us to have doe's and don'ts. But for such reasons, there is all around hue and cry about accountability of judiciary also. This seems to be need of the hour and we must accept to go ahead for this.

Out of many, one of the sad experiences in courts, where the court deliberately deprived of the suffering petitioner-in-person his due justice is worth mentioning here. He was kept waiting for the whole day in the courtroom by giving three pass-over and was finally told at 4 pm that he had forgotten to deposit process-fee. The petitioner was sticked to the courtroom having an apprehension whether his name may be called any time. If he leaves the courtroom for natural calls for a short while and his name is called, the case would have met any fate in his absence. Such a shabby conduct on the part of judicial officer created doubt on the integrity of judicial officer without any reasons as the judge had taken his authority unchallenged and had become very personal to please the other party. Such a callous conduct has to be restrained by virtue of declaring certain open rules and regulations for judicial officers.

In this context, it shall be justified by coming forward with few more examples of autocratic conduct of courts. Finality of the courts is many times not challengeable. To prove themselves a final authority beyond merits of the case they at times do not hesitate to satisfy their personal ego in the name of court procedures. A petitioner-in-person is the worst victim of high handedness of such courts because the courts finds him alone and unsupported by the Bar Association. So, he is most unsafe. Presently, there is no control over such upsetting conduct of the judicial officers as there is no place to file a complaint against such a conduct. In order to justify the above views, few parallel instances are here:

1. In the year 1991, stay orders were passed against Delhi Police, for continuing of nude cabarets running without proper permission by saying that 'people go to these shows of their own.' So, running such shows even without proper license remained for the court. This stay took nine years to be vacated by the senior court. The said judge who gave such socially condemnable stay, later, rose to the status of chief justice in the apex court.

2. In the year 1989, a Double Bench in higher court passed technically wrong orders by issuing Rule DB admitting a writ without passing any interim orders on either party. The case appeared in the court after 18 years and was dismissed on frivolous grounds because the case was being fought by the

litigant himself and there was no fear of protest by Bar Association for mishandling the case by the court. The first judge of this Double Bench happened to be the first lady judge who later rose to the status of Chief Justice of two High Courts.

3. In the year 2005, in another case No. 81/03 in a north district trial court, one of the civil judges vacated stay when he was requested to give decision in little faster pace of time by old-ailing senior-citizens. The preceding civil judge dismissed two consequent contempt applications also ignoring photographic evidence of contempt. Not only that the civil judge got so annoyed by the above prayer that he invited application from opposite party u/s 340 Cr.P.C. (perjury) and trying to trap the appellant RWA to teach the in-person president of the registered RWA a lesson. The case is pending and the very civil judge as a routine has rose to the next rank of Metropolitan Magistrate now.

4. In the year 2005, a lady presiding officer in Delhi School Tribunal did not allow file inspection, refused to give certified copy of certain documents, returned a draft of Rs. 500/- as a fee of certified copies required, for five months, misguiding the suffering litigant saying that the office of Law Secretary is not covered under RTI.

5. In the same above case the same presiding officer did not entertain a written complaint against the court clerk of the Tribunal, who removed stake documents from the case-file to the advantage of respondents. The presiding officer repeated entire hearing thrice to lapse a period of two years and still evaded passing any orders, even after announcing a 'date for orders'. She got annoyed with the litigant who requested her not to allow any more adjournments asked by the respondents again and again. The 17 years old case of ex-parte termination is still pending since 1991. This presiding officer is now one of the judges in Delhi High Court.

6. In the year 1995, presiding officer in Distt. Consumer Forum at Kashmere Gate dismissed a case on the grounds of maintainability after four years of its filing and allowing at least twenty adjournments.

7. In the year 2005, a PIL pleading 'unconditional release of over-staying under trials in Indian Jails' and 'to appoint a commission to study the factors that are delaying justice to the countrymen and the question of absence of Mass Legal Education Programme by the government for the last 60 years, was dismissed.

8. In the year 1991, another Double Bench did not pass any orders on respondents to issue experience certificates to the petitioner after 18 years of his regular job and dismissed his three applications one by one by single word 'Dismissed' without justifying, why these certificates cannot be given to the petitioner.

9. In the year 2005, on 2nd January, another Double Bench comprising then officiating chief justice dismissed a large number of old admitted pending cases in default, without notifying the litigants after a gap of two decades of pending these admitted cases. One admitted writ was dismissed after the maturity of 18 years. This judge is now the Chief Justices in a Union territory of North India.

10. In the year 2006, a newly constituted Double Bench ignored 52 paged written arguments with 14 citations (five from the apex court) telling the litigant that he is not going to read 320 pages of the file and the petitioner must tell the case in nut shell orally (in presence of written arguments) to confuse the litigant for dismissing an eighteen years old pending case in a hurry, to get rid of this old case.

11. In the year 2007, recently Justice B.J. Sethi and Justice PB Majumdar of Gujarat High Court beat up each other like school boys and the news was highlighted in the press.

In this way, we can have numerous other instances of high handedness of judicial officers at all stages because there is no accountability of judicial wrong by the officers and they use unlimited discretion for passing orders as well as to satisfy their personal ego. The ultimate sufferer is the litigant. If innocent sufferers are invited to tell horrifying stories of harassment by the courts, more revealing incidents will come to the fore.

Telling truth is no 'Contempt of Court'. The courts are for meant of bringing the truth out.

Peoplism has studied the situation with many details when and how certain judicial officers have been misusing unchallenged discretion. Therefore, in such an untidy situation the need of a 'Judicial Code of Conduct' for lawyers as well as judicial officers at all levels has become necessary. It is very unfortunate that the politicians feel more threatened for their own existence and stability in public life due to political instability than ordinary unprotected citizens. Most of their time and energy is wasted in maintaining themselves. To look into people's problems is a remote priority for them. For such reasons, they have no time and intention to look into such serious problem of using personal hunch by judicial officers while making decisions on personal priorities than on the merits of the case. They cannot afford to reason why this way of working is getting more and more popular day after day in the name of unlimited discretion?

Beyond unlimited liberty to use free discretion without any guidelines to pass judicious order in courts, the judicial officers are suffering from government's negligence of different nature. Irrational and unorganized disbursement of work to the courts is one of the negative factors. In trial courts, a magistrate is supposed to handle 60 and some times 100 cases a day. In high court also, a judge is to deal with almost the same number of cases by a Bench of two judges. Here, the work load is shared by two judges. So the pressure is divided to half. In apex court the work is over by lunch hours in most of the chambers. This situation is comparable to work load of a school teacher and a college lecturer with that of university professors. A college lecturer is not work-loaded to the extent of a school teacher. For example, in a college a teacher is supposed to take 2 to 3 classes a day while in schools this number is 6 to 7 without a vacant period to relax and revitalize. Such a principle of disbursement of work is coming from the time of British Raj. If we look at the nature of work at these three levels, it is the same. Lesser work at higher places, perhaps, had been assigned with a psychology of being more specific and meticulous with greater responsibility. But no body takes it in that light. College lecturers have eased themselves by not taking their classes regularly and do not turn up to colleges for days as there is no attendance compulsion for them. They have not to maintain a teacher's diary and are not accountable for bad results as a school teacher is. They have a number of other privileges like university professors such as promotion up to the level of asstt. Professor, visit to foreign countries, project allocation from UGC and so on. The only difference in essential qualification between the two is that one does two years B.Ed and another does Ph.D of three years. Otherwise the academic level of senior secondary classes is no less than the graduation classes in any form. No one has looked at this difference and continued with over-burdening and over expecting from school teachers. The situation is just same to the lower courts with higher courts. The number of cases at all levels of judiciary has to be the same. Why the judges in higher courts leave for their homes after 2 pm and why the magistrates in lower courts should take courts till 4.30 pm, needs a sincere look? Solution to this problem of over loading the workers and expect results is not justice. If we need justice from courts, we need to have justice with them first. In the higher places neither judges nor professors take their work with more responsibility and take advantages and privileges as their right and mode of their service condition which absolutely wrong and a self generated misconception. This needs to be clarified and amended. One of the best solutions to reduce work load and rational allocation of work is appointing more judges but to look into such misconception is equally important while reorganising work of judiciary at different level. Out of many reasons of congestion in courts, one is unjust distribution of work.

Delhi School Tribunal is a unique court. Before May 2007, it used to be a quasi-judicial court that used to sit for one hour only, on Tuesday and Thursday. The presiding officer used to be the Law Secretary of Delhi Administration. The P.O. used to have other departments and other responsibilities parallely. This Tribunal was set-up after 1973 after Delhi Education Act came into being and was meant for hearing and deciding the cases of termination of school employees. Other matters like transfers, promotions, selection grade were out of its jurisdiction. Due to these reasons the P.O. was brought from lower judiciary, mostly from Tis Hazari court. Only favourite officers were brought here on deputation of two years. Since this was a post for special people, so the post of presiding officer was reserved to give way to Delhi High Court and thus, this office used to work as a launch pad from back door to give promotion to certain privileged judicial officers. The rate of disposal of cases here has ever been one or two in a year.

Seeing the Tribunal functioning highly autocratic and bureaucratic, high court passed orders on Delhi Administration to set-up this Tribunal as an independent full time court with all powers to deal with all matters related with employees of schools and the management.

Now, it is full time court but the situation of it is as it was ever before. The presiding officer starts its court at 11.30 am instead of 10 am and takes up only eight to 13 cases per day on an average. He leaves the Tribunal at 12.30 pm before lunch to the place of his choice. The dates of adjournments even in long pending cases of 1979 or 1991, etc. are given no less than 40 days to three months. The Tribunal is in no hurry to pass orders in cases where the final arguments were concluded in the year 2003 after submitting written arguments, in some cases. The present presiding officer is of view, 'why to make haste in passing orders? It is the lowest court and either of the parties shall go into appeal and the case may take another 10 to 20 years even after going out of here so, there is no harm in going slow.'

The present judicial officer took all privileges granted that are provided to him and his salary cheque reaches to him in time. Why should he/she bother for those who have been illegally removed from their permanent jobs and are in a pitiable condition due to criminal high-handedness of managements on teachers and employees? The entire attitude of such judicial officers is negative as he has guts to ignore directions from the apex court to decide certain cases on priority basis before hundred days back. He was adjourning the dates for one or the other pretence.

Finally, after being directed by the hon'ble apex court, the tribunal decided the case against the appellant ignoring Constitutional obligations, on whimsical and illegal grounds, as he fells that appellant can go into appeal, thus believing in more litigation, rather, deciding the case on merits. The biggest reason to become callous to the sufferers in absence of accountability of judges for their deliberate wrong and proving them to be absolutely invincible is to remain connived.

Over loading courts is bad, not for the judicial officer only but finally to the litigant. The total situation may suffer from a sense of uncertainty due to high work pressure on court administration. In such disordered situation, we shall have to pay acknowledgment to those who still maintain their cool and use their best faculty to impart justice to the sufferers taking the challenge as their responsibility with a balanced approach. Judicial officer disposing off maximum number of cases in a specified period needs to be publicly awarded by the government and be given out of turn promotion, may increase work efficiency of other onlooker officers. Such great officers really need to be acknowledged to set inspiring example before the junior officers. Hearing cases and deciding them on merits is not a kind of mechanical work. It is of highly intellectual nature, as every case cannot be covered by a blanket decision. It needs cool and stable mind and serenity at heart so deserves justified treatment from higher ups.

There can be strict and uniform rules to draft and file cases at all levels throughout the country. At present, the rules for drafting and conveyencing are developed according to the court Rules at trial court level as well as at the highest court level. It is confusing, for the lawyers who ought to take up cases in other States as well as for the judges when they are transferred to other States. To make the work simple and understandable, there is no harm in making uniform rules throughout the country about drafting and conveyencing. For the reason of security and reasonable due justice, all the case-files are to be physically maintained by 'Record-Section' under specific guidelines. To prevent tempering of the file, all the pages must be given court-folio-number and be stamped (by using some machine) to check any kind of tempering. The lawyer may also put the same page numbers in his file for reference in the court during arguments.

One of the biggest targets in Peoplism will be clearing cupboards even in government offices including judicial services. Only those cases will be on hold, which need opinion of more than one authority. Rules will be framed on how to dispose of work in a time bound manner outside judiciary also. The doctrine of 'time bound working' will not be confined to judiciary only but shall be spread in all areas of Public administration. In spite of investing public funds for public representatives and government officer's comforts, public money shall be diverted to appoint sufficient staff to affect time bound working of different government agencies. If teachers who are most qualified section of society, at all levels, can plan and execute their work in a given time-table, why any part of government should be let loose to delay the disposal of their work for unlimited period for no valid reason. So, every post needs to be bound by the policy of time bound working.

***Alternative Democracy syn. PEOPLISM:** It is a new proposed programme of governance which is aimed at the masses of third world and underdeveloped countries to understand the social and national responsibilities before adopting the best system of governance, i.e. the Democracy.*

Consequential Punishment

9

If you are acquitted from a graft of police in the court of law, why the court cannot punish the erring cop for his criminal manipulation consequently? Who stops him?

Defamation suits on the fake contender may exhaust one's remaining lifetime after coming out clean. These measures will minimise artificial and frivolous litigation on innocent people. It is a simple misfortune that the existing Law does not provide "Consequential Punishment" to the party that pleaded 'Cause of Action', in the court of law in a failed-case. A large number of acquittals in cases filed by the police and other executive agencies are evidence that large number of perky cases overload the judicial system for ulterior purposes, unnecessarily. By imposing consequential punishment, the load of courts may be reduced to its minimum. It will not only give relief to overloaded courts but also minimise the chances of official harassment by police that file fake-cases as its right. Besides bringing the provisions of consequential punishment into force, Section 181 to 211 of IPC (excluding S. 180) provides punishment for filing fake documents in a case. Section-340 of CrPC is also sufficient to prosecute the presenter of false papers on affidavit, which is one among many other provisions of prescribed law. Also, inherent powers through Section-151 of the CPC and *Suo motto* powers of the courts may be possible alternatives to begin with 'Consequential Punishment'. But still one needs to file an independent suit for damages on the doer of fake case and has to pass through all the stages of legal proceedings afresh.

Besides filing a separate suit for damages, can it be made consequent when the filing party loses the case? Most of the innocent sufferers do not afford filing a suit for damages due to cumbersome nature of judicial proceedings and due to exhausted lifetime in defending their innocence for many years. The most frequent victims are poor and unpatronised citizens who cannot rebut the police atrocity due to their limited resources will get great relief from police crime on them. This preference of not approaching the court of law for a filing a suit for damages will discourage the real offender, police who filed fake cases against an innocent citizen or subordinates. The crime of planned offence of filing a fake case on innocents by police or by an official authority, always remain unchallenged and unpunished. Identifying such officers who dare use their official statue for their ego satisfaction is equally important to be brought to books of the punishing authority, i.e. courts in a consequent manner. The basic principle of implementing and adopting the policy of 'Consequential Punishment' is very clear. If the accused is proved innocent, the guilt of filing agency is consequently and automatically proved. If accused cannot be prove guilty of charges leveled on him/her and he cannot be prosecuted, the police, who implanted an innocent person, shall be held responsible for filing a fake case. Such police officer shall be taken seriously by the attending court and will pass orders on the erring cop as per law in Peoplism to prosecute him of his criminal manipulation. Such a measure shall definitely reduce the number of fake cases filed, exhausting precious time and human resources of judiciary. Consequential punishments will be of many types which will include the following salient features of Peoplism. This is more relevant, in case when the case is filed

(i) by any government agency including the police,
(ii) by the harassed person.

The second possibility is a kind of suit for damages. But the first possibility is something extraordinary. Here, the case is to be filed by acquitted person who was trapped on artificial grounds. Consequential *punishment* shall be imposed in the case of acquittal in a criminal case but consequential *compensation* shall be imposed on the impostor party in a civil case. Such impositions are very relevant in a situation when the acquitted person needs to be given justice by the court in the form of punishment on the guilty police. To be more specific the police officer may be directed to pay a substantial sum as compensation amount to the acquitted person. This amount may be deducted from the salary of the errant cop in the years to come. If proved not guilty, the filing party automatically proved wrong due to acquittal of the accused. To stop intentional harassment of an innocent person for many reasons proves that the authorities were guilty of filing this case against him/her. They are liable to be punished. In this proposal the guilty party has to be punished consequently at the time when the innocent accused is acquitted in the same order by the court.

In a civil case, the harassed party who was deprived of his rights will be paid all his/her losses by the filing party but the other hidden losses in his family shall be placed on record for final slap on such a guilty party. The winner will be paid a consequential fine on filing party, as compensation. Consequential punishments will create a fear in the minds of wrong doers who take advantage of over-loading of the courts to continue litigation for ten or fifteen years and torturing an innocent person during pendency of case. This complementary provision with Time Bound Justice is to make judiciary really effective and respectful.

The dose of consequential punishment is no doubt small but very effective. It will not only reduce the number of fake cases by police on innocent citizens but shall reduce harassment of hardworking honest workers in government offices. Officers in private and public sectors shall understand well that they cannot harass any person out of rules and regulations and cannot transfer, suspend of terminate an innocent person who is not to their personal liking and who refuse to submit to their illegal and immoral comforts. Citizens will be able to lead a dignified life and shall concentrate to their duty in spite of flattering their boss for seeking their due attention and undue privileges. By implementing the provision of Consequential punishment as well as consequential penalties on the erring senior, who practice corruption in their official clout, shall not be able to harass honest and devoted employees will have a relief from immoral conduct of their bosses. Discipline and order can be maintained without boasting cadre before the immediate juniors. Most of the juniors surrender to make a compromise with a situation, when their errant immediate boss hurling a fake cases on him. In Peoplism creating a situation of inaccessibility by a powerful superior by using unfair and illegal means, shall be taken as a criminal offence. Officers too have to be at ground in their conduct while dealing with juniors. Peoplism shall improvise the process of preparing and publishing lists of 'good' and 'to be good' officers in all departments that have public dealing. This list will be maintained by special cell in 'Promotion Department'. Any person having sad experience with an officer in this list can object to this list. The Promotion Department in every office may be central or specific to a particular office, depending on the number of employees in the office. The boss has not to be a part of this team. Merits for promotion shall be calculated mathematically only.

Things will not only improve as per design of a particular office but also a large number of unnecessary malpractices will come to a halt. To a corrupt officer the seniors will be able to impose consequential penalties and compensation on their officer for their wrong and unlawful act which has cause damage or loss to the department to a junior person by immediate boss. As far as punishment is concerned, it may be the jurisdiction of the criminal court but the civil courts can also use this doctrine to impose penalties and fines on the erring party as it is still done by courts in rare case. After implementing the provision of consequential punishment it will become a part and parcel of the law and will be in practice to improve the over all atmosphere in organisations.

It may also be provided with such punishment that if the guilty officer on whom consequential punishment is imposed by a court of law or by a senior officer shall first pay the amount imposed on him/her as a fine and then go into appeal. This amount shall be deposited into the government treasury and will be paid after the appellant's appeal fails. If the errant officer is awarded punishment in the form of a sentence, and he/she wants to go into appeal, he will remain suspended until the appeal is disposed off. Such sentenced officer if along with sentence directed to pay compensation to his victim, he will have to deposit the fine before going into appeal or this sum will be paid to the victim from his provident fund or other such securities and assets.

Mediation Cell versus Middleman

10

Lawyers, police, ministerial staff of the court, touts and the likewise shall get away seeing things happening faster and better, without them.

Middlemen shall get discouraged by the functioning of newly established 'Mediation Cells' in trial courts. Maximum number of people must take advantage of it. By resolving their disputes at an early stage, one can save himself from further humiliation of being a regular visitor of court; preparing for the next date of hearing and remain in hang over of uncertainty, is no good to end up your dispute, than negotiating it in the Mediation Cell at an early stage. Mediation Cells can prove to be an effective measure to reduce the number of litigations in courts, provided these are organised scientifically with great care and practically function with great commitment.

The mediation team needs to be acquainted with specific techniques and strategies to handle an odd situation. Addl. ACP, can be an effective member of the negotiation team. Making negotiations and persuasion friendly and amicable, has to be the first motto and to reach a point of compromise and settlement, to be the final. Members of the negotiation team must include certain law experts who can make both the parties aware of legal complications at the first place which may follow to include people of social recognition or marriage councilors or counselors trained in specific discipline by virtue of their educational qualification as well as their practical experience in the field. To avoid a regular litigation in the court of law and let the effected parties suffer for a long, it is preferable to go under the shelter of these mediation cells.

The only fear with this new idea of mediation cells is that these cells should not be converted into full-fledged courts as happened in case of consumer forums. The presiding officer must be accompanied by few assistant officers. These assisting officers may be three. One may be the area Addl. ACP, who was authorised to maneuver general complaints to register FIRs as described earlier and two, a social worker and three a law expert on the issue being taken up. The (MO) mediation officer must invite the affected parties separately and directly, without any lawyer. The first out-burst of both the parties must be taken in written format in advance along with brief of the case in maximum one page text.

After studying the written complaints and replies, these will be entered in the case file of the Mediation Cell. It will be managed on the same rules as a court case, like putting a folio number and a court stamp. Bringing both the parties face to face should be done with care and respect to each other on separate dates to avoid direct confrontation. Both the parties be advised and negotiated by the team of Mediation Cells on separate dates who will try to bring them to the common point of compromise. The party doing wrong to the other party also deserves equal opportunity and respect. After negotiating both the parties separately towards a common point of agreement, if situation allows, both of them may be invited for face to face for final negotiation.

1. Clarification of misunderstandings,
2. Feeling sorry and tendering apology,
3. Agree to make a compromise, the office will also decide the terms and conditions of final compromise and to this respect ask such compromised from the parties, on affidavit.

On the basis of such affidavits it will give its decision which will be a legal binding on both the parties. The Mediation Cells have to be different from the regular courts in order to have independence from the pressure of lawyers and touts. The processing of papers has to be very simple and understandable to a layman. There has to be no compulsion to get the papers typed in any defined format and in the form of a legible handwriting as allowed in consumer forums. Judicial stamps, blank sheets and other stationary materials must be available on the reception counter easily. It is only the affidavit which has to be authenticated by the appropriate authority prescribed by the Cell. All ministerial services needed, must be available in the premises to minimise the exercise of the litigants. A computer system, laser printer and a photostat machine must be available to help contestants near the reception or counselor's desk.

These Cells must discourage third party in the form of a lawyer or middle-man or a professional agent, who may promise to get the dispute settled by making the dispute more strategic by unfair means, covering themselves and thus delaying the settlement.

Early disposal needs to be formulated with details stipulating every possibility. The norms and techniques to mediate between the affected parties shall be defined and worked-out by taking different kind of research and studies, into consideration. Parallel cases settled in other countries and places may have to be worked out to make the process of negotiation direct and simpler. The mediating officer has to be sufficiently acquainted with such cases from law cases whose example may be cited before the parties to convince them. These experts have to be acquainted with the psychological condition of both the parties genuinely, to create a point of compromise between them as per circumstances of each case. Peoplism may make mediation process a mandatory part of court proceedings and every civil case will have to pass through the process of mediation before entering into litigation.

Touts have a business to stand in the way of early disposal and make things difficult for their own interest. So, they have not to be allowed to join any negotiation through a settled law. Self-styled god fathers in the system are not difficult to be identified to escape their participation in any form to avoid any pressures from unwanted lawyers, police personnel, ministerial staff of the court, outside touts and the likewise, in presence of a 'guide' (counselor) sitting outside the Mediation Cell to help contestants to prepare documents and process them and guide those who need help. However, in the times of internet and laser printing, all the documentation and proceedings shall be available to the contesting parties in English as well as in regional language in all States or as the need be. Their availability in hard copy form must also be made much easier for those where internet is not available.

There has to be a straight and direct way to come to the shelter of mediation officer, who will discourage unwanted persons to join the parties. Petitioners in person/sufferers/defendants will have direct accessibility in the Mediation Cells. The nature of cases falling under the jurisdiction of Mediation Cells will be the cases of civil nature only. These may cover disputes of

1. Matrimonial,
2. Financial transaction,
3. Family disputes,
4. Tribal issues (Locality disputes),
5. Tenant-land lord's disputes,
6. Loan recovery disputes,
7. Miscellaneous minor disputes.

Cases of different nature out side the jurisdiction of the Mediation Cell shall be referred to the relevant mediation center or department for its progress after informing the effected parties. In case the mediation team finds the case certain issues to be of criminal nature, it will be referred to a criminal court. Criminal cases of physical assault and non-cognizable offense against the State shall not be dealt here. But if any accuse appeals to the Mediation Cell for his innocence, he may be heard in person against a graft. In case of the complaint of an accused against the police is found to be genuine. The mediation cell can summon the officer to explain his basis/logic to frame a case on the applicant. The Cell shall have right to question the reasons for filing a FIR against an innocent person. But finally, if the cell finds the complainant innocent, it will prepare a report of his innocence and send that to the higher ups in police department. In case, the persuasion with the police officers fails to withdraw the same, the Cell shall refer such complaints to the 'Human Right Commission' for further action beyond Section-16 of National Human Right Commission Act. Basically, clear cut cases that are subject to crime against the State shall not be handled by the Mediation Cells.

Peoplism can infuse its basic programme to give quick justice without the help of a paid person. Civitals will work for those, who are illiterate and without means and can be parallelly set up with Mediation Cell office in the same premises. The sufferer will be attended to immediately as he/she approaches a Civital or the members of some classified NGOs attached to a particular Civital. Staff will provide immediate help and the aggrieved party shall be granted immediate relief as first-aid is given in a hospital. Through different stages, the helpless aggrieved sufferer shall be granted interim relief until a regular case is registered and proceeded for routine litigation.

Restoring Faith in Judiciary

11

Implementing Time Bound Justice through a Bill in Parliament shall change the scene.

Faith is a wide word. It cannot be imposed by using force. Faith emerges from within when the credibility is proves to be consistent. Citizen's faith in justice delivery system had been continuously eroding for yester-years. Present situation is no better. Rather, the situation is deteriorating day by day. High handedness and autocratic decisions by courts along with other shortfalls in the working of present judiciary, made judicial system least dependable. Since people are not provided with any alternative to seek for justice, it is our compulsion to go to the courts to seek justice for our grievances. Despite of a number of lacunae in the present judicial functioning, there is still a silver-lining to upgrade the infra structure and functioning culture of judiciary. If the efforts to improve judiciary are positive without having ill will to anyone, people can start having faith in judiciary once again. And if the judges (judicial officers at all levels) are allowed to work in a dignified and respectable way, with space to work in far conducive conditions required to the basics of this noble profession. There may be more than one factor that can create conditions for a dignified, honest and committed judiciary. Politicians of any developing country must realise the vital importance and significance to have a really dignified and well equipped judiciary to create a progressive and just society. The civil administration has to be corrected from both the higher and lower ends. If economic strengthening against poverty may be our fight to make countrymen economically independent on one side, it is necessary to look into the need of correcting justice giving system by harnessing it with all its necessities and essential requirements and amending stale laws to this effect, on the other side. To expect too much from present state of affairs of our present judicial system without filling all vacancies of judges and changing the entire system encouraging to the judges, is not justice to either side, i.e. the judiciary as well as the litigants. Present overloaded judiciary is not only unfair treatment to the existing judges but to the democratic framework of our society and the suffering citizens also.

This promising work can be done without special or hard exercise within our presently available means. But it needs a positive outlook to preserve Constitutional guarantees of fundamental rights (civil rights) and human rights of underprivileged common citizens at large. The judicial officers have to be trained to develop a positive attitude to protect aggrieved and already harassed parties, who are depending on his decision to get out of the situation he/she is a victim of. As far as fundamental rules and basic ethics of judicial officers is concerned, a judicial officers must be confident to contain the following forces in mind when conducting a court:

1. I am the full and final authority of my court.
2. I owe responsibility to impart justice to the deserving party.
3. The litigants have come to my court from a distance investing time and money with a hope that the case will forward ahead.
4. Seeking adjournment in my court is a difficult thing.
5. I have been entrusted by the President of my country to be the first custodian of Constitution.
6. I shall never try to establish any precedence that can be taken as a usual practice of judiciary against the reputation of judiciary as well as the interest of the party in trouble to protect my coming generation from such uncalled for gesture of court when I shall not be there.

7. I can always be not present in all the courts all the times and let my near and dears even my kith and kens must not face a frustrating practice or uncalled for attitude of the court.
8. I am a son of God who is watching my work and me.
9. I am not a lord. I am being addressed so in order to give respect and acknowledge my authority.
10. I am a part of society and my family has every right to interact with my relations and outside.
11. I am always answerable to myself as well as to the Judicial Commission.
12. For any wrong, I may be subject to Judicial Commission that has powers to create a situation against my position and respect.
13. I wish to have a constrain-free progressive life for me and my family.
14. I shall maintain balance in my gesture, utterance and dictation while in chair.
15. By no means, I shall be personal in my approach and shall decide things on merits.

Article-50 of the Constitution separates judiciary from executive. It further explains the role of a judicial officer as under (from Constitution of India):

(a) A judge should not allow his judicial position to be compromised at any cost.
(b) This is essential for maintaining the integrity of the institution and public confidence in it.
(c) The credibility of this institution rests on the fairness and impartiality of the judges at all levels.
(d) It is the principle of highest importance, for the proper administration of justice.
(e) Judicial powers must be exercised impartially and within the bounds of law.
(f) Public confidence in the judiciary rests by the judge of recognized objective principles which owe their existence

to a system as distinguished from subjective moods, predictions, emotions and prejudices.

(g) Judges must always ensure that they do not allow the credibility of the institution to be eroded.

(h) Unwarranted harsh treatment or prejudices is not meted out to those who need care and attention has been laid down in case titled *Chetek Construction vs. Om Prakash AIR SC 1855-pg 1859-60* and *Chenena Jagdishwar vs. State of AP-1988 Cr.L.J. 549.*

Time bound justice is such a remedy in itself that will repose people's faith in judges and working of courts. Measures like 'Civitals', 'Mediation Cells' and 'Direct Action Cells', etc. if allowed to work for the justice delivering system, these will minimise the load of regular courts for many reasons. DAC System shall help to reduce a number of filing as it works before things ripe for legal filing (log on the website of the author for details of Civital and Direct Action Cell).

Courts have to primarily believe police through the challans, it is filed in the court to give us a crime-free society. The court issues summons and warrants on its behalf. The dependence of courts on police actions is so firm that in traffic police courts, the magistrate does not even give a chance to the so-called offender, whether the challan is right or a fabrication and passes orders on the so-called violator. Here, the court believes the police blind folded and imposes fine on the drivers as per particular Sections of the Motor Vehicle Act. People pay the same silently and avoid legal complications by challenging the challan. But in other criminal cases where police might have joined the other party to graft a case, for an ulterior purpose of extorting comforts from the grafted accused or to create a pressure to withdraw a complaint against them, or for any other similar purposes, is very much in practice.

Courts have not to be a party with the police while pursuing a criminal case against any person and have to be sure

---

***Civital and DAC System:** Both these programmes are available on author's website www.intl.societyforhr.org.*

for the authenticity of the FIR and the challan. Court means upholding the truth. And police may not be holding the truth. So, it is the prime duty of every court to be very classified and independent for its intuition and legal considerations when handing a criminal case. The example, gross misuse of Section 107-150 of CrPC in a blanket way by the police is found to be very frequent. This is illegal and also negligent, on the part of law framing bodies, who gave police unchecked powers to conduct a court of their own (the court of Special Executive Magistrate run by the area ACP and defend police action whether right or wrong). Such blind folded gross misuse of power by the police shall not exist in Peoplism. Rules shall be framed to protect innocent citizens and not to harass and demoralise them in Peoplism. The police will be restrained to misuse this clause on apprehension only. Breach of peace will not be a coarse word rather, it will be explained widely in the interest of senior citizens, RWAs, registered organisations, registered companies, reputed citizens, sick and physically challenged persons, women and children, etc. which are not excluded in this section at present. This is one of the most absurd laws since British time which is still being misused by the police to create their terror in the minds of law abiding citizens.

Every enquiry report by different investigating agencies shall help the court in a faster way as these will come before the court after getting scrutinized at three stages in Peoplism. The IO and the attached legal experts shall sign the Challan jointly with the SHO. It will be placed before the court only when the case is found strong on merits. In case of failure of the police in the court of law the liability of failure will be shared by all the three officers equally.

The police vigilance department shall not investigate complaints against any police officer. An **'Independent Body'**

Independent Body: *It will be a form of appointed body or a Commission like (IPCA) Independent Police Complaint Agency. It shall not be under Police control but can independently make their own decisions. Ministry of Vigilance shall have control on IPCA and it will not be accountable to the Ministry of Home.*

shall take up this work. This body (Commission) shall be independent directly under Ministry of Vigilance and its findings shall be recommended to various action taking effective agencies as per schedule prepared for the purpose. Such a body can be named as IPCA which has already been in reference earlier here. This Commission shall not have its own courts like CBI, TADA and SEM Court of police. Fair trial is not possible in these courts as the Challan comes from their own department who had already prejudged the issue against a person for a number of outside reasons. These departmental courts work hardly disbelieving any other story that they fabricate on the accused, which is mostly totally unlawful and illegal from all angles. Therefore, purity and accountability of judiciary is one of the important milestones to bring true justice to the aspirants.

Besides constituting with 'Judicial Commission' to look into the complaints against misconduct of judicial officers, it will also have other functions like maintaining 'Track Records' of all judicial officers; prepare its report for the purpose of promotion and the likewise. Rule and Performa, through which a complaint can be lodged before the judicial commission, shall be available to litigants on internet also. In Peoplism, all the judicial officers shall have binding of a 'Code of Judicial Conduct'. This code is in two parts. The first part covers all the practicing lawyers and the second part covers the judicial officers. Judicial Commission will be empowered to entertain complaints from any aggrieved person if the conduct of a lawyer or a judicial officer is not in accordance. The commission shall have the power to go into the technicalities of any order passed by any judicial officer, including the merits of the case. Such an order shall be scrutinised by a specially constituted board of retired judges that can consequently recommend getting the impugned order quashed by a senior judicial officer. The process of taking decision on such order will be of administrative nature and shall be devoid of normal process of charges, cross examination, counters and so on. It all will be affected on fast track and will be almost the same as 'Judicial Review' is held under Article-32 of the Indian Constitution.

Undesirable Lingering

12

Lawyers or police cannot skip dates by seeking adjournments on murky grounds to linger on the suffrage of innocent.

Rules are made to simplify difficult multi-faceted tasks. Procedures are made to homogenise and coordinate the work to get it faster. Rules and procedures are framed for convenience and scientific functioning. Still working is supposed to be coarse due to making own rules and priorities, sidelining the existing rules. In the rove, it is difficult to care for what is in practice and what is in rules. There is no law yet to bring a person to books that evades set rules and does things as personnel preference. Simple matters some times take a big and difficult shape that might put the whole department under a question mark. Tactics to escape a date in the court by way of seeking adjournment are counted which the court also knows. Since adjournment may damage the cause of the sufferer only. All other parties see benefit in it. It is a common practice that courts at all levels are generous to grant frequent adjournments until any hue and cry is made by the sufferer. In an adjournment, every one gets relieved except the party who is suffering by lawlessness. In such circumstances when the adjournment takes place after a gap of six to eight months two dates are enough to suck up one year after years. Life slips from hands, litigants retire from job, litigants die in lurch but the date of final hearing does never arrive, signifying each day dreamy for a trace of relief from the court. His day dreaming is repeatedly shattered by the tremors of adjournments. Life period, left out energy and money are wasted bit by bit when you return home with a long date. Technique to use adjournments to lapse important and limited years of your job, works as deadly weapon against the sufferer. Still the courts do nothing specific to give justice quickly. Compensating the lost years is out of fashion when court is empowered to take suo motto decisions to do so. Adjournment is the biggest curse on the sufferer in today's judiciary. Adjournments are also used as a court craft by smart lawyers to linger on the litigation for years together or to wait for a suitable judge to come to the Bench. It is a sharp edged weapon in the hands of manipulators.

For seeking and granting adjournment, there are no rules. It is affected by the mutual understanding between the respondent lawyer and the judge. There are rules that if the respondent seeks adjournment, it has to pay expenses to the other party, is almost out of practice in courts, ignoring such rules available in the law, due to intervention of Bar Association. Since adjournments make the work of lawyer easier, the Bar Association supports its voters and ignores the interest of litigant.

Frequent-long-adjournments is a serious lapse in today's judiciary. This has been seriously dealt with, in a defined manner in Peoplism. The strategy on adjournments had already been given in schedule 2 in 13th Chapter. More details are available in these tables to minimise the number of adjournments where the number of adjournments has already been fixed by seeing the nature of litigation. The court has to be very classified and clear while granting an adjournment and must look into the adverse effect of asked adjournment in the case or on the suffering party. Adjournment may be allowed in rarest to rare cases when it becomes a must and no other alternative is available. Waste of the entire human resources on the day of adjournment is a national loss.

No one shall take advantage of the leniency of the court to fetch an unnecessary adjournment. Fragile rules shall not do. Rules regulating granting of adjournment need change. Lawyer busy in other court shall have to pay fine in case; he/she needs an adjournment for this purpose. Lingering on litigation beyond permissible number of adjournments will be taken as misconduct of the judicial officer in Peoplism. A case may be dismissed if the lawyer is not present and no proxy should be entertained to grant an adjournment. An advance application with a receipt of fine decided by the court (as per nature of the work on that date) be deposited with the advance application, if the lawyer is unable to attend the court and take part in court proceedings. The client should not be forced to pay that fine and client's complaint on this matter to the same court shall be taken seriously by the court which may be subjected to referring the complaint to the Bar Association.

It is a general observation that most of the lawyers want to engage as many as clients at a time. They do not want to free the clients and make no efforts for early disposal of the cases he/she has in hands. More number of cases in pocket far big is the lawyer. Therefore, lawyers are more interested to linger on cases. By the lapse of few years, they start demanding another round of fee. Most of the lawyers have juniors with them. These juniors are some time students of law or some poorly educated Munshi only. Most of the lawyers do not appear in the court until the situation to argue arrives. For that stage also, they take each case so lightly that they seek few adjournments to skip the day of argument. Some times, the proxy lawyer who is an unauthorised person beyond the status of Power of Attorney with the court is allowed to argue in the guise of a lawyer. Credentials of such proxy are never questioned by the court. Winning or losing the case, is the concern of the parties and not that of the lawyers. A lawyer is concerned only with payments from parties. He is a professional and occupies a place in open market. Lawyers are not bothered for the fate of the case. Even a lawyer thinks if the party loses a case in lower court he will get another contract to move to the higher court. So, a lawyer cannot be treated as well wisher of his client. He is a professional person who has been hired to work for you. And in this contract, he keeps the neck of the client in his fist to behave in any manner that suits him. He has no moral or legal binding to be loyal to the client as no code of conduct exists to set right his working. Merely covering lawyers under Consumer Act is not sufficient. There has to be a separate Code of Conduct with defined clauses in it with proposed penalty for these violations. It is important and a must, to make them accountable for a misconduct within the Code. Therefore, in Peoplism, a photograph of the lawyer shall be pasted on every Power of Attorney, which the lawyer will submit at the time of filing the case. Magistrates and Judges, who start their career as a lawyer came up practicing in the conventional method of lawyers. Therefore, this becomes the foremost duty of all judicial officers to go against such malpractice of lawyers in the interest of quick disposal of cases and giving justice to the sufferer. The 'Judicial Commission' shall be empowered to recommend suspension of license of such lawyers who tease already aggrieved and already harassed sufferers.

Written complaint against any lawyer presently comes to Bar Association, but in Peoplism it shall be submitted to the concerned judge who is attending the case and finding substance in the complaint the judge may direct the Bar Association to take action against the erring lawyer. If the charges on the counsel are grave of higher magnitude and of criminal nature, the case may be referred directly to the Judicial Commission or put the matter to the area police station. Peoplism shall frame laws to initiate criminal breach of trust in such cases.

By seeking long adjournments the lawyers have enough time to manipulate with the opposite party during prolonged pendency of the case. There have been instances, when a lawyer changed its party; returned the case file to the petitioner and started arguing from the side of respondents. The case is on record of Delhi School Tribunal where the lawyer is a former Deputy Director of Education, Delhi Administration. Such a conduct should be treated as a contempt of court and the court should have not allowed the lawyer to do so. But it did not happen in absence of any code of conduct for lawyers.

This is true that the courts are over-loaded but allowing adjournment in a free manner shall increase more piling up of cases and it shall finally amount to more pressure on judiciary itself. So, in spite of giving frequent adjournments one must try to disposing off as many as cases possible during his/her tenure. Adjournments must be discouraged by the courts keeping the forthcoming chaos in view.

There seems to be an inadvertent chaos in day-to-day functioning of courts. 'No early decision' in criminal cases encourages crime in society. A vital question in such atmosphere emerges in minds whether prolonging of cases is attached to sustaining the crime in society? The answer depends on individual. Proceedings may be exhaustive and time consuming but delay in justice must not be prolonged by adjournments.

We must keep succession of crime in society and the role of courts has to be final to terminate it. After a crime spurts out in the society, it continues to grow unnoticed by the onlookers for long time, including the police. It grows to a big cactus for years. But when a matter finally come before the court, the termite of adjournments could have eaten up timely justice to the extent that either the sufferer makes a compromise with the crime or dies out in frustration. If the sufferer is young and self-respecting, he can retaliate the failure in the courts becoming a rebellious/criminal or even a avenging terrorist to take revenge on them who ruined him and his family and the very shelter of court failed to give the sufferer a dignified life by not punishing the criminals in time. He leaves a life of suffrage and frustration due to long pendency of cases or frequent adjournments for petty reasons and finally takes law in his own hands creating a threat to others unconcerned and innocent citizens around him. So, it is only the police and judiciary to preserve the fabric of society by taking timely action in a process of disposing of any offence or crime from the society.

It has always been very much in the knowledge of courts that by the time a stage of orders would reach, evidences could be tempered or destroyed and witness be killed or made hostile. Still the entire handling remains so stretched that even in millions of fake criminal cases, the courts normally have lukewarm attitude as far as disposing of the case is concerned. Courts may use their *suo motto* powers for humanity sake, in highly belated cases, realising limited resources of the government and cumbersome procedures of the courts. There are cases where no guarantor is available to get bail of an accused or a witness has become hostile or has died, the accused is supposed to languish in jail for ever. There has to be specific rules for such a situation where the courts may be empowered to act *suo motto* in order to decongest over packed jails taking the convincing period of detention in view as per offence charged on under-trial.

Millions of under-trials are languishing in jails for years unattended and progressing there cases a bit only. They have to be taken into consideration for their release. The apex court has been repeatedly prayed to do some thing to take care of them. Releasing over-staying accused as early as possible will be noble, keeping in view that ours is not a perfect system at all levels and is not strong enough to take judicious care of citizens by the police and the bureaucrats.

In these long years of sixty years, offence continued deep rooting into the society and the criminals proved their power on innocents. Time is the most important factor in a criminal case. Court cases are not just paperwork of court clerks. Lives of the citizens are on stake. It is really a very serious matter and the responsibility of the court becomes more serious to give a clean and a crime free society. The duty of a judge does not end by keeping the case running for many years but to dispose of case quickly also. Disposing of cases with shortest period of time must be the first priority for every judicial officer. Timely justice shall minimise shelter to crime under the umbrella of pendency of the case in courts.

The judiciary has to be conscious to dispose of cases than to shift liability by allowing adjournments. All the courts must dispose of cases to reduce the piles of files by continuously proceeding forward defying all tactics by the lawyers. If the cases are disposed of quickly, it is natural that the work load of courts will be reduced and obviously they will have to attend lesser number of cases a day by increasing the rate of disposal *at par* to the number of filing of new cases.

The provision to add an 'Adjournment sheet' in each case file will remind the judicial officer how many adjournments are possible in this type of case. The design of adjournment sheet will reveal the type of the case and number of adjournments allowed.

Terms in use Here

Police Establishment Board: will exclusively handle three subjects viz. confidential reports, transfer within the State and outside the State and promotions of all policemen below the rank of IPS officers.

Court Police: In peoplism the police force has been classified with specificity with their defined duties in theat particualr department. The court police is specially trained to ensure safety and security of the premises along with lives inside the premises and working as marshals to help the court.

Coordination Committees: A body to look into allocation, disbursement and utilisation of public funds to various projects for general good of people. Its composition shall be decided as per requirement. Comprising with scheduled non-political members from the actual users of a policy in the society, taken from People's Forum.

Special Commission: A temporary Commission constituted for specific purpose to formulate certain policies beyond political interference on the issues the politicians are always illogical and unfair like on reservation, salaries of peoples representatives and so on.

Citizen's Forum: An independent body of citizens who represent certain registered body like RWA or certain NGO who will be elected for cotozens furum at the time of any kind of general elections through a separate ballot.

Spervisory Committee: A legal body constituted by Bar Association and memebers of court administration Block to look after performance of various services within the premises of court.

Schedules to Dispose of Cases in Time

13

Peoplism is not an alternative to democracy in developing third world countries only but a primary training to honour and own a true democracy.

Why the citizens are deprived of justice in many ways? Why the entire system of governance works at the mercy of people who are in power? Why law does not overrule the unexplained discretion? Is the answer of this questionnaire stand to be 'accountability'? Most probably, the answer is, yes! The tools of accountability remain unused as those in power; want to rule the society unquestioned for their wrong or for their connivance with politicians, judicial officers, police and the executive machinery. It needs to be scrutinised and be penalized, in case they are found guilty for deviation from their defined and mandatory functioning.

A system termed as Peoplism is that where ordinary people (beside elected representatives) participate in every activity of the government. The chosen public men shall participate in planning and become members of a number of government's watch-dog committees. These participants will be independent from elected politicians. Such non-governmental bodies may be termed as 'Citizen's Forum' which will be free from politicians and political influence of any kind. Their members will directly come from registered Resident Welfare Associations and other such NGOs and may be directly elected during general elections. Such bodies shall not have any office except membership of 'Citizen's Forum' that shall work as watch dogs on the functioning of different organs of system. They are given assignment of different kinds by the Governor/LG of the State.

Their members may be taken as a member of Jury in the courts. No politician shall be taken as a member of these forums. It shall be a kind of social work and for each attendance the members may be paid honorarium only. Members shall make a report of a particular assignment and it will be submitted to the LG/Governor. It is only ordinary citizens of our society, who will help the government machinery and the courts in the form of members of 'Jury' as mentioned earlier, to decide people's fate in Peoplism.

For quick and proper justice, the following schedules numbered from 1 to 6 needs to be adapted and practiced under the surveillance of a 'Jury' in Peoplism. These Schedules have been drafted especially for Peoplism and can be used anywhere in the world after certain modulations as per requirement.

The various schedules have been planned keeping the significance of time limit in view in each case. Various stages of litigation have been scheduled and have been planned in a manner to complete all necessary stages of litigation from filing to final orders. From drafting to conveyancing and the final virdict. The schedules are:

The First Schedule: Classification of offences in relation to maximum time limit for litigation.

S.No.	Type of Offence	Maximum Time Fixed
1.	Constitutional	One month
2.	Political	2 months
3.	Between two or more States	one month
4.	Public Interest Litigation	3-6 months
5.	Criminal	6-9 ,,
6.	Civil	5 ,,
7.	Service Matters	3 ,,
8.	Revenue	3 ,,
9.	Consumer	3 ,,
10.	Marriage	2 ,,
11.	Petty Tribal issues	one month
12.	Miscellaneous	2-4 months

NB: The time limit is proposed by keeping the nature of the dispute in view.

The Second Schedule: Maximum number of Adjournments in each classified cases has to be defined as per nature of case and events and stages a case passes through. The court has to maintain the number of adjournments which are given below in the form of a table. The number of maximum adjournments will be written on the adjournment sheet in the case-file after order sheet on second page:

S.No.	Category	Maximum No. of Adjournments
1.	Constitutional	six
2.	Political	six
3.	Disputes of States	six
4.	Public Interest Litigation	three
5.	Criminal	six
6.	Civil	four
7.	Service matters	four
8.	Revenue	three
9.	Consumer	three
10.	Marriage	three
11.	Petty Tribal issues	two
12.	Miscellaneous	three

The court has to maintain the number of adjournments which are written by the litigant on the file in the form of a format on the front page or inside on the second page.

The Third Schedule: Service Rules for Judicial Officers will include:

1. Pay Scales and Perks
2. Leave Rules
3. Protocols
   (a) Judicial officer can deny more than one portfolios.
   (b) No judicial officer shall carry more than one court.
   (c) No judicial officer shall carryout any bureaucratic work.
   (d) No judicial officer shall be placed on deputation.

(e) No judicial officer shall appear in public function and avoid public gatherings and shall not ignore security arrangements.

(f) May attend to Govt. functions as a VVIP.

(g) Shall not appear in routine celebrations and mix up with public for security reasons.

(h) Can entertain invitation to attend public functions and preside over as Chairman under satisfactory security arrangements.

(i) May conduct emergency court at his residence.

(j) In case of travel it shall be privileged special arrangements by the government (Security and facilities).

(k) Shall continue to be a member of Bar Council but not of Bar Association.

(l) Shall join 'All India Judicial officer Council comprising of sitting and retired judges.

4. Appointments and Promotion Rules: Minimum age of Appointment in the lower court: 30 years.
5. Retirement: Age of retirement 65 years.
6. Miscellaneous.

The Fourth Schedule: Rules for Disciplinary Action:

I Stage: Complaint by authority to Senior Authority

II Stage: Enquiry

III Stage: Explanation on Affidavit in written

IV Stage: Appointing Disciplinary Authority (Mostly members of Jury appointed by the Judicial Commission)

V Stage: Show cause

VI Stage: Written reply submitted

VII Stage: Categorical opportunity to be heard on schedule time, day and place and before whom to be informed by registered AD

VIII Stage: Statement and explanations to be recorded

IX Stage:	Departmental resolution
X Stage:	Decision communicated by the competent authority
XI Stage:	Appeal if new facts to be placed or be placed with new approach
XII Stage:	Decision confirmed/quashed by appellant authority in the department

Maximum Time limit is Twelve months

The Fifth Schedule: From drafting to conveyancing and final verdict the schedules are:

Common Stages to all kind of legal proceedings: Drafting Rules:

1. Cover pages

a. Paper size:	Legal
b. Margins:	Left 2" Right 1" Top 1" Bottom 2"
c. Line Space:	Double
d. Font:	Courier New/Manual Type-writer Type

2. Sequence of pages

e. I Page-	Blank
f. II page-	Adjournment sheet
g. III page-	Order Sheets

3. Running pages

IV page-	Index with page Numbers and references
V page-	Memo of Parties with full postal address
VI page-	List of dates in succession
VII page-	Synopsis of the case, justifying what provision of prescribed law is violated and categorically mentioning 'Cause of Action'
VIII page-	Prayer in one paragraph (Max. 6 lines)
IX page-	1 to.... Main writ petition a. Question of Law b. Background of the case (History)

c. Main Petition (body)

d. Grounds

e. Grounds for interim relief

f. Prayer for interim relief

g. Main Prayer

X page- Citations, evidence and support materials

XI page- Annexures

Though different applications, writs and SLP, suits, etc. are drafted in a specific pattern these have to be made uniform throughout the country. Discrepancy in drafting should not create any problem for a lawyer or a litigant of different States. The Ministry of Law shall issue document to such effect in Peoplism and law procedures shall be seen to be uniform in all the courts of the country.

The format of Special Leave Petition and Public Interest Litigation must remain the same at all level of courts from the lowest court to the final court. There is no harm in it. Civitals will be responsible to guide people (both lawyers and the petitioners-in-person) to get clarification on procedures and other problems in conveyencing the documents (often printed guidelines) in the interest of justice.

The Sixth Schedule: Various stages of litigation have been planned and scheduled in a manner to complete all necessary stages of litigation from the stage of filing to the stage of final orders of court proceedings, keeping time limit in view:

Stage One: Filing

a. Directly by petitioner-in-person
b. Through a lawyer
c. Through an authorised representative
d. By the State such as police, revenue officer or the like wise.

Stage Two: First hearing—Appellant heard for maintainability Notice to the respondents/arrest warrant/summons.

Stage Third: Hearing both the parties and followings to be decided by the court

a. Question of maintainability
b. Recording primary pleadings of both the parties even in criminal case (*Prima facie* available or not)
c. Bail, if qualified
d. Deciding number of issues
e. Deciding maximum numbers of hearings (on adjournment sheet)
f. Deciding maximum numbers of adjournments within a parameter of time prescribed as per First Schedule.

Stage Fourth: Court proceedings includes

a. Reply
b. Rejoinder
c. Evidence
d. Arguments

The maximum number of 'part arguments' (heard partly) from both the side, must not exceed by three dates (two adjournments).

e. Decision.

Comments: In case both the parties file 'written arguments' no personal arguments shall be necessary and the court will be bound to give its decision within a specified period in different classes or within a period of seven days after the arguments are concluded. The conclusion of the arguments shall be recorded in the order-sheet and the date of decision shall be announced in the open court. What has been announced in the open court has to be brought on record in the order-sheet. Any discrepancy recorded by the litigants and brought into the knowledge of the same or a senior court or Judicial Commission shall amount serious repercussions on the career of the judicial officer.

What Others Claim

14

(Only relevant Part (Articles/Sections) have been given here without changing their given numbering for brevity.)

The constitutional claims by few developed, developing and underdeveloped nation need a look for justification of our claims.

It is a wishful thinking to incorporate the concept of Peoplism through which 'Time Bound Justice' will be the first application. Constitutional guarantees to impart timely justice are claimed by all the nations but these could be actualized by few nations only. They can be called developed not only for economic richness reasons but they have up-to-date judiciary on one side and effective reliable police on the other. Let us examine the specificity in the Constitutions of few countries and find out how much careful these are for perseverance of human rights and natural justice for their citizens.

1. ARGENTINA

Section-5: Guarantees of the national Constitution, ensuring its administration of justice.

Section-14b: (1) Protection against arbitrary dismissal; stability of the civil servant; free and democratic labour union organizations recognized by the mere registration in a special record.

(3) The State shall grant the benefits of social security, which shall be of an integral nature and may not be waived. In particular, the laws shall establish: compulsory social insurance, full family protection; protection of home stead; family allowances and access to a worthy housing.

Section-16: All its inhabitants are equal before the law, and admissible to employment without any other requirement than their ability.

Section-18: The prisons of the nation shall be healthy and clean, for the security and not for the punishment of the prisoners, shall render the judge liable for the bad condition of the prisoner.

Section-28: The laws that regulate their enforcement shall not modify the principles, guarantees and rights recognized in the preceding sections.

Section-111 (4): To decide the opening of the proceedings for the removal of judges, when appropriate to order their suspension, and to make the pertinent accusation. Comment: This recalling the judicial officer and this can apply to politicians also.

2. MORROCCO

Morocco is a constitutional, democratic and social monarchy. The new Constitution superseded those of 1992, 1972, 1970 and 1962.

Art. 63: The Government shall be answerable to the King and the Parliament. Decrees endorsed by the Prime Minister shall be countersigned by the Ministers responsible for the implementation thereof.

Art. 64: The Prime Minister shall be responsible for the coordination of ministerial activities.

Art. 65: The Prime Minister may delegate some of his powers to the ministers.

Art. 66: The Cabinet shall be notified of the following, before any relevant decision is taken: (a) Matters related to general policies of the State; (b) Declaration of martial law; (c) Declaration of war; (d) Requesting confidence from the House of Representatives to allow the Government to carry out their responsibilities further; (e) Draft bills, before they are brought to one of the two Houses; (f) Statutory decrees; (g) Decrees mentioned in Articles 40, 41, 45 and 55 of this Constitution; (h) Draft plan; (i) Projects for revising this Constitution.

3. FRANCE

Article-2: [State Form and Symbols] (1) France is an indivisible, secular, democratic, and social Republic. It ensures the equality of all citizens before the law, without distinction as to origin, race, or religion. It respects all beliefs, or religion. It respects all beliefs.

(5) The Republic Motto is "Liberty, Equality, and Fraternity".

(6) Its principle is government of the people, by the people, and for the people.

Article-54: Constitutional Revisions for Ratification] If, upon the demand of the President of the Republic, the Prime Minister or the President of one or other Assembly or sixty deputies or sixty senators, the Constitutional Council has ruled that an international agreement contains a clause contrary to the Constitution, the ratification or approval of....

Article-64: Title VIII; The Judiciary [Independence]

(1) The President of the Republic shall be the guarantor of the independence of the Judiciary.

(3) An organic act shall determine the status of members of the Judiciary.

(4) Judges may not be removed from office.

Article-65: [Conseil Superieur] (a) The Conseil Superieur de la Magistrature shall be presided over by the President of the Republic. The Minister of Justice shall be its ex officio Vice-President. He may deputize forthe President of the Republic. (b) The Conseil Superieur shall, in addition, comprise nine members appointed by the President of the Republic under the terms laid down by an organic act. (c) The Conseil Superieur shall make proposals for appointments of Judges of the Cour de Cassation and of Presiding Judges of the Courts of Appeal. It shall give its opinion, under the conditions stipulated by the organic act, on the proposals of the Minister of Justice relative to appointments of other judges. It shall be consulted on questions of pardon under conditions determined by an organic act. (d) The Conseil Superieur shall act as the disciplinary council for judges. In such cases, it shall be presided over by the Presiding Judge of the Cour de Cassation.

Article-66: [Personal Freedom] (1) No one may be arbitrarily detained. (2) The Judiciary, guardian of individual liberty, shall enforce this principle under the conditions stipulated by legislation.

Article-67: [Membership] (1) A High Court of Justice shall be instituted. (2) It shall be composed of members elected in equal number by the National Assembly and the Senate from within their ranks after each general or partial election to these Assemblies. It shall elect its President from among its members. (3) An organic law shall determine the composition of the High Court, its operating rules and the procedure to be followed before it.

4. BHUTAN

Mere adoption of a Constitution does not mean the establishment of a true representative democratic system. China, Myanmar and Pakistan, all have Constitution minus a true representative democratic system.

Before Bhutan resorted to democracy in March 2008, Royal decrees were still the laws. There would be no real freedom and all the rights promised by the drafting committee were impossible to achieve in Bhutan.

Committee: The Royal Government of Bhutan (RGOB) did not include any member from Nepali-speaking Lhotshampa community in the drafting committee, thus, muting the minority voice was there in its formulation. Thus, the Constitution always remained a subject of debate and controversy even after its adoption. The Chairman of the drafting committee and the RGOB have frequently told the international media that the people do not want Constitution and are happy with the present system. In real terms, Bhutan would be no different from the erstwhile Panchayati Raj in pre-1990.

Personal freedoms: Bhutanese people did not enjoy even basic personal freedoms like wearing the dresses of their own choice. The Royal government infringed personal freedoms with the prescription of dress code.

There was no Election Commission. There used not to be qualified judges with legal educational background to interpret the Constitution and uphold the independence of the judiciary. People had no right to freedom of expression and press, which are the basic pillars under which the Constitution and a democratic society stand. Without the right to freedom of expression and press, how are the people expected to deliberate on the Constitution and express their views?

The basic flaw in the Bhutanese society, system and the government is not the lack or absence of a Constitution, but their intolerance to any kind of criticism before the recent general elections were held in order to bring democracy in the country.

A rebel is born, if he is prevented from speaking. There are still hundreds of political prisoners in Bhutanese prisons incarcerated for their criticism of the government policies and voicing concern for political and human rights.

Refugees: The new Constitution will now solve Bhutanese refugee problem, rather it will exacerbate their situation. If the discriminatory Citizenship Act, 1985, which is responsible for the generation of refugees, is incorporated in the new Constitution, it will encourage the return of Bhutanese refugees permanently. The RGOB may not be likely to keep this Act. If the elections are held before the repatriation of refugees this will eventually block the return of refugees. Since their names will not be included in the electoral roll or voter's list it will make them non-citizens permanently.

Despite of these facts, no genuine and visible efforts with commitments on the repatriation of Bhutanese refugees have been taken by the International community and the United Nations. International community has not done anything even after a year of the completion of verification, besides the fact that even the verification results have not been published yet. However, by the newly acquired democracy hopes have emerged for a just society.

5. CYPRUS

Article-1: The State of Cyprus is an independent and sovereign Republic with a presidential regime, the President being Greek and the Vice-President being Turk elected by the Greek and the Turkish Communities of Cyprus respectively as hereinafter in this Constitution provided.

Article-8: [No Inhuman Punishment] No person shall be subjected to torture or to inhuman or degrading punishment or treatment.

Article-9: [Social Security] Every person has the right to a decent existence and to social security. A law shall provide for the protection of the workers, assistance to the poor and for a system of social insurance:

1. No person shall be held in slavery or servitude.

2. No person shall be required to perform forced or compulsory labour.

3. For the purposes of this Article the term "forced or compulsory labour" shall not include: (a) any work required to be done in the ordinary course of detention imposed according to the provisions of Article-11 or during conditional release from such detention; (b) any service of a military character if imposed or, in case of conscientious objectors, subject to their recognition by a law, service exacted instead of compulsory military service; (c) any service exacted in case of an adversity/emergency.

Article-10: [No Slavery, Servitude, Forced Labor] Emergency or calamity threatening the life or well-being of the inhabitants.

Article-11: [Liberty and Security of the Person]

1. Every person has the right to liberty and security of person.

2. No person shall be deprived of his liberty save in the following cases when and as provided by law:

(a) the detention of a person after conviction by a competent court; (b) the arrest or detention of a person for non-compliance with the lawful order of a court; (c) the arrest or detention of a person effected for the purpose of bringing him before the competent legal authority on reasonable suspicion of having committed an offence or when it is reasonably considered necessary to prevent his committing an offence or fleeing after having done so; (d) the detention of a minor by a lawful order for the purpose of educational supervision or his lawful detention for the purpose of bringing him before the competent legal authority; (e) the detention of persons for the prevention of spreading of infectious diseases, of persons of unsound mind, alcoholics or drug addicts or vagrants; (f) the arrest or detention of a person to prevent him effecting an unauthorised entry into the territory of the Republic or of an alien against whom action is being taken with a view to deportation or extradition.

3. Save when and as provided by law, in case of a flagrant offence, punishable with death or imprisonment, no person shall be arrested save under the authority of a reasoned judicial warrant issued according to the formalities prescribed by the law.

4. Every person arrested shall be informed at the time of his arrest in a language, which he understands of the reasons for his arrest and shall be allowed to have the services of a lawyer of his own choosing.

5. The person arrested shall, as soon as is practicable after his arrest, and in any event not later than twenty-four hours after the arrest, be brought before a judge, if not earlier released.

6. The judge before whom the person arrested is brought shall promptly proceed to inquire into the grounds of the arrest in a language understandable by the person arrested and shall, as soon as possible and in any event, not later than three days from such appearance, either release the person arrested on such terms as he may deem fit, or where the investigation into the commission of the offence for which he has been arrested has not been completed, remand him in custody and may remand him in custody from time to time, for a period not exceeding eight days at any one time: Provided that the total period of such remand in custody shall not exceed three months

of the date of the arrest on the expiration of which every person or authority having the custody of the person arrested shall forthwith set him free. Any decision of the judge under this paragraph shall be subject to appeal.

7. Every person who is deprived of his liberty by arrest or detention shall be entitled to take proceedings by which the lawfulness of his detention shall be decided speedily by a court and his release ordered if the detention is not lawful.

8. Every person who has been the victim of arrest or detention in contravention of the provisions of this Article shall have an enforceable right to compensation.

Article-12: [Habeas Corpus, Double Jeopardy, Proportionality of Punishment, Presumption of Innocence, Right to Defense]

1. No person shall be held guilty of any offence on account of any act or omission which did not constitute an offence under the law at the time when it was committed; and no person shall have a heavier punishment imposed on him, for an offence other than that expressly provided for it by law at the time when it was committed.

2. A person who has been acquitted or convicted of an offence shall not be tried again for the same offence. No person shall be punished twice for the same act or omission except where death ensues from such act or omission.

3. No law shall provide for a punishment which is disproportionate to the gravity of the offence.

4. Every person charged with an offence shall be presumed innocent until proved guilty according to law.

5. Every person charged with an offence has the following minimum rights: (a) to be informed promptly and in a language which he understands and in detail of the nature and grounds of the charge preferred against him; (b) to have adequate time and facilities for the preparation of his defense; (c) to defend himself in person or through a lawyer of his own choosing or, if he has no sufficient means to pay for legal assistance, to be given free legal assistance when the interests of justice so

require; (d) to examine or have examined witnesses against him and to obtain the attendance and examination of witnesses on his behalf under the same conditions as witnesses against him; (e) to have the free.

6. A punishment of general confiscation of property is prohibited.

7. Primary education shall be compulsory for all citizens of such school age as may be determined by a relevant communal law.

Article-24: [Duties]

1. Every person is bound to contribute according to his means towards the public burdens.

2. No such contribution by way of tax, duty or rate of any kind whatsoever shall be imposed saves by or under the authority of a law.

3. No tax, duty or rate of any kind whatsoever shall be imposed with retrospective effect: Provided that any import duty may be imposed as from the date of the introduction of the relevant Bill.

4. No tax, duty or rate of any kind whatsoever other than customs duties shall be of a destructive or prohibitive nature.

5. The members of the armed forces, of the police and of the gendarmerie shall not have the right to strike. A law may extend such prohibition to the members of the public service.

6. Every person has the right: (a) to be informed of the reasons why he is required to appear before the court; (b) to present his case before the court and to have sufficient time necessary for its preparation; (c) to adduce or cause to be adduced his evidence and to examine witnesses according to law; (d) to have a lawyer of his own choice and to have free legal assistance where the interests of justice so require and as provided by law; (e) to have free assistance of an interpreter if he cannot understand or speak the language used in court.

Article-48: [The executive power] Powers exercised by the President of the Republic consists of the following matters:

(a) Designation and termination of appointment of Greek Ministers; (b) convening the meetings of the Council of Ministers as in Article 'provided, presiding at such meetings and taking part in the discussions thereat without any right to vote; (c) preparing the agenda of such meetings as in Article-56 provided; (d) right of final veto on decisions of the Council of Ministers concerning foreign affairs, defense or security as in Article-57 provided; (e) right of return of decisions of the Council of Ministers as in Article-51 provided; (f) right of final veto on laws or decisions of the House of Representatives concerning foreign affairs, defense or security as in Article-50 provided; (g) right of return of laws or decisions of the House of Representatives of the Budget as in Article-51 provided; (h) right of recourse to the Supreme Constitutional Court as in Articles 137, 138 and 143 provided; (i) right of reference to the Supreme Constitutional Court as in Article-141 provided; (j) publication of the communal laws and decisions of the Greek Communal Chamber as in Article-104 provided; (k) right of reference to the Supreme Constitutional Court of any law decision of the Greek Communal Chamber as in Article-142 provided; (l) right of recourse to the Supreme Constitutional Court in connection with any matter relating to any conflict or contest of power or competence arising between the House of Representatives and the Communal Chambers or any of them and between any organs of, or authorities in, the Republic as in Article-139 provided; (m) the prerogative of mercy in capital cases as in Article-53 provided; (n) the exercise of any of the powers specified in Article-47 conjointly with the Vice-President of the Republic.

Article-50: 1. The President and the Vice-President of the Republic, separately or conjointly, shall have the right of final veto on any law or decision of the House of Representatives or any part thereof concerning:

(a) Foreign affairs, except the participation of the Republic in international organisations and pacts of alliance in which the Kingdom of Greece and the Republic of Turkey both participate. For the purposes of this sub-paragraph "foreign affairs" includes: (i) the recognition of States, the establishment of diplomatic and consular relations with other countries and the interruption of such relations. The grant of acceptance to diplomatic representatives and of exequatur to consular representatives. The assignment of diplomatic representatives and of consular representatives, already in the diplomatic service, to posts abroad and the entrusting of functions abroad to special envoys already in the diplomatic service. The appointment and the assignment of persons, who are not already in the diplomatic service, to any posts abroad as diplomatic or consular representatives and the entrusting of functions abroad to persons, who are not already in the diplomatic service, as special envoys; (ii) the conclusion of international treaties, conventions and agreements; (iii) the declaration of war and the conclusion of peace; (iv) the protection abroad of the citizens of the Republic and of their interests; (v) the establishment, the status and the interests of aliens in the Republic; (vi) the acquisition of foreign nationality by citizens of the Republic and their acceptance of employment by, or their entering the service of, a foreign Government.

(b) the following questions of defense: (i) composition and size of the armed forces and credits for them; (ii) nomination of cadres and their promotions; (iii) importation of war materials and also explosives of all kinds; (iv) cession of bases and other facilities to allied countries.

(c) The following questions of security: (i) nominations of cadres and their promotions; (ii) distribution and stationing of farces; (iii) emergency measures and martial law; (iv) police laws.

It is specified that the right of veto under sub-paragraph (c) above shall cover all emergency measures or decisions, but not those which concern the normal functioning of the police and the gendarmerie.

2. The above right of veto may be exercised either against the whole of a law or decision or against any part thereof, and in the latter case such law or decision shall be returned to the House of Representatives for a decision whether the remaining part thereof will be submitted, under the relevant provisions of this Constitution, for promulgation.

3. The right of veto under this Article shall be exercised within the period for the promulgation of laws or decisions of the House of Representatives as in Article-52 provided.

Article-51: 1. The President and the Vice-President of the Republic shall have the right, either separately or conjointly, to return any law or decision or any part thereof of the House of Representatives to the House for reconsideration.

2. On the adoption of the Budget by the House of Representatives the President and the Vice-President of the Republic, either separately or conjointly, may exercise his or their right to return it to the House of Representatives on the ground that in his or their judgment there is discrimination.

3. In case a law or decision or any part thereof is returned to the House of Representatives as in paragraph 1 of this Article provided, the House of Representatives shall pronounce on the matter so returned within fifteen days of such return, and in the case of return of the Budget as in paragraph 2 of this Article provided the House of Representatives shall pronounce on the matter so returned, within thirty days of such return.

4. If the House of Representatives persists in its decision, the President and the Vice-President of the Republic shall, subject to the provisions of this Constitution, promulgate the law or decision or the Budget, as the case may be, within the time limit fixed for the promulgation of laws and decisions of the House of Representatives by publication of such law or decision or Budget in the official Gazette of the Republic.

5. Whenever the President or the Vice-President of the Republic exercises his right to return as provided in this Article he shall immediately notify the other of such return.

6. The right of return under this Article shall be exercised within the period for the promulgation of laws or decisions of the House of Representatives as in Article-52 provided.

Article-52: The President and the Vice-President of the Republic shall, within fifteen days of the transmission to their respective offices of any law or decision of the House of Representatives, promulgate by publication in the official

Gazette of the Republic, such law or decision unless in the meantime they exercise, separately or conjointly, as the case may be, their right of veto as in Article-50 provided or their right of return as in Article-51 provided or their right of reference to the Supreme Constitutional Court as in Articles 140 and 141 provided or in the case of the Budget their right of recourse to the Supreme Constitutional Court as in Article-138 provided.

Article-80: 1. The right to introduce Bills belongs to the representatives and to the ministers. 2. No Bill relating to an increase in budgetary expenditure can be introduced by any representative.

Article-84: 1. Representatives receive from the Public Revenue remuneration defined by law. 2. Any increase of such remuneration shall not become operative during the term of office of the House of Representatives in which such increase has been made.

Article-85: Any question with regard to the qualifications of candidates for election and election petitions shall be finally adjudicated by the Supreme Constitutional Court.

Article-87: 1. The Communal Chambers shall, in relation to their respective Community, have competence to exercise within the limits of this Constitution and subject to paragraph 3 of this Article, legislative power solely with regard to the following matters: (a) all religious matters; (b) all educational, cultural and teaching matters; (c) personal status; (d) the composition and instances of courts dealing with civil disputes relating to personal status and to religious matters; (e) in matters where the interests and institutions are of purely communal nature such as charitable and sporting foundations, bodies and associations created for the purpose of promoting the well-being of their respective Community; (f) Imposition of personal taxes and fees on members of their respective Community in order to provide for their respective needs and for the needs of bodies and institutions under their control as in Article-88 provided; (g) in matters where subsidiary legislation in the form of regulations or bye-laws within the framework of the laws relating to municipalities will be necessary to enable a Communal Chamber to promote the aims pursued by municipalities composed solely of members of its respective community; (h) in matters relating to the exercise of the authority of control of producers' and consumers' co-operatives and credit establishments and of supervision in their functions of municipalities consisting solely of their respective community, vested in them by this Constitution: Provided that—*(i)* any communal law, regulation, bye-law or decision made or taken by a Communal Chamber under this sub-paragraph (h) shall directly or indirectly be contrary to or inconsistent with any by which 'producers and consumers' co-operatives and credit establishments are governed or to which the municipalities subject, *(ii)* nothing in paragraph (i) of this provison contained shall be construed as enabling the House of Representatives to legislate on any matter relating to the exercise of the authority vested in Communal Chamber under this sub-paragraph (i): in such other matters as are expressly provided by this Constitution.

2. Nothing in sub-paragraph (f) of paragraph-1 of this Article contained shall be construed as in any way curtailing the power of the House of Representatives to impose, in accordance with the provisions of this Constitution, any personal taxes.

3. Any law or decision of a Communal Chamber made or taken in exercise of the power vested in it under paragraph-1 of this Article shall not in any way contain anything contrary to the Fundamental Rights.

4. Interests of the security of the Republic or the constitutional order or the public safety or the public order or the public health or the public morals or which is against the fundamental rights and liberties guaranteed by this Constitution to any person (Communal Chamber means Parliament).

Article-111: Subject to the provisions of this Constitution any matter relating to betrothal, marriage, divorce, nullity of marriage, judicial separation or restitution of conjugal rights or to family relations other than legitimating by order of the court or adoption of members of the Greek-Orthodox Church or of a religious group to which the provisions of paragraph-3 of Article-2 shall apply shall, on and after the date of the coming into operation of this Constitution, be governed by the law of the Greek-Orthodox Church or of the Church of such religious group, as the case may be, and shall be cognizable by a tribunal of such Church and no Communal Chamber shall act inconsistently with the provisions of such law. Nothing in paragraph-1 of this Article contained shall preclude the application of the provisions of paragraph-5 of Article-90 to the execution of any judgment or order of any such tribunal.

6. IRAN

Iranian society based on Islamic principles and norms, which represent an honest aspiration of the Islamic Ummah. The judiciary in the Constitution: The judiciary is of vital importance in the context of safeguarding the rights of the people.

Islamic Government: The plan of the Islamic government as proposed by Imam Khomeini "Independence! Freedom! Islamic Government!". Koranic verse "This community is a single community; The Economy is a Means, Not an End Woman in the Constitution. Through the creation of Islamic social infrastructures, all the elements of humanity that served the multifaceted foreign exploitation shall regain their identity and human rights. As a part of this process, it is only natural that women should benefit from a particularly large augmentation of their rights, because of the greater oppression that they suffered under the old regime. The family is the fundamental unit of society and the main center for the growth and edification of human being. Compatibility with respect to belief and ideal, which provides the primary basis for man's development and growth, is the main consideration in the establishment of a family. It is the duty of the Islamic government to provide the necessary facilities for the attainment of this goal. This view of the family unit delivers woman from being regarded as an object or instrument in the service of promoting consumerism and exploitation. Not only does woman recover thereby her momentous and precious function of motherhood, rearing of ideologically committed human beings, she also assumes a pioneering social role and becomes the fellow straggler of man in all vital areas of life. Given the weighty responsibilities that woman thus assumes, she is accorded in Islam great value and nobility. An Ideological Army Koranic verse [8:60]. "Prepare against them whatever force you are able to muster, and strings of horses, striking fear into the enemy of God and your enemy, and others besides them" The Judiciary in the Constitution Koranic verse [4:58]. "When you judge among the people, judge with justice".

Executive Power: The system of bureaucracy, the result and product of old forms of government, will be firmly cast away, so that an executive system that functions efficiently and swiftly in the fulfillment of its administrative commitments comes into existence. Mass-Communication Media Koranic verse [2:143] "Thus We made you a median community, that you might be witnesses to men" Article-1 [Form of Government] Koranic justice, in the referendum of 29 and 30 Mar 79.

Article-2: [Foundational Principles] Koranic Principles: The Islamic Republic is a system based on belief in: (1) the One God; (2) divine revelation and its fundamental role in setting forth the laws; (3) the return to God; (4) the justice of God in creation and legislation; (5) continuous leadership and perpetual guidance; (6) the exalted dignity and value of man, and his freedom coupled with responsibility before God; in which equity, justice, political, economic, social, and cultural independence, and national solidarity are secured by recourse to: (a) continuous leadership of the holy persons, possessing necessary qualifications, exercised on the basis of the Koran and the Sunnah, upon all of whom be peace; (b) sciences and arts and the most advanced results of human experience, together with the effort to advance them further; (c) negation of all forms of oppression, both the infliction of and the submission to it, and of dominance, both its imposition and its acceptance.

Article-3: [State Goals] In order to attain the objectives specified in Article-2, the government of the Islamic Republic of Iran has the duty of directing all its resources to the following goals:

(1) the creation of a favorable environment for the growth of moral virtues based on faith and piety and the struggle against all forms of vice and corruption;

(2) raising the level of public awareness in all areas, through the proper use of the press, mass media, and other means;

(3) free education and physical training for everyone at all levels, and the facilitation and expansion of higher education;

(4) strengthening the spirit of inquiry, investigation, and innovation in all areas of science, technology, and culture, as well as Islamic studies, by establishing research centers and encouraging researchers;

(5) the complete elimination of imperialism and the prevention of foreign influence;

(6) the elimination of all forms of despotism and autocracy and all attempts to monopolize power;

(7) ensuring political and social freedoms within the framework of the law;

(8) the participation of the entire people in determining their political, economic, social, and cultural destiny;

(9) the abolition of all forms of undesirable discrimination and the provision of equitable opportunities for all, in both the material and the intellectual spheres;

(10) the creation of a correct administrative system and elimination of superfluous government organization;

(11) all round strengthening of the foundations of national defense to the utmost degree by means of universal military training for the sake of safeguarding the independence, territorial integrity, and the Islamic order of the country;

(12) the planning of a correct and just economic system, in accordance with Islamic criteria, in order to create welfare, eliminate poverty, and abolish all forms of deprivation with

respect to food, housing, work, health care, and the provision of social insurance for all;

(13) the attainment of self-sufficiency in scientific, technological, industrial, agricultural, and military domains, and other similar spheres;

(14) securing the multifarious rights of all citizens, both women and men, and providing legal protection for all, as well as the equality of all before the law;

(15) the expansion and strengthening of Islamic brotherhood and public cooperation among all the people;

(16) framing the foreign policy of the country on the basis of Islamic criteria, fraternal commitment to all Muslims, and unsparing support to the freedom fighters of the world.

Article-6: [Administration of Affairs] In the Islamic Republic of Iran, the affairs of the county must be administered on the basis of public opinion expressed by the means of elections, including the election of the President, the representatives of the Islamic Consultative Assembly, and the members of councils, or by means of referenda in matters specified in other articles of this Constitution.

Article-13: [Recognized Religious Minorities] Zoroastrian, Jewish, and Christian Iranians are the only recognized religious minorities, who, within the limits of the law, are free to perform their religious rites and ceremonies, and to act according to their own Canon in matters of personal affairs and religious education.

Article-19: [No Discrimination, No Privileges].

Article-20: [Equality before Law].

Article-21: [Women's Rights] The government must ensure the rights of women in all respects, in conformity with Islamic criteria, and accomplish the following goals:

(1) Create a favorable environment for the growth of woman's personality and the restoration of her material and intellectual rights;

(2) The protection of mothers, particularly during pregnancy and child-rearing, and the protection of children without guardians;

(3) Establishing competent courts to protect and preserve the family;

(4) The provision of special insurance for widows, aged women, and women without support;

(5) The awarding of guardianship of children to worthy mothers, in order to protect the interests of the children, in the absence of a legal guardian.

Article-22: [Human Dignity and Rights] The dignity, life, property, rights, residence, and occupation of the individual are inviolate, except in cases sanctioned by law.

Article-23: [Freedom of Belief].

Article-24: [Freedom of the Press] Publications and the press have freedom of expression except when it is detrimental to the fundamental principles of Islam or the rights of the public.

Article-30: [Education] The government must provide all citizens with free education up to secondary school.

Article-31: [Housing] It is the right of every Iranian individual.

Article-32: [Arrest] No one may be arrested except by the order and in accordance with the procedure lay down by law. In case of arrest, charges with the reasons for accusation must, without delay, be communicated and explained to the accused in writing, and a provisional dossier must be forwarded to the competent judicial authorities within a maximum of twenty-four hours so that the preliminaries to the trial can be completed as swiftly as possible. The violation of this article will be liable to punishment in accordance with the law.

Article-34: [Recourse to the Courts] It is the indisputable right of every citizen to seek justice by recourse to competent courts. All citizens have right of access to such courts, and no one can be barred from courts to which he has a legal right of recourse.

Article-37: [Presumption of Innocence] Innocence is to be presumed, and no one is to be held guilty of a charge unless his or her guilt has been established by a competent court.

Article-38: [Torture] All forms of torture for the purpose of extracting confession or acquiring information is forbidden. Compulsion of individuals to testify, confess, or take an oath is not permissible; and any testimony, confession, or oath obtained under duress is devoid of value and credence. Violation of this article is liable to punishment in accordance with the law.

Article-43: [Principles-Citizen's rights] (1) The provision of basic necessities for all citizens: housing, food, clothing, hygiene, medical treatment, education, and the necessary facilities for the establishment of a family; (2) ensuring conditions and opportunities of employment; (3) leading to all-round development, full use of his creativity; (4) respect for the right to choose freely an occupation; (5) the prohibition of extravagance and wastefulness; (6) the utilization of and the training of skilled; (7) prevention of foreign economic domination over the country's economy; (8) emphasis on increase of agricultural, livestock, and industrial production in order to satisfy public needs and to make the county self-sufficient and free from dependence.

Article-44: [Sectors] (1) The economy of the Islamic Republic of Iran is to consist of three sectors: state, cooperative, and private Article-90: [Complaints, Petitions] who so ever, has a complaint concerning the work of the Assembly or the executive power or the judicial power can forward his complaint in writing to the Assembly. The Assembly must investigate his complaint and give a satisfactory reply. In cases where the complaint relates to the executive or the judiciary, the Assembly must demand proper investigation in the matter and an adequate explanation from them, and announce the results within a reasonable time. In cases where the subject of the complaint is of public interest, the reply must be made public.

Article-97: [Attendance in Parliament] In order to expedite the work, the members of the Guardian Council may attend the Assembly and listen to its debates when a government bill or a members' bill is under discussion. When an urgent government or members' bill is placed on the agenda of the Assembly, the members of the Guardian Council must attend the Assembly and make their views known.

Article-140: [No Immunity] Allegations of common crimes against the President, his deputies, and the Ministers will be investigated in common courts of justice with the knowledge of the Islamic Consultative Assembly.

Article-165: [Public Trials] Trials are to be held openly and members of the public may attend without any restriction unless the court determines that an open trial would be detrimental to public morality or discipline, or if in case of private disputes, both the parties request not to hold open hearing.

Article-167: [Rule of Law for Judiciary] The judge is bound to endeavor to judge each case on the basis of the codified law.

In case of the absence of any such law, he has to deliver his judgment on the basis of authoritative Islamic sources and authentic fatwa. He, on the pretext of the silence of or deficiency of law in the matter, or its brevity or contradictory nature, cannot refrain from admitting and examining cases and delivering his judgment.

Article-171: [Liability of Judges] Whenever an individual suffers moral or material loss as the result of a default or error of the judge with respect to the subject matter of a case or the verdict delivered, or the application of a rule in a particular case, the defaulting judge must stand surety for the reparation of that loss in accordance with the Islamic criteria, if it be a case of default. Otherwise, losses will be compensated for by the State. In all such cases, the repute and good standing of the accused will be restored.

Article-174: [National General Inspectorate] In accordance with the right of the judiciary to supervise the proper conducting of affairs and the correct implementation of laws by the administrative organs of the government, an organization will be constituted under the supervision of the head of the judiciary branch to be known as the National General Inspectorate. The powers and duties of this organization will be determined by law.

7. MEXICO

Article-1: Elementary education shall be compulsory.

Article-2: All education given by the State shall be free.

Article-4: No person can be prevented from engaging in the profession, industrial or commercial pursuit, or occupation of his freedom.

Article-7: Freedom of writing and publishing writings on any subject is inviolable.

Article-8: Every petition shall be replied to in writing by the official, to whom it is addressed.

Article-14: No person shall be deprived of life, liberty, property, possessions, or rights without a trial by a duly created court in which the essential formalities of procedure are observed and in accordance with laws issued prior to the act.

a. In criminal cases no penalty shall be imposed by mere analogy or by prior evidence. The penalty must be decreed in a law in every respect applicable to the crime in question.

b. In civil suits the final judgment shall be according to the letter or the juridical interpretation of the law; in the absence of the latter it shall be based on the general principles of law.

Article-17: No one may be imprisoned for debts of a purely civil nature.

Article-18: Arrest is permissible only for offenses punishable by imprisonment. The place of detention shall be completely separate from the place used for the serving of sentences.

Article-19: No detention shall exceed three days without a formal order of commitment, which shall state the offense with which the accused is charged; the substance thereof; the place, time and circumstances of its commission; and the facts brought to light in the preliminary examination. These facts must be sufficient to establish the *corpus delicti* and the probable guilt of the accused. All authorities who order a detention or consent thereto, as well as all agents, subordinates, wardens or jailers who execute it, shall be liable for any breach of this provision.

a. The trial shall take place only for the offense or offenses set forth in the formal order of commitment. Should it develop, during the course of the proceedings, that another offense, different from that charged, has been committed, a separate accusation must be brought. This, however, shall not prevent the joinder of both proceedings, if deemed advisable.

b. Any ill-treatment during arrest or confinement; any molesting without legal justification; any exaction or contribution of the judiciary. If the offender is a day laborer or a workman, his punishment cannot consist of a fine exceeding the amount of his wages, for one week. An advisory board composed of five organic laws; consequently, the law shall punish severely and the authorities shall effectively prosecute every concentration or cornering in one or a few hands of articles of prime necessity for the purpose of obtaining a rise in prices.

Article-38: The rights or prerogatives of citizens are suspended: persons to be appointed by the President of the Republic and who shall perform the functions specified in the Constitution:

I. Through failure to comply, without sufficient cause, with any of the obligations imposed by Article-36. This suspension shall last for one year and shall be in addition to any other penalties prescribed by law for the same offense;

II. Through being subjected to criminal prosecution for an offense punishable by imprisonment (*pena corporal*), the suspension to be reckoned from the date of the formal order of commitment;

III. Throughout a term of imprisonment;

IV. Through vagrancy or habitual drunkenness, affirmed in the manner prescribed by law;

V. Through being a fugitive from justice, the suspension being reckoned from the date of the order of arrest until the prescription of the criminal action;

VI. Through final sentence imposing such suspension as a penalty;

VII. The law shall specify those cases in which civil rights may be lost or suspended.

Article-101: The ministers of the Supreme Court of Justice, the circuit magistrates, the district judges, and their respective clerks in Violation of this provision to seek other employment shall be punishable by loss of office.

Article-104: The federal courts shall have jurisdiction over:

I. All controversies of a civil or criminal nature;

II. Cases in which the Federation is interested, the laws may provide for appeals to the Supreme Court of Justice against judgments in second instance or against those of administrative courts created by federal law, provided that such courts are granted autonomy to render their decisions;

III. Those that arise between two or more States, or one State and the Federation, and those that arise between counts of the federal District and those of the Federal or State;

IV. Those that arise between a State and one or more residents of another State;

V. All cases that involve members of the diplomatic and consular corps.

Article-106: The Supreme Court of Justice shall likewise have the power to settle questions of jurisdiction that arise between courts of the Federation, between the latter and State courts, or between the courts of one State and those of another

Article-125: No individual may fill two popularly elected federal offices at the same time, nor one federal and one state office, also by popular election; but an elected candidate may choose which of the two he desires to hold.

8. TURKEY

Article-9: Judicial Power: Judicial power shall be exercised by independent courts on behalf of the Turkish Nation.

Article-10: Equality before the Law:

(1) All individuals are equal without any discrimination before the law, irrespective of language, race, colour, sex, political opinion, philosophical belief, religion and sect, or any such considerations.

(2) No privilege shall be granted to any individual, family, group or class.

(3) State organs and administrative authorities shall act in compliance with the principle of equality before the law in all their proceedings.

Article-13: Restriction of Fundamental Rights and Freedoms:

(1) Fundamental rights and freedoms may be restricted by law, in conformity with the letter and spirit of the Constitution, with the aim of safeguarding the indivisible integrity of the State with its territory and nation, national sovereignty, the Republic, national security, public order, general peace, the public interest, public morals and public health, and also for specific reasons set forth in the relevant Articles of the Constitution.

(2) General and specific grounds for restrictions of fundamental rights and freedoms shall not conflict with the requirements of the democratic order of society and shall not be imposed for any purpose other than those for which they are prescribed.

(3) The general grounds for restriction set forth in this article shall apply for all fundamental rights and freedoms.

Article-14: Prohibition of Abuse of Fundamental Rights and Freedoms:

(1) None of the rights and freedoms embodied in the Constitution shall be exercised with the aim of violating the

indivisible integrity of the State with its territory and nation, of endangering the existence of the Turkish State and Republic, of destroying fundamental rights and freedoms, of placing the government of the State under the control of an individual or a group of people, or establishing the hegemony of one social class over others, or creating discrimination on the basis of language, race, religion or sect, or of establishing by any other means a system of government based on these concepts and ideas.

(2) The sanctions to be applied against those who violate these prohibitions and those who incite and provoke others to the same end shall be determined by law.

(3) No provision of this Constitution shall be interpreted in a manner that would grant the right of destroying the rights and freedoms embodied in the Constitution.

Article-15: Suspension of the Exercise of Fundamental Rights and Freedoms

(1) In times of war, mobilisation, martial law, or state of emergency, the exercise of fundamental rights and freedoms can be partially or entirely suspended, or measures may be taken, to the extent required by the exigencies of the situation, which derogate the guarantees embodied in the Constitution, provided that obligations under international law are not violated.

(2) Even under the circumstances indicated in the first paragraph, the individual's right to life, and the integrity of his material and spiritual entity shall be inviolable except where the death sentence has been decided upon; no one may be compelled to reveal his religion, conscience, thought or opinion, nor be accused on account of them; offences and penalties may not be made retroactive, nor may anyone be held guilty until so proven by a court judgment.

Article-71: Declaration of Assets: Declaration of assets by persons entering public service, and the frequency of such declaration, shall be determined by law. Those serving in the legislative and executive organs shall not be exempted from this requirement.

Article-74: Right of Petition:

(1) Citizens have the right to apply in writing to the competent authorities and to the Turkish Grand National Assembly with regard to requests and complaints concerning themselves or the public.

(2) The result of the application concerning himself shall be made known to the petitioner in writing.

(3) The way of exercising this right shall be determined by law.

Article-100: Parliamentary Investigation:

(1) Parliamentary investigation concerning the Prime Minister or other ministers may be requested with a motion tabled by at least one-tenth of the total number of members of the Turkish Grand National Assembly. The Assembly shall consider and decide on this request within one month at the latest.

(2) In the event of a decision to initiate an investigation, this investigation shall be conducted by a commission of fifteen members chosen by lot on behalf of each party from among three times the number of members the party is entitled to have on the commission, representation being proportional to the parliamentary membership of the party. The commission shall submit its report on the result of the investigation to the Assembly within two months. If the investigation is not completed within the time allotted, the commission shall be granted a further and final period of two months.

(3) The Assembly shall debate the report with priority and, if found necessary, may decide to bring the person involved before the Supreme Court. The decision to bring a person before the Supreme Court shall be taken only by an absolute majority of the total number of members.

(4) Political party groups in the Assembly shall not hold discussions or take decisions regarding parliamentary investigations.

Article-108: State Supervisory Council:

(1) The State Supervisory Council which shall be attached to the office of the Presidency of the Republic with the purpose of performing and furthering the regular and efficient functioning of the administration and its observance of law, will be empowered to conduct upon the request of the President of the Republic all inquiries, investigations and inspections of all public bodies and organisations, all enterprises in which those public bodies and organisations share more than half of the capital, public professional organisations, employers' associations and labour unions at all levels, and public benefit associations and foundations.

(2) The Armed Forces and all judicial organs are outside the jurisdiction of the State Supervisory Council.

(3) The members and the chairman to be designated from among the members of the State Supervisory Council shall be appointed by the President of the Republic from among those with the qualifications set forth in the law.

(4) The functioning of the State Supervisory Council, the term of office of its members, and other matters relating to their status shall be regulated by law.

9. FINLAND

Judicial power shall be exercised by independent courts of law, at the highest instance the Supreme Court and the Supreme Administrative Court.

All persons shall be equal before the law.

No one shall, without acceptable grounds, be afforded a different status on account of sex, age, origin, language, religion, conviction, opinion, state of health, disability or any other reason related to the person.

Section-6: No one shall be sentenced to death, tortured or otherwise treated in a degrading manner. There shall be no interference in personal integrity, nor shall anyone be deprived of his liberty in an arbitrary manner and without grounds prescribed by Act of Parliament. All penalties entailing deprivation of liberty shall be imposed by a court of law. The lawfulness of other forms of deprivation of liberty may be submitted to judicial review. The rights of persons who have been deprived their liberty shall be secured by Act of Parliament.

Section-8: The secrecy of correspondence and of telephone and other confidential communications shall be inviolable.

Section-15a: Everyone who is unable to procure the security required for a dignified life shall have the right to necessary subsistence and care.

Section-16: The publicity of proceedings and the right to be heard, to receive a decision with stated grounds and to appeal against the decision as well as other guarantees of a fair trial and of good public administration shall be secured by Act of Parliament.

Section-16a: Public authorities shall secure the implementation of fundamental rights and of international human rights.

Section-17: If a representative does not arrive in time for a parliamentary session or if, without the permission of Parliament, he fails to appear and has no acceptable excuse; Parliament may impose as a sanction the forfeiture of the whole or a part of his salary. If the representative does not thereafter amend his conduct, Parliament may revoke his mandate. If a representative is serving a sentence of imprisonment, he shall forfeit his salary for the same period. An initiative may be withdrawn when there are grounds for so doing.

Important and Relevent part in the Constitutions

Argentina	Section-111 (4)
Moracco	Art-63
France	Art-64-66
Cyprus	Art-11(b), 5, 6, 7, 12
Iran	Art-32, 34, 37, 43, 90, 165, 14(a)
Italy	Art-15, 71, 74
Finland	Section-6

What Obstructs Quick Justice

15

Research and analysis reveal certain hard facts that come in the way of quick justice.

Frustration is the product of multiple failures beyond the capabilities of a hardworking person. If it is maintained for some time it transforms into hopelessness by and by resulting into a negative attitude. It is a slow but successive process, which takes firm footing into us overriding our capabilities. On the contrary, to remain hopeful even in odd conditions suffers no stage of deterioration. Positive attitude makes a man succeed at last and keeps him/her physically active and mentally fit. Judicial officers for their professional liability, to the cause, need to occupy chair in the courtroom with a positive attitude to finish their work in a balanced way to help the sufferer as well as to his own conscious.

To be politically conscious, while working has become latest fashion for judicial officers in third world countries. Highlighted cases are decided as per the expectation of media. Recently, high court in Delhi hearing two murder cases are the evidence. On the other side, the court dismisses hundreds of old admitted cases of its own, in camera, as done to decide old admitted cases in the first week of January 2005. The court is not justified to have such dual standards. Priority to decide highlighted cases is highly objectionable for the waiting litigants, who are in queue for the last few decades. On one side, the court admits a writ without asked for and on the other side; the court dismisses it of its own reasons, ignoring the merits of the case.

Over-loaded judicial-officers due to irrational distribution of cases and imbalanced allocation of work create displeasure among magistrates and judges. The judicial officers understand the situation well that the negative attitude of government by keeping thousands of posts of judicial officers vacant, are on one side and balanced, honest, committed judges are on the other. Citizens must be thankful to most of the judicial officers who are handling more cases every day properly and judiciously than a judicial officer should handle.

To boost the moral of judicial officers, Peoplism shall not allow reservation in judiciary. Also, the various discrepancies shall also be ruled out in the appointment procedure and all the reasons and factors that pervert a judicial officer from his work shall be taken into account making the atmosphere more conducive and clean to work efficiently.

All the vacancies in judiciary shall be filled on first priority. We can afford to hold postings in any other department but to keep vacancies unfilled for years together in judiciary is proving highly damaging to the entire system. Law shall be framed to affect this concept and special exchequer will be allocated for this purpose in Peoplism. Judiciary in Peoplism has been placed at second place after Ministry of Defense.

After Article-21 of the Constitution, ensured premises to Bar Association in/near court premises, the Association acquired more rights to take the entire premises under their control. So much so, allowing venders within the court building in lower courts have converted the court building into a mess. The trial courts at other places also, are the worst example of grabbing of court building by all kind of venders. Touts are rampant there. The ways of staff of trial courts are so bold that they ask fee for every work they are supposed to do as a part of their official duty. They are so confident in getting a tip that they did not hesitate to ask for it, even in presence of the magistrate.

The client becomes unsupported and helpless inside the courtroom. In court-premises, he cannot oppose any of the atrocities by the lawyers, vendors and staff of the court, if he wants to get his work done. He will have no option than to submit to them. Accountability of lawyers and the judicial officers shall bring positive changes in their attitude. More responsible and reliable conduct shall help early justice to the litigants. Appointing sufficient number of judges, filling all existing vacancies, increasing the number of judges by abolishing multiple duties to one judicial officer, creating subordinate courts below the level of trial courts such as small cause courts, forums, Mediation cells, Civitals, independent Tribunals, cells for women, dowry cells, labour disputes, family disputes and many ad-hoc courts set up for special purpose for defined period and more internal administrative measures shall make judicial officers more efficient, confident, relaxed, honest, fast and respected. We shall create new vacancies where competent lawyers will be appointed as ad-hoc judges shall be the first priority of Peoplists.

To give judiciary its due honourable place; adopting above relieves; rehabilitate innocent citizens protecting them from crime and use of force by offenders, is the sole motto of this new system of governance. Research and analysis reveal certain hard facts that come in the way of quick justice:

1. Lack of positive attitude: The success of metro railways in Calcutta and Delhi gives a clear message that we still have capability to do things if we really want to do. So, to redress prolonged problems also need attention. If we can do metro, what we cannot do? We can do anything, if we really want to do. The only trait, we lack, is an intention to do things. We all qualified and well placed citizens must realise to leave our footprints on the stones not only to inspire our coming generations but to solve our present problems which have made our lives miserable.

2. Political agendas and priority of politicians: It is a common vote that politicians do not want to do any thing substantial for the poor. Rather, they want to keep people ignorant and deprived of economically and academically so that they can befooled for a long. But this theory seems to be a flirt now. Continuous efforts of serious top politicians have succeeded in bringing changes in the standard of lives of our countrymen in many fields. Industrial and marketing boost is evident. But the politicians have yet not taken education, legal justice, internal security, electioneering on their agenda which are still suffering from political neglect. If talk about one service i.e. education, we have lost good education after letting free from adequate government control. Gross corruption in education and unethical approach of teachers, especially at senior school level, is getting uncontrolable day by day in private school and colleges. The quality of education is continuously falling day by day. Inspiring stories of Munshi Prem Chand and literary legends have been replaced by film clips. Poetic lines of modern Hindi poets and English poets are missing from the syllabus. No one can deny that on the screen of juvenile mind, meaningful lines used to register for ever to inspire the disciples throughout their lives. I very well remember a number of verses from Hindi poetry that still inspire me to fight corruption in my life. The lines are *Veer tum badhe chalo, dheer tum badhe chalo, samne pahad ho singh ki dahad ho. Na tum jhuko kabhi na tum ruko kabhi, Veer tum badhe chalo* gives a versatile message of courage, sustenance, positivity and determination and this cannot be compared with a photograph of a seminude cinema actress on the school bags.

The first priority of politicians is any how to remain in power, no matter how low you need to go leaving aside the theory of morality and ethics. Today's politics is totally based on opportunism. To form government you often need to beg from opponents with adverse political ideology. Everyday collision governments may be minority governments are in sight these days. For such blending political parties have to give up their political ethics and morality to please the participants immorally abandoning national programmes approved by the Parliament. Therefore, a large number of development plans are left in the midway hindering national progress. There can be no un-interrupted national policy, programme and plans in such combination of political parties for national development in a time bound frame work. All such programmes which are essential for the poor countrymen like investment in uplifting standard of education, medical services, legal justice, police system, properly maintained roads and other development plans that need investment are kept in cold begs. Issuing license to more and more liquor shops is being practiced. One can imagine that the Delhi Government spending a lot of public money of Prohibition advertisement and Nasha Bandi (Prohibition) camps but opening liquor shop in industrial slums. Recent liquor shop at the corner of gali number 4, on New Rohtak Road at Anand Parbat Industrial Area became the first priority for unethical Delhi Government to spoil the families of labour and never thought of a small dispensary to treat poor labour and their family members. Present Delhi is the exact mirror of immorality of our politicians, who are increasing their salary for such nice job for the citizens. For politicians, all voters are equal, irrespective of their legal status. It is better if these voters are land grabbers and encroachers and form a bigger vote bank. Politicians also misuse public funds to spend in illegal colonies by giving facilities in slums and unauthorised colonies to those who have grabbed public land. But here the question of legality and illegality does not arise when there are no rules about spending this public money. Timid or corrupt bureaucrats work with such politicians thick and thin to please them. And politicians work to please such voters irrespective of their legal status. Public funds are for development in the lawful areas. But politicians do not hesitate to build lane and roads in these illegal colonies and show the expenditure in legal area. On the contrary, they take least care of the legal areas as the number of voters matters more for them. So, political will to follow rules and work legally is rare in today's politicians at least at lower levels of Municipal Corporation and Legislative Assembly.

3. Vacant posts for many years due to laxity: If on one side the judicial officers are difficult to access on the other side cumbersome judicial procedures make a litigant impossible to approach courts in case of emergency. For a poor person legal aid cells prove to be an eye-wash and there is total negligence and humiliation at the hands of workers and office bearers of legal aid cells. Even in the last court, the legal aid cell is suffering from bureaucracy and red tape-ism. Here, the lawyers on penal, prejudge the issues and turn it down saying that 'not a fit case on merits'. They take up only those cases which feed bribe or use approach. If the suffering litigant wants to see the officers, they refuse to see the litigant.

In the apex court, on December 14, 2006 at 3 pm, in his office of Secretary, when a litigant wanted to see the Joint Registrar cum Secretary of the Legal aid cell, he said that he is not working on that post now. When prayed, he said it is not the time to see him and he is busy. Finally, he refused to help the litigant for assigning some lawyer from the penal, to go through his SLP drafted by him, on prescribed payment mentioned in the SC Rules 1998. He said 'No'. A litigant if not in position to afford a private lawyer and is refused legal help from government sponsored legal aid cells should not hope for justice in such country and for him the entire judicial system is a fraud on other innocent citizens also. Thus, the very purpose of having free legal aid is completely forfeited when this service is under firm grip of office bearers who humiliate and insult the poor helpless litigants coming to them for legal aid. What to talk of legal services in trial courts and high courts.

If the politicians are not inclined to deal with heavy litigation in courts, the bureaucrats controlling the affairs in courts are confident to ignore the interest of suffering litigants in different manners. If political leaders are not inclined to allocate sufficient funds to fill a post of judicial officer, the bureaucrats too have no hurry to affect the appointment of judicial officers generating serious repercussions of having no judge in a court for years together. Judicial officers are also at ease as their salary cheques are released in time and for them they have to deal with a number of files without any human feeling while deciding the fate of sufferers mostly by ignoring the merits of the cases.

Since the top bureaucrats at secretary level in the government are comfortable with good salary, perks heavy paraphernalia from public funds. They never try to imagine the magnitude of suffering innocent accused in jails that had been trapped by the police in connivance of some white collared criminal. He is carefree, negligent, authoritarian, inaccessible and a big boss that feels to diminish his authority in clearing a file. Such negative attitude must be punishable making it a criminal offence to eradicate such callous attitude from our system. Negligence of duty flouting time bound framework shall be a criminal offence in Peoplism.

It is not just the shortage of funds to fill nearly 40,000 vacant posts of judicial officers in India for the last five years but the truth lies with bureaucratic tangle and their unquestionable absurd British legacy that has been reared in their minds being in very comfortable position in office. For instance, the Law Secretary was appointed in Ministry of Law, in Delhi administration. This officer has to be an IAS officer being a bureaucratic cadre in nature. But the Law Secretary is brought from judiciary from trial courts as he/she has to be delegated powers of presiding officer of Delhi School Tribunal to decide court cases of termination of school teachers from the school run under the jurisdiction of Delhi Education Act 1973. The tangle in this case is that the appointment of Law Secretary is affected by the L.G. on the recommendation of Principal Secretary, Delhi Administration and the judicial power to be a Presiding Officer of DST are delegated by the High Court of Delhi. So, the entire process of bringing a Presiding Officer in the Tribunal is full of legacy and fantasies of bureaucrats at various levels unnecessarily.

In the year 2003, July 30th, new Law Secretary was appointed on the very date on which the previous Law Secretary left the Law Department on transfer. But the new Law Secretary kept waiting for powers from the Delhi High Court and the work of Delhi School Tribunal remained suspended until the judicial powers came after a lapse of about six months. Now the question is why the powers were delayed by six months? Here the question of funds was not involved as the law secretary was being paid her salary since the first day of her joining. But the question of good intention and positive attitude was there which lacked. She too behaved accordingly, after taking charge and acquiring judicial powers practiced delaying tactics for postponing hearing. During her stay of 27 months as Presiding Officer of the Tribunal, she did not decide more than two cases and most of the times she lapsed service period by two more years of the terminated teachers unnecessary by adjournments. For such reason, there are more than twenty years old cases still rotting in the Tribunal. In one case file dated 1979, the teacher has died waiting for justice but his case still remains undecided in this tribunal till 2008. However, this Presiding Officer has now been promoted to the post of a high court judge in the Capital as per plan.

The number of vacant posts is not small. It is nearly 40,000 or more. That means if a judge hears 30 cases a day, by filling all these vacancies, the judiciary will be equipped to hear 12,00,000 (1.2 million or 12 lakh cases every day) or more cases a day through out the country, making the function of present judiciary much faster. Though, it needs a special exchequer from the central government but it can be spared from the reserves of the nation to practically serve the end of legal and other form of justices to more than 30 crore sufferers of judiciary of the country increasing the efficiency of present judges, who shall work freeing themselves from over-loading their extra burden in real sense. But it needs positive intension in right direction which we are still lacking.

4. Absence for periodic review of existing law: This has been our culture to be lithargic and negligent to take existing laws perfect, as we believe that these are working well since long. But the truth is different. There are number of situations and laws, where law, rules and regulations need to be framed (see the book by author titled 'Wanting Law'). But the practice is that we think of framing rules when an accident takes place causing heavy loss of life and property.

Parliamentarians keep sleeping on vital issues of safety of human lives and the apex court has to come forward to frame rules and laws as done in case of School buses, school admissions, and many more issues through PILs. Incompetent and inefficient politicians call it 'Judicial Activism'. Not only that if the court wants to correct an illegality, feel threatened, they amend laws as happened in case of sealing residential accommodations being used for commercial purposes. Under the grab of votes and power, criminal mentality in politics, at unit level keep doing and encouraging illegality in the society making life of law abiding citizens a hell. They never bother to amend law in the interest of law abiding citizens and if the court is doing its duty they are revengeful. If they do not do some one has to do and the courts are doing it.

Courts play a role of guardian of Constitution under which the Laws and Acts the Parliament frames. Then what is the fuss on court's preserving the prescribed and defined law? Courts cannot do work of legislation. If they are protecting legislation why the politicians feel challenged? Like ever before politicians always have double standards. The judiciary that is why have lost their credibility among law abiding citizens and silent supporters in the country whose number is the largest. This is one of many reasons that no one relies on corrupt politicians who are not doing any service to nation and are busy in serving their own ends only at the cost of good of the nation. It is highly condemnable. And we deplore them for such misconduct.

There are clear cut laws of Municipal Corporations through out the country that residential houses cannot be used for commercial purpose. These rules were framed decades back in different district corporations independently. It provide basic protection to our residential dwelling. Politicians never bothered to implement Master Plans they chalked out as a constitutional document and keep encouraging unscrupulous voters to distort law during their tenure to keep the voters in their pocket. Could a single politician come forward to tell us that he has reported to the police or civic authorities about illegal construction in his constituency or reported the police after 10.30 pm against playing loud speaker in Jagrata throughout the night or against a person who became overnight rich to the income tax department or any other investigatory agencies? The truth is that who boast of goodness in their speeches are only for talking and not taking problems of the country seriously. We have to pay by our nose to send wrong people to the legislative temples for such a long period of five years. But now, we have not to see the party stamp on a candidate but see personal conduct of a candidate, may be one solution.

5. Corrupt or faulty appointment procedure: There is a lot of corruption in appointments and recruitments in government.

If caste-reservation is also eating quality like a termite, the invaded corruption is making the situation worst. No one has any right to scrap quality for vested interest through reservation. What quality of work, what standards are set for acquiring just and rational use of authority and what has been achieved by consistent handwork, determination and devotion is a national property and by no political party no political goal can be achieved through handing-over quality and merits of the country in the name of reservation.

Beyond the concept of caste reservation, faulty recruitment procedures, political appointments and promotions tagged with seniority, ignoring deserving merits and no refresher periodical acquaintance of law, rules and regulations bring undeserving candidates to top posts, which have no inclination to be true to their work. Appointment of a judicial officer with this approach has to done with great care and it needs strict implementation of rules.

6. Least number of ad-hoc appointments and deputation posts: It has to be in practice to classify small cause disputes (court cases) and appoint ad-hoc judicial officers from the list of lawyers in 'Legal Aid Cells' throughout the country. It is unfortunate that for senior lawyers who enjoy a number of privileges under Article-21 of Constitution, few years have to be given to the paid social service as mandatory assignment to legal aid cell services and serve the poor in order to reciprocate the nation what is being shared as special privileges to them through constitutional advantage. In spite of appointing most junior and inexperienced lawyers, every senior lawyer has to have chance to run a ad-hoc or small cause court. There is no harm to appoint new lawyers on the penal but the presence of senior lawyer in the Legal services has to be made mandatory after a practice of 25 year's practice. To guide the juniors and look after the quality of service by the Legal Aid services, will certainly add to this national cause.

7. No Civitals: The concept, composition and functioning of Civitals has already been given in website of the author Civitals will prove to be an effective tool to get a FIR or a complaint registered with effective authority to reach the police, which a big fights these days. To get a case reported by the police is as important right of citizens as equally the right to justice by the courts.

During these sixty years, if police have taken it as their granted right to register a case or not; the courts also have reached at such a pass to decided or not to decide a case in time or not. Right to justice promised as a fundamental right now lies with the courts and not with the suffering citizens. While drafting the working of Civitals, it has been made mandatory to bring the complaint on record through electronic means or manually by third party like an NGO on behalf of the sufferer if the sufferer in not in a position to report the matter himself/herself and asks the registered NGO to report for him/her. Civitals if on one side enables a sufferer to get his/her report bringing on record, it also promises to give instant interim relief to the suffer by the attending magistrate like first aid is given to an injured person in the hospital.

8. No provision of consequential punishments in law: If those who file fake cases against innocents or harass subordinates to prove their authority on them and entangle them in legal complications, remain unpunished after the innocents are acquitted by the court, it amounts to injustice to the sufferer. This practice is very frequent with those who are in power and have no legal bar to misuse this power. If those who initiate the 'cause of action' fail in the court of law are punished being proved guilty of misusing authority and causing irreparable injury to innocent, getting punishment immediately at the time of acquittal of the innocent, fake filing shall be minimised which is not in practice now.

9. No 'Judicial Commission' to hear against misconduct of judicial officers: Concept, structure and operation has already been discussed earlier. It is true that every case has its own facts and figures and even similar cases need to be reviewed a fresh from law view-point, to pass specific order. Even in similar looking disputes a blanket decision some times does not solve the purpose. Presently, Absolute, undefined and unlimited discretion to judicial officers to hear and decide the cases is doing a lot of delay and straying the purpose of litigation. In such cases where a judicial officer is not handling a case properly and expeditiously as per decided guidelines framed by the Judicial Commission to an early and timely disposal of cases, may be cross-checked by such commission, if the litigant is not satisfied with the progress of the case. A litigant may also bring its other grievances against the unlawful intentions of a judicial officer with evidence, if he/she apprehends a foul play in the entire progress of his litigation. Such commission will not only hear the grievances of litigants but also from and maintain policies of appointing, recruiting, promoting and penalising the judicial officer as per clauses of 'Code of Judicial Conduct' adapted by the Commission.

10. Incompatible number of courts to the increasing population and the volume of increasing number of filed cases: It is so simple to calculate whether the number of courts has increased along with increasing population and number of cases filed rationally. The ratio formula between population and the number of courts needs to be revised and meticulously shrunk. Also, this revision needs a look into the fact that the bifurcation and ramification creating more profiles in judiciary, also needs to be taken into consideration. Presently, the courts are under heavy pressure of workload. It is worth quoting that the trial courts, civil courts and even high court of Delhi, try to avoid reading each and every word of the documents filed by parties, and especially the written arguments; they do not have time due to go through heavy number of the cases every day. How this can be possible for any efficient judicial officer to read and hear about one hundred cases every day, when every case is different from each other. In one case, a Double Bench in Delhi High Court, on 24th August 2006 refused to go through a 325 pages of case file, written arguments annexures along with provided citations and forced the petitioner in person to narrate his main points orally. The court heard the case very coarsely apparently overlooking all supplied annexure, arguments and decided court cases and passed orders against the litigant to get rid of it.

Over burdening the court is injustice to judges the fact is that hearing and passing orders is absolutely an intellectual and highly academic work needs extras intelligence. Such work can be carried out only when the judge is not in a hurry and feels entrusted and confident from free mind to make justice with a situation. Our judicial officers are not compensated nicely and properly due to not good remunerations and insufficient perks but at least we can give them space to work properly. It will certainly go in our favour. You cannot expect a good lecture from a teacher who is over-burdened by unnecessary pressures of many kinds on his head. To have a good teacher we have to provide space to work and conduciveness to the doer. So judicial officers too need justice in justified and rational allocation of daily assignments, less burden (nobel number is 40 cases a day), complete strength of colleagues, one to one department, no multifarious liabilities, and so on.

11. Multifarious jobs by one judicial officer: Judiciary has been placed near the status of highest office of President of India as it deserves for the nature of its work. We have to be submissive and yielding before a court. A judge deserves the highest place in the society. And it has to be, because he/she has been authorised to make his/her decision judiciously in the name of God without fear and favour. A judge is the first architect of our society. It is there to protect constitutional rights of the people. It has been given such power. Its work is not only intellectual but full of diligence and close to divinity. This stature has to be maintained by not only litigants but by the judicial officers themselves also. If on one hand, we have to keep check on the conduct of judicial officers by making new laws, we have to preserve their supreme place in the society. They are to be honoured as divine representatives. But to maintain them, they shall have to face penalty if they want to go down their dignity and their place. We want to see them in high places, adore them but set them right to be in their place if they want to slip-down.

12. Exclusive unlimited discretion in passing orders and adopting own procedures by courts: There are courts where the presiding officers have been given rights to frame its own rules.

Most of the tribunals are provided such rights. But what did happen here? Presiding officers, start functioning, as per convenience of staff which may be illogical and against the litigants. Here whosoever joins the post, starts working with no defined and open to all, democratic ways. Every thing goes as per hunch of the new coming presiding officer and the court clerks. Since the presiding officers come here for a limited period on deputation he/she takes up their work negligently. Here the PO is changing but the clerical staff continues for more than ten years or may be for ever. The clerks have has become the master of procedures in the tribunal. Written complaints to higher authorities in bureaucratic arena were thrown into dust bin. Had there been uniform law for maintenance, drafting, processing and conveyencing through out the country, people who do not want to engage any lawyer would also feel convenient to proceed independently. By making variation from place to place is wrong and prone to corruption and exploitation of sufferers.

13. Absence of accountability through a 'Code of Conduct for lawyers and judges': There has to be a code of conduct for every post not in judiciary but in Government also. There is no harm in formulating a list of liabilities, duties, jurisdictions, limitations and privileges to abolish slavery in government departments and treat every employee not as per discretion of the immediate boss but to be dignified citizens. Every person working in government must be known to his arena of working and should not be the victim of 'whatever duty is assigned by the officer'. Let us make things categorical, classified, clear and transparent with honesty and respect to others.

14. No existence of small cause court for specific purposes: Establishing ad-hoc courts for disposing of small cause disputed for a short period shall reduce burden of regular courts. Often, such petty cases consume considerable time of the regular courts and jumble with the busy working of more serious proceedings there. Regular courts have to be classified and specific to hear defined nature of matters and miscellaneous functioning must be discouraged. But this will be possible only when we intend to appoint all judicial officers and bring more judicial officers in vacant places.

15. Misuse of powers feeing unchallenged: In absence of accountability, the judicial officers often misuse the provisions of Article-226 under which they issue ***Rule D.B.*** Admitting a case on long list in presence of rejoinder and all documents, is manipulative to harm the litigant for ulterior motives of particular judicial officer. Keeping the ***decision reserved*** or running dates for many years ***case in orders*** for a certain sensitive period and ***ignoring the question of law*** properly raised by the litigants, are good source of generating loss of faith in judiciary by the suffering litigants. The courts have to be so transparent that even in case when the case is liable to be dismissed at the time of admission, the points of 'question of law' need to be explained by every court.

No dismissal can be genuine and scientific until it is dismissed by negating all questions of law prove to be violative of certain settled law. Here, it will be interesting to mention a court case in the apex court where the petitioner's transfer was decided after 18 years by the high court against the petitioner. The apex court refused to entertain the case saying it is belated. In this case the questions of Law raised through this SLP were as follows:

1. Whether the right of employer to transfer has to be an express condition of service which has to be duly agreed upon by both the employer and employee to be subsequently binding on such employee?
2. Whether the petitioner can be transferred despite of the fact that there is no such condition in his appointment letter?
3. It is justified for the high court to hold that there is no bar on transfer in Delhi Education Act?
4. Whether it is justify holding that the termination of the petitioner's service is the genesis of transfer and saying that after termination the issue of transfer has become academic?

In this case the apex court did not take it ill that:

a. Rule was issued withoutganting any interim relief, like granting the 'stay'.

b. Not issuing experience certificate by the employer as well as by the high court till date.
c. Terminated the services of petitioner *ex parte* without holding any enquiry (Mandatory under Article-311 of Constitution).
d. Holding the admitted writ for two decades and finally dismissing it without giving any relief to the waiting petitioner who was removed from his job *ex parte*.
e. Without quashing two fabricated Circulars allegedly saying issued by the Directorate of Education when the question of their being ultra vires was raised by the petitioner during argument in written arguments, rather took these documents as the basis if dismissal of the writ in a situation when the Directorate of Education never came forward to defend these circulars.
f. And so on so forth....

In the above case the provisions of settled law were jeered by the high court and the apex court as the apex court did not take any action against the high court for not entertaining five citations from the apex court supplied by the petitioner with his written arguments under the provisions of Article-41 of the constitution and passed one page orders saying that the apex court see no infirmity with high court orders without justifying how the apex court is supporting the above anomalies by the high court, is totally illegal and personal by the apex court.

Deferring the date of decision for months and years together has been taken as a liberty by the judicial officers. There are no rules about it. If the arguments have been concluded on a date, it must be mentioned in the order sheet and why not? The judicial officer must by all means pass orders within a prescribed period. This practice of keeping the orders reserved or deferring the date of decision must not be at the mercy and convenience of judicial officer generating a possibility of corruption and manipulation.

Article-141 (Indian Constitution): Law declared by Supreme Court to be binding on all courts: *The law declared by the the Supreme Court shall be binding on all courts within the territory of India.*

ADDENDA

Sad Experiences with Judiciary

16

Model cases of delayed justice that caused disaster for individuals and the masses at large.

ONE: Notified land grabbed, sold and constructed to change land-use deliberately: Place of event: Anand Parbat, Karol Bagh, New Delhi, India: Selling of notified land during litigation and change land-use to the point of no return. Delhi Government notified a large number of lands all around Delhi for acquisition under Section-4 of the Delhi Land Acquisition Act, for Development of Master Plan 2001. Till the arrival of year 2005, Delhi shows its fast changing face because the marked lands were finally taken over by DDA (Delhi Development Authority) and developed into new colonies and other structures built for the citizen's users as per schedule. Out of much litigation with DDA the present case is a great mockery of this entire development plan.

Exceptionally foreseeing the power of the erstwhile owner, the government which is impaired within own cobweb of cumbersome and outdated rules and procedures. The land owning NGO learnt how to delaying tactics in court of law can fail government plans. Succeeding in failing to even take-off any of development plans like Master Plan 2001, due to repeated filing of cases and appeals after appeals till year 2000 after handing over the taken over land till date. They knew much earlier that by going under the shelter of Judiciary they would get sufficient time to manipulate a notified land for selling it off. Having a mischievous purpose, the NGO could succeed to hold this land through a stay from high court in the year 1973 to take any action against them.

The government antagonized for about two decades. All government agencies were approached by the previous NGO owner, to become mute spectator to dispose of this notified land to un-scrupulous manufacturers and petty traders to manufacturer fake automobile components here. Due to litigation all government agencies like development authorities, corporation, land department and police were kept silent to set-up an illegal industrial slum on this notified land earning lakhs of rupees as rent from these allottees. Most manufacturing units produce spurious-duplicate products here till today. At least 40 per cent industries are pollution prone including electroplating, foundry; casting of iron, copper, aluminum; polishing and buffing; used oil filtration and packing; lathe, turning and forging, plastic molding and casting, etc. posing serious threat to the lawful residents living in the vicinity of this industrial slum. Complaints to pollution department fall on deaf ears. This notified land was sold of in the form of small plots in an un-approved and unplanned manner ignoring prescribed norms of town planning and pollution department. Since the origin of these industries was illegal, the owners never wanted to be on record of the government evading excise and other taxes to the government. Factories run here without any license from civic authorities. This notified land was sold off in the form of small plots in an unapproved and unplanned manner ignoring prescribed norms of town planning and pollution department. Since the origin of these industries was illegal the owner never wanted to be on record of the government evading excise and other taxes to the government. Factories run here without any license from civic authorities. This notified land was handed over to these unscrupulous industries without any open public-policy. Civic authorities provided electricity, telephone and water connections. Soon, the barren land was tagged as a 'light industrial area' as was shown in the Master Plan. Though agriculture was impossible on this rocky bed, still the notified erstwhile owners took precaution to allot land piece to these industries, in the name of 'agricultural plot' taking a written understanding from the allottees binding them by the statement "It is an agricultural land piece and any construction by the allottee shall be done at risk of the allottee." Soon, a 'Manufacturers Welfare Association' got registered by the Registrar societies who without verifying the title of these illegal industries allowed that to be registered. To hush up illegality of the whole development, owners allotted land-pieces to the effective politicians. In the mean time when the litigation was in progress, the land grabbers too grabbed vacant land in the nearby areas where the notified owners were unable to protect it.

At a stage when almost 85 per cent of this land was occupied. It was built by encroachers, land grabbers and scrupulous industries. Delhi Municipal Corporation also did not demand the registry of these plots and started talking of house tax on these illegal constructions facilitating them water connections and cleansing services. So is with the telephone and electric connections. In the absence of any national policy of not granting water, telephone and electricity services to unscrupulous land grabber and illegal constructions, slums are becoming growing eye-sores all around.

The area would have been cleared from grabbers but the court delayed decision and litigation continued for about six decades. Can any policy remove more than 2000 illegal colonies on government land all over Delhi? Removing all these colonies in a blanket way, means up-rooting more than 4 million people in one stroke. Today, entire Anand Parbat area is a big slum where land grabbers are being protected as vote bank of politicians and it has joined one of the 2000 unauthorised colonies of the Capital which wait to be regularized. Among the total built up area, it is only the teacher's houses where the staff of former owner is still living which had been built by the lawful owner. All the tenants in these quarters were paying rent or HRA and receipts were being issued to them. These teachers are living here since 1935 or earlier.

To rear growing slum on vacant land, the politicians diverted water supply of these teachers to the unauthorised grabbers as their number is much bigger than the number of lawful residents. The DDA officials have been influenced to show these illegal occupants with the residents of teacher's lane to justify their occupancy under political pressure. The MP of the area being member of planning of DDA succeeded in suspending development plan at Anand Parbat and it was kept on hold till date. The politicians also managed to postpone the raising of both DB Gupta Road and Arya Samaj Road to Anand Parbat in order to maintain their vote bank which has to be removed to materialise this project of construction of these roads to connect Karol Bagh with west Delhi.

Had stay would have not been granted in the year 1973 against land acquisition, DDA could develop this vast land according to Master Plan 2001 for the lawful 350 families residing here since pre-freedom period. But due to prolonged litigation, no government plan could take shape here; rather, this prime, centrally located and costly land had been constructed and inhabited by grabbers and encroachers under the protection of successive politicians in last sixty years.

TWO: Stay against Delhi Police to run nude cabarets: Delhi Police sealed a private owned restaurant for running vulgar nude cabarets without any license. The sealing was removed by Delhi High Court by saying 'people came to see these shows of their own' and stayed the action of Delhi Police. The stay continued for nine years and more nude shows were opened in every nook and corner of Delhi. The police had to exert for nine years to get the stay vacated but till than many girls would have been converted into prostitutes as their fate. The Judge giving stay later raised the status of Chief Justice in the apex court.

THREE: Encroachment and illegal construction: Making traffic impossible by occupying footpaths. There is no one who can stop shopkeepers to extend and encroach on the footpath, which is named and meant for walking of passerby. Throughout the country, in each State big or small, the footpaths are treated as personal possession of the shopkeepers. Inspectors from corporation, police and other agencies take regular bribe from these illegal users to take footpath into their possession creating extreme hardship for the genuine users. Since there is complete nexus of the shop keepers and action taking agencies they are organised but the walkers are sporadic and cannot organise. It is only the authorities to provide clear and clean foot paths to walk on them. Word hawker means a person who sells his goods by roaming all around and who does not settle at a place. On the opposite side of shop, on foot paths certain venders occupy space for running a tea stall, scooter repair works, helmet selling or the like wise with the connivance of police and corporation inspectors. Since the pedestrians are sporadic and unorganized they cannot get together to make their Association to forcefully ask for a safe and clear footpath, but the shopkeepers are organized and some times have got themselves registered with registrar societies. Such grabbing is a usual practice of shopkeepers throughout the country. The rules of corporation are so loose that the grabbers of public land are treated legal by either getting alternative land allotted to them against the land they grabbed. If after legalization such allotted place is assessed for market price, it comes to more than hundred times of the goods kept in this looted public property. This story is almost the same in all the cities. Go to any city big or small, you will see this. It is very well on record that the situation at Janpath and Panchkuya Road where footpath snatchers were to sit with their sellable on the footpath on both the sides of the road. These grabbers could not succeed on one side of the road as this side belonged to Railways and they finally erected boundary wall to protect their land. But the scene on the opposite side changed totally to the advantage of the grabbers. For less than 12 years, these grabbers used footpaths as their shop and got regularly challaned by the civic authorities and kept police at bay by giving regular hafta. Finally, MCD allotted this public property to these footpath grabbing shop keepers. So, is the story of grabbed public land and develop an unauthorised colony in almost the same. Civic authorities have their fee for such grabbing and illegal unauthorised construction on public land. And this *modus opprendi* to become land owner/property owner is far simple and easier than to get a group housing flat booked and pay throughout life in installments. Unauthorised colonies are regularized by corrupt politicians as a large part of population lives here creating an effective vote bank. There is no law in the country, more surprisingly; it is really unbelievable that grabbers have succeeded in grabbing national monuments like Lal Quila, Old Fort at Nabi Karim-Paharganj; Lado Sarai and other Sarais in south Delhi. For a bold crazy citizen, law is a trash and if he wants, he could grab any land he wants. No law can stop a grabber. The government badly failed to tackle this problem due to its lukewarm handling under the influence of local politicians and people are allowed to grab these national monuments too.

Coming back to foot-paths, we can see practically no footpath available in Daryaganj, Chandani Chowk, Khari Bawali, Paharganj, Baratooti, Sadar, Panchkuiya Road, Moti Nagar, Patel Nagar, Karol Bagh, Vikas Marg, Green Park, Lajpat Nagar, Hauz Khas, where you can see people managing to walk through roadside as the footpaths are occupied by venders or shopkeepers. **Blue line buses are killing those people who are walking on roads finding no place to walk on foot paths. No blue line was noticed crushing pedestrians on footpaths. All their victims are crushed on the road.** Can you imagine that the registrar societies are so careless or say manipulative to enroll and register associations of those people who are doing illegal activities like capturing foot paths? The apex court that demands all the approaching parties with PILs, to be registered does not know that registration of any kind is sold here at a price in Registrar society's office. The limit of corruption is so high in this office that they allow an illegal alliance to register an association of footpath vendors as "Patrikhokha Shopkeeper's Association" of Fountain at Chandni Chowk. The Khokha market one can see opposite to Majistic cinema outside Gandhi ground (Ramlila Ground) and in the back of Bhagirath Palace which have been allotted by the Corporation. There is practically no footpath left on the sides of the road in many cities. One has no option than to walk on the road as footpath is filled with goods of shopkeepers or vendors. When police tried to remove them, the registered association got 'stay' from the court and the police had to retain them there. The stay continues till date as the police got silent. The police are comfortable as it has been taken as a way of life. Peoplist shall constitute a special Legal Cell in Police Head Quarters that will fight such court cases. The shopkeepers are so daring that at some places the shopkeepers have encroached and engulfed the entire footpath into their shops extending the side walls of the shop and putting a shutter in the front nearing the road. Peoplist is also committed to make laws to get all the footpaths in the country clear for unauthorised users especially the shop keepers in its front.

FOUR: Destroying the entire career of an innocent litigant by holding the case for 18 years and dismissing it at last: We often come across news about service matters settling a court case after thirty years, i.e. much after retirement of the employee. A teacher was transferred from one school to another within Delhi. Both the schools were run by an NGO, which used to impart only 5% of all the expenditure of these schools. The appointment letter did not have any clause of transfer. The transfer order was challenged in High Court in 1988 within limitation of 90 days. The respondent lawyer was the son-in-law of one former judges of this court. The court read the date of approaching the court as 31.10.1988 instead of 13.10.1988 and did not grant stay saying application belated but admitted the writ for future. The teacher was left with only option to execute the challenged orders making his admitted writ infructuous. Three subsequent applications till 1991 for early hearing asking subsistence allowance, early hearing and issuance of experience certificate were dismissed by the court one after another.

The teacher did not join the place under protest as the jurisdiction of the other school was under question through the admitted writ. During pendency of the case the NGO terminated the permanent services of the teacher one sided. The case of termination was filed separately in the Delhi School Tribunal in the year 1991 with a reference of writ petition admitted in the higher court. The hearing of the case continues till date. One can imagine how many adjournments and dates of hearings would have been affected in these twenty years. The teacher used to appear on every date as his non-appearance could give opportunity to the Tribunal to dismiss the case in default as it had already done once. The NGO bribed the staff of the Tribunal to remove original documents from the case-file. The court master did not put-up subsequent application dated 21.5.1991, before the presiding officers in last 20 years and notice was not issued on them. Inspection of case-file were not allowed; certified copies of the orders were not given till six months, orders were not passed in accordance of the events in the courtroom and documents submitted to the court in person were not brought on record nor mentioned and acknowledged in the orders passed on that day. The Tribunal judges after a repeating hearing in 17 years passed no orders saying the case is pending in the Delhi High Court. The relief sought in higher court is 'whether the transfer is legal or not' while relief sought in Delhi School Tribunal is 'whether termination by a school whose jurisdiction is yet to be decided by the High Court is legal or not' and 'whether the termination has been affected by following mandatory disciplinary procedure or not'. But the Tribunal preferred to continue the case for more years till the date of retirement of the teacher approaches in 2008.

Coming back to the events in High Court, the teacher was surprised to inspect the case file in February 2005 and found that the case had been dismissed in default in January 2005 itself. The Delhi High Court did not bother to issue summons to inform the petitioner-in-person who used not to visit the court every day to see the cause-list. Application for restoration took one year lapsing this one more year from the remaining two years of service period of the petitioner. The court fixed 24th August 2006 for final hearing and dismissed the admitted writ without hearing the case properly ignoring submitted 'written arguments' and five citations from the apex court violating Article-141 of the Constitution of India and 9 more citations from other courts, which were submitted with written arguments in photostat form for the convenience of the court.

In service matter especially, there is need to frame separate rules for not lapsing the entire service period for small matters.

The functioning of Tribunal has to be more scientific and unquestionable than the regular courts. Tribunals should not be allowed to make their own rules. Uniform law needs to be made applicable in all the courts throughout the country. It is unfortunate that in the circumstances to have liberty to make rules and to run tribunal, certain tribunals prefer not to make any rules and use their discretion the way the Presiding Officer or the tribunal staff wants to work, creating inconvenience to the litigants and generating corruption.

The clerk and the Presiding officer, who happens to be the Law Secretary, prefer to be autocratic ruler to run this Tribunal. Every Presiding Officer works here with his/her hunch ignoring normal rules prescribed in CPC, CCA and CCS Rules which are applicable in service matters. Tribunal is headed by the bureaucrats coming from executive or *vice versa*. Judicial officer from trial-court is appointed as Law Secretary on deputation in place of an IAS officer. The top bureaucrats have invented a novel method to promote the judicial officers of trial court to depute them as Presiding Officer of the Tribunal as well as work as Law Secretary in the administration. So that after completing two years of deputation this Law Secretary may be promoted to higher court as a Judge. The administration equates these two posts on the basis of salary structure which is illegal. The principal Secretary, LG of Delhi and other higher officials in Delhi administration preferred to promote the staff against whom complaints were pending. Today, when the DST has been elevated to a full fledged full-time court at a different venue, the oldest case filed in 1979 was placed on cause list after two long dates of its functioning. On the first day of hearing, after two years of silence (2005-2007) on 3.10.2007, the respondent party again sought adjournment which was resented by the petitioner but the Tribunal adjourned the hearing for about two months again.

After the high court dismissed 18 year-old admitted writ in the year 2006 without taking written arguments in consideration and ignoring five decisions of the apex court and nine decisions of other high courts, the apex court did not go into the merits of the case and dismissed the 20 year case, saying 'it is an old matter'. It is interesting that the same court No. 10 had already passed orders on 27.7.2007 that 'the litigants are not to pay for the delay by the courts' dismissed the SLP ruining the entire career of the innocent teacher whose entire career was lost in waiting for justice. So, where is the justice? The apex court has inconsistency in its verdicts and couldn't stick to its own verdict.

FIVE: At the top level: Some of the important PILs are being dismissed by the highest court of the country not on merits but on technical clerical lapse. If the apex court wanted to evade real and serious issues in the name of procedures, who else should not? Procedures are framed to achieve quick and quotable justice. No justice should be evaded in the name of procedures, especially, when the petitioner is a layman but has been cleared by the technical staff of the filing-section that finding the petition in accordance. In such circumstances, the court might have ordered for the redrafting of the PIL which was being presented by petitioner-in-person or the court might have appointed a lawyer from Legal Aid Cell. But it was not done. In other words, the highest court was in the know of the incompetence and incapability of the government to give relief prayed by the petitioner, so the court preferred to turn down the PIL on the ground of its multifarious nature. For brevity, the entire text of this PIL with annexures is on our website along with orders of court.

Such a grave bureaucratic decision by the apex court of the country is really not ignorable. This PIL which had been prepared by studying the working of our judicial system, police and bureaucratic system exposing various ills therein and finally suggesting workable measures. It also covered facts and figures of the entire system by conducting seminars and workshops, for about ten years by author's NGO. But all the work had been thrown into dustbin in one stroke. The main issue of this PIL was to seek immediate release of over-staying under-trials for more than the period of their would-be-sentence, if convicted, was dismissed on the pretext of technical grounds that the NGO was not a registered one. In this PIL the petitioner was not a beneficiary personally in any manner, rather, he was trying to bring favour to the unfortunate under-trials in the name of God. But he failed.

Surprisingly, the litigant was told in the mid of the scutinisation of this PIL that the entire six copies of the PIL have been lost in the PIL section. He doubted that such immense research work had been lost in the section or handed over to some one. The petitioner was asked to file the case again after a period of about six months after first filing. It came on first hearing after 14 months of its filing. The petitioner doubts truly that the text of this petition was included a letters from the two former Prime Ministers in the name of the petitioner to come together to solve the problem of over staying under-trials. Finding the text material of immense importance some one had used it for his advantage. The evidence to this doubt is that after few months of rejection of this PIL, the government constituted a special body for 'Legal Mass Education' with the same terminology, used for the first time in this PIL. A big seminar was organised. The CJI was the main host and the PM inaugurated this function announcing the constituting of such a body. A banner had been put on the entry gate No. 4 of Delhi High Court to make people aware of government's intention to constitute a body for legal mass education programme. More banners were displayed near courts and pump and show was done.

Later, the programme died its own death as it lacked any soul being a snatched concept, i.e. in absence of any knowledge of practical approach that was conceived by the petitioner nobody could carry it out further. In this PIL, such a question was categorically raised by the Petitioner is already on our website for evidence for the readers. The litigant though, had a copyright of this PIL much before filing it, being apprehended of such pilferage a year before, is on record.

SIX: Under-trials: There have been repeated unchallenged reports in the press where challans were not filed by the police for 10-15 years in petty criminal offence of theft of Rs. 30 only. There are more than 2.4 million under-trials in Indian jails in very bad shape. The jails are over crowded and with substandard maintenance. The treatment of jail staff and police is callous and uncalled for with these unfortunate detainees. In such a time of extreme hardship and grave crisis, the police inside the jail does not refrain to extort comforts from these innocent under-trials otherwise, they are put to maltreatment. We must always keep in mind that all the under-trials are not culprits and convicts. We have no right to treat them at par with convicts. In absence of quick justice and delayed trial, the lives of these under-trials have become a curse for uncertain period. Their families wait for them everyday. Life partner usually die waiting her innocent husband who was trapped by a biased boss or an avenging cop. He is one of many who are in jail for the last few decades.

A large number of cases may be brought to light where due to slight difference of opinion the management trapped an innocent person in some criminal case or removed him from job illegally and so on. In service matters, sole bread earner of a family either put behind the bars for trial or is roaming from pillar to post in search for livelihood of his family. Children could not get good education and strayed accusing honest fighting/defending father for their untimely ruin. Not to accuse the total judicial system that has indifferent attitude of criminality for not deciding cases in time and a sufferer is justified in saying: 'Hell with such justice and such a system that is playing with the lives of innocent citizens'. Litigants/ accused now are so harassed that they pray not to delay justice any more.

Judicial officers should not treat cases merely as one of the case-files and must consider the suffrage of the injured party before any official formality. There is no harm to bring the economic condition of both the parties on record so that the amount of suffrage may be assessed to look into the possibilities of events mentioned in the case file. It is reasonable to know by the 'System' what is happening to the family of a person engaged in litigation grafted by the police who are failing to bring bread and butter to its dependents. In certain developed nation, the government has arrangement for the juvenile children abandoned by a convicted mother. Can we do some thing to innocent children who have never been a part of crime and save them from getting astray without a guardian?

Behind a person being tried in court, there is a complete family. Therefore, it is expected that the courts have to be merciful in service matters where the lone bread earner has lost his job. By virtue of a law there is a need of interim relief to the innocent family members. Such subsistence amount may be imparted by contesting party till the litigation is over.

There cannot be any person who does not need quick justice or timely justice. No one ever imagined that the work of judiciary will become so slow in five decades that justice will become a rare phenomenon. Otherwise, it would have been improvised at the time of drafting the Constitution. But it is never late. To preserve Constitutional guarantees we must make laws for time bound justice. There is enough information available on the issue of delayed justice as everyday we come across Press clips on this issue. Belated, ignored, unattended, unprocessed cases have been high lighted by Press to expose extreme negligence on the part of justice delivery system in the country. Out of numerous unnoticed cases, few are here:

First instance: Under-trial dies under Mysterious circumstances (Covered by Times of India dated 6.5.2000).

Second instance: Under-trial gets one year imprisonment after thirty years (Covered by Indian Express dated 13.3.2000).

Third instance: Charges to be framed in 28 years old case (Sunday Times (TOI) most witness have retired, three accused absconding dated 15.2.2004).

Fourth instance: Under-trial tried after 40 years and prosecuted for one day (Hindustan Times dated January 2007).

Fifth instance: Look who's waiting for justice for 12 years—a judge: (Indian Express dated 7th January 2007 in Sunday Magazine section).

It writes "Additional Session Judge Sujata Kohli filed a case of physical abuse against a lawyer 1994; she now wants to withdraw it (as a sign of protest against prolonged delay in justice). Once the application to withdraw the petition was dismissed; now she is filing an appeal in High Court. The case was filed when she was a practicing lawyer in Tis Hazari Court at Delhi. An office bearer of Delhi Bar Association was charge sheeted u/s 323 causing hurt and u/s 506 criminal intimidation to the modesty of a woman, under Indian Penal Code. In last para of the article, it states "If a judge does not believe in the judicial system, who will?" Now the judge has been shifted to a lower rank court has a mark of punishment to go to the press and the same lawyer has been again elected an office bearer of the Bar Association by our learned lawyer community.

Unforgettable negligence: The first two cases were cited in PIL by the author in the apex court on 5th April 2005 and last two above cited cases after dismissing the PIL. Had the PIL was entertained or taken seriously, these innocent citizens would have got justice. Worthy to mention in the fourth case is relevant here as the court refused to send the accused to jail for one year rigorous imprisonment and held in her orders that if he is sent to jail at this stage when he is brought to this court on a stretcher due to bad shape of his health, he may die. Later, he is ordered two hours conviction in the court room itself.

SEVEN: Implanting innocent people in criminal cases and detaining them till they die: Out of numerous cases of under-trials, the famous case of Dr. Subramanian of a government research institute, who was charge with espionage charges. Press over-reacted prejudging the issue before anything was established and painted him as a traitor. His remaining service period was taken over in deciding the case and his reputation changed into humiliation and disgrace. He was finally discharged from the charges leveled on him in a mischievous way by the rival scientists in connivance of police. Thus, here an Individual was destroyed for his career, professional reputation, social status and irreparable loss of peace of mind and his official position for ever. Everyday fake cases are being filed by the police against innocent citizens. Police had been entrusted by Britishers to the extent of blind faith. The coordination of police and judges is worth watching. For example, if one has been wrongly challaned by traffic inspector and you decide to contest the case. You can have a look of the court proceeding making yourself presented before the court. The court is asking every accused the same question as 'Did you commit the mistake?' Your lawyer advises you to say 'yes'. So, everyone is saying yes. The judge announces the fine and you are acquitted after paying the same. In this court, you have no say and what has been charged on you by the constable on road, is taken granted and correct by the court. Thus, in a criminal offence, the magistrate primarily takes it granted that the challan presented is genuine. It is your wisdom and luck if you are acquitted. In court, you are not *at par* with a policeman or the Public prosecutor if you have no lawyer.

There are thousand of women and men who have no guarantor or security to get themselves released on bail. The procedure and policy for such cases is uncertain. Until there is no guarantor, such accused will remain behind bar. It has always been a privilege of police to put innocent people behind bars before the Hon'ble Supreme Court ordered to deduct the detention period from the period of conviction. But in such cases where the case is not forwarding even an inch, what will be the fate of such detainees even after years of detention. There are no rules framed yet on such situation.

EIGHT: Religious disputes: Two religious communities developed hatred/tension, if their disputes are pending in the court of Law for decades together. That sums up by and by and finally explodes in the form of terrorism and communal riots. All governing authorities have inherent liability to refrain from creating situation that can sum up into mass frustration; otherwise, the democracy is taken over by military rule which is no less than official dictatorship as in neighboring countries.

NINE: No law exists to stop it as it suits to all higher ups: Money comes money goes by its own feature. Here money does not go. It is one-sided flow when it comes illegally. All the money-collected by unfair means, is stored for future fearing its knowledge to others. But, the courage of today's mongers is so perfect that black money now comes to the fore in the form of investment in property. People are pumping black money in property and it is very difficult to locate it. The ownership may be fake. Investment in property is no serious gamble. It is a sure business as it is the best way to multiply fast. More daring people invest such money to build houses without any fear as according to them the machinery to check up such investment is very weak. To invest in property is repeatedly done after its demolition and rebuilding the same. People who could grab public land like parks and lane bravely pump available black money in property. Courts pass such orders once in blue moon and no verdicts are issued on illegal property. It is a lengthy process and enforcement of such orders no less than a futile and cumbersome exercise to demolish an illegal structure. So, municipal officers, policemen, bureaucrats in DDA prefer to play safe for a considerably long period without taking any action. People who multiplied money overnight are dealing in property and builder's business. Property of politicians, IPS officers, judicial employees, businessmen and higher ups are in the form of farm-houses and empty plots all over the country, some times in isolated state. There is no effective measure to check such investment of black money in property. Block Development Officers must sign all registries and Power of Attorney before going to registrar properties. The Block Development Officer of the area must have some legal compulsion by a newly framed Law in Peoplism, of having a record with details of each and every property and his report whose copies must go to local police and to the income tax officer of the area. If the owner is not located, the property should be taken over by the Government.

TEN: Police court is run by ACP of the area: This is called SEM Court means the ACP of the area acts here as Special Executive Magistrate. Here, the police justify its own action. The complaints and FIRs lodged by the police are stamped of as "TRIED and OK" seal by this police court. In a fabricated case the ACP/SEM helps the SHO by convicting the accused, he brings before his ACP/SEM. Police court is a complete fraud and not solving any problem of hooliganism in the area.

ELEVEN: The high court gives stay to nude cabarets against police action but not to an illegal transfer orders of a teacher: The morality of court is before us all. It tells us that the courts are misusing their authority and are sellable through costly lawyers while aggrieved petitioners in person hardly get any relief from there.

TWELVE: Inconsistent verdicts by the apex court: The apex court can grant bail to rich convicts but dismissing Special Leave petition of a teacher against illegal orders of high court to up hold illegality against Constitutional duty to impart justice to the aggrieved party: The apex court often is criticidsed for its over rech and negative activism. In a case the apex court No. 10 on 14.12.2007 gave diecision against his own orders showing inconsistency of court against the universality of Law. The apex court preferred to release rich people like actor Sanjay Dutt and cricketer Navjot Singh Siddhu and can hear them on Fast Track but dismiss a Public Interest Litigation praying immediate release of over staying under-trails in stinking jails.

The Final Face Lifting Globally

17

a. International Human Right Commission, b. The Charter of United Nations, c. International Trade, d. International Games and Cultural Exchanges, e. UN Sanctions, f. Quick Natural Justice, g. Practicing Peoplism, h. Resident Welfare Associations.

Out of many essential features of true democracy, few are (i) Perseverance of Human Rights, (ii) Government by People's true representatives, (iii) Equality, (iv) Freedom of expression, (v) Right to choose religion, (vi) Free movement, and (vii) Justice to all.

a. International Human Right Commission: More than thirty Human rights have been accepted by the Human Right Commission at the international level. These have been drafted and forwarded through a well known international NGO named 'Amnesty international' to the United Nations through a Charter. Beyond physical rights of being a human, these rights include rights that preserve human dignity and natural traits one can promote for his growth and development and that of his society. Human Rights do not discriminate between men and women and confer equal rights to women also. Countries, where women still fight for their existence are violating these rights. Human Rights cover Natural Justice by those who hold governance of a society.

There has been hue and cry by the developed nations on gross violation of human rights in dictatorial and military regimes of the world. United Nations has also expressed its displeasure on violation of human rights in developing countries by having sluggish judiciary. Courts are bound to handle pending cases of millions of under-trails. International Monetary Fund (IMF) has raised objection to such a high number of detainees and pending court cases in some of the oriental developing countries, while assessing the substance of democracy, before funding.

b. The Charter of United Nations: Foundation of United Nations is one of the most important milestones of human civilization. Beyond few important negatives of UNO, it has become indispensable in the present context. The six organs of UNO have been designed and nurtured by all the member nations that keep vigil of various executions suggested by the authorised signatories. Its important organs include 'International Monetary Fund' that has a control on world bank to support many world nations financially with sufficient amount to run various developmental programmes related with health, education and constructions also on the basis of honesty of the local authorities and a positive report of previous tenure. Other agencies raise funds for child programmes. International Labor Organisation (ILO) is another important organ that looks into the position and save labour from exploitation by suggesting governments of these nations. UNICEF is another important organ to look after interest of world children and their welfare.

c. International Trade: This is a very important event in the lives of nations around the world. This is not only the index of world economic growth but also a medium to come close to each other by developing trade relations. It does not only make various products of one country available to others but also helps to develop passion for each other, its people and cultural pursuits. Exports and imports between two countries create a bridge between people of nations around world. We feel that we are not alone in this world. We are one of others who need us.

The trade practices also encourage exchange of new technologies giving a chance to new common culture and life style to emerge from such relations. Internet, computer technology, research and development shared by counterparts are making world to be a small place to live in. International

Television channels have opened new vistas before us to know people in far off places and develop a uniform culture and lifestyle to bring people of different foci together and to understand humanity in a better way. America played a significant role to abolish apartheid from this planet. This gives us support to sustain life even when we are at low note of life.

The boost in banking trends opened new possibility to have sufficient funds even in developing countries is another achievement of the recent years. Passport and visa system is fast changing and world is developing in such a uniform manner that we are looking for no visa required to move any where in the world.

d. International Games and Cultural Exchanges: Olympic and other international game events make us feel that we are a member of world family. People outside Indian wish us to join together in all international joint activities. Various forums have been constituted to frame various agreements for regional peace and developments. Developed nations or friendly nations always keep trying to bring two conflicting countries to resolve their differences to establish peace and progress. But there will be a time when countries shall copy best systematic change in their internal matter like giving a good government to its people and time bound justice will become a part of the constitutions of all the nations.

e. UN Sanctions: UNO and other care taker nations are alert to watch the internal affairs of developing countries that have been entrusted to have funds from International Monetary Funds. Observers ensure themselves by inspecting these countries personally. They have every right to suggest these nations to mend their ways and preserve human rights. The Charter of 'Human Rights' has 'Natural Justice' as one of the important rights of every citizen. UN observers can impose sanctions of different kinds on the countries who are not cooperative to the expectations of UNO. Some times, UN sanctions are so harsh that it develops into conflict. This is an important activity to bring countries together and make citizens feel that they are being taken care by the biggest power of the world and they have a bright future.

f. Quick Natural Justice: There can be no two definitions of natural justice. The justice which is balanced and acceptable to all gives chance to be heard before a decision is natural justice. Human race have always been suffering from discrepancy of resources in different times and in different nations. But for all human beings justice at all level gives peace leading to progress. Disparity in economic condition, social preference, legal equality, sex discrimination, apartheid factor make society bifurcated into different sections. Economically deprived of sections need economic justice, society deprived of in the name of caste; creed and race need social justice and suffering from lawlessness need legal justice. It is the duty of all citizens to create a country with least discrimination of different kind and enable countrymen to enjoy equality of all kind.

Justice in time is a relative term. But belated justice has no meaning. Justice coming when not required is absurd. Timely justice is the necessity of all human beings and countries that are careless about giving different types of justice to its people at the right time are on the verge of collapse and civil war. Most of the developing countries are passing through such turmoil and have become sensitive zones encouraging offence over innocent citizens by ignoring the timely delivery of justice. It is bursting into increasing trends of suicides local unrest and terrorism. United Nations agencies are worried about the condition of judiciary in developing countries as it has reached an alarming state now. So, beware of the need of quick justice in a natural way.

g. Practicing Peoplism: Peoplism is the last alternative to restore real democracy in developing nations where the power as been captured by few white collared terrorists. They are filling their pockets at the cost of poor and down-trodden. They claim very high to come to the power and join the other block of exploiters after come to coterie of privileged citizens. Peoplism is the answer of such a gimmickry democracy where the politicians do not want to implement recommendations of the various Commissions and even those of the apex court to establish accountability of police and judicial officers, dismissing Public Interest Litigation to release over staying under-trials and passing technically wrong orders in guise of finality; where police refused to file cases of death and murders and file fake cases on innocents and bureaucrats are running their show from air-conditioned offices and never bother to go to the site and pay personal visits to their areas. The bitter pills offered by Peoplism are for these white collared culprits, who are no lesser than parasites on us.

Let all the right thinking citizens depend on Peoplism for those who is crippled to bring necessary and inevitable changes in different organs of democracy. Let the unchallenged and unaccountable judiciary be set-right first to have command on criminal-friendly police, autocratic bureaucrats; wolfy politicians and irresponsible and immature media.

h. Resident Welfare Associations (RWAs): Another great hope in our entire efforts, to bring the situation normal, is the emergence of 'Resident Welfare Associations' besides registered Non-Governmental Organisations. RWAs have upper hand over any kind of organisation. There can be some fake NGOs, eating up government funds in the name of welfare schemes; government wants to get done through NGOs. But there cannot be a fake RWA. As far as bungling of funds are concerned, that is the remotest possibility in a RWA because every RWA runs well by the culture of leg pulling more and constructive work less. Still these are more dependable to implement many government's welfare schemes where government spends lots of money. The representation to various government bodies from RWA will always be genuine. The government must frame rules to organise RWA in all residential colonies even in villages, to look after the welfare of citizens without depending on corrupt politicians. Membership of registered RWA must be mandatory and monthly payments must be made mandatory through established law that decides how the RWAs are to run. Besides 'Memorandum of Association' there have to be some essential clauses in the RWA document and they should be encouraged to maintain and fight for the rights of residents. Such Associations must be given a legal status, and financial support for improving the colony from MP/MLA funds by virtue of being a legal entity.

Judicial Code of Conduct in Peoplism

18

(Basic concept of proposed codes for lawyers and judges is taken from such Codes in Canada and America.)

The essentiality of code of conduct is not confined with the police or lawyers or judicial officers only but it must run for every post that has public dealing. Accountability of those consuming public funds is a part of Democratic society.

Historical Perspective

Legal profession is recognizable since 13th century in England. Professional legal heritage may be said to have originated at the end of the 13th century. David Lemmings indicated as in the reign of Edward I (1272-1307) "reveal the existence of professional lawyers whose services were tendered to litigants." Pleaders and attorneys—the two classes of lawyers practicing in the Royal and Provincial Courts were first subjected to regulation.

The modern English Bar could be said to have formed, was about the year 1730. Lemmings Harkens refers to writings in 1615 of Sir John Davies, a future Chief Justice, in which Davies argued that the lawyer's vocation-dependent role of wage earner, and beyond the mere pursuit of money, for his fees and not "duties given to a learned Counselor is called 'honorarium' being indeed a gift of honor as well to the Takers by the giver." Today's contractual principles are purely professional.

However, in pursuing its historicity the question arises: why have a legal profession? According to F.A.R. Bennion "Advisory services (including concomitant executive functions) on matters requiring expert intellectual knowledge provided by a private practitioner whose competence and integrity are vouched for by an independent body representative of such practitioners."

The link between English concepts of professional/legal conduct and those which have evolved in Canada is undoubtedly to be found in the United States of America. Michael Birks records that the steps taken to regulate the profession in America during the first half of the 18th century followed contemporary trends of thought in regard to such matters in England. A society of lawyers became established as early as 1797 in Upper Canada. With its establishment and the founding of other similar bodies came standards of conduct that were used, *inter-alia,* to both guide and discipline their members.

Integrity, Competencc and Quality of Service

Personal qualities have been viewed by Canadian lawyers as comprising good professional legal conduct. One jurist has indicated that in his view, the qualities of honesty, integrity, and trustworthiness and respect make-up the necessary elements of conduct for a lawyer.

In a Convocation address delivered at the University of Toronto in 1986, Chief Justice Dickson of the Supreme Court of Canada used the term "**compassion**" as a further desirable element in a lawyer's make-up. His Lordship used the term in the sense of it being "a feeling of empathy or sympathy for the hardships experienced by others a feeling, which extends to a sense of responsibility and concern to alleviate hardships at least in some measure".

"To these qualities, the Canadian Bar Association has added those of loyalty and competence, synthesized into a triplet of terms: integrity, competence and a concept called "quality of service". These three terms keep appearing singly or together in relation to the Canadian legal profession in conduct codes, cases and writings. Thus, we find that the term "integrity" perforce includes honesty, trustworthiness, competence" and skill to coin the term "quality of service". By the approach of Industrial Revolution in Europe, a new spate of clients being manufacturers and traders, the uncalled for behaviour of solicitors and attorneys could not be achieved by the tricks and nice ties. To be successful, he had to acquire reputation for integrity and a straight dealing. Evidence of a professional's integrity is confined in the preservation of confidentiality, the display of impartiality, taking of full responsibility, the exhibition of competence, fairness and fearlessness. It is one to quote that a decided thrust toward a high degree of integrity being required of lawyers is found in an Act of Parliament passed in England in 1729. Entitled "for the better Regulation of Attorneys and Solicitors", it and its two extending Acts, states Birks, did much towards promoting a higher standard of honesty and integrity among the profession at large. As to competence, Bennion refers to it as "the giving of the hallmark" by a professional person is that the public looks for in the services of a professional person.

The word "quality" becomes allied with the criteria now set-out in the codes of professional legal conduct as to what does or does not comprise competence amongst lawyers. It is the "spirit" of profession that alone derives success of a profession. To place the interests of his client before his own, and to give of his utmost without regard to material reward, is a most precious concept.

Professor J.H. Baker, arguably England's leading present day legal historian, goes back much further, the late 1400s, to at least the 15th century of writing in. The Order of Serjeants at Law the form of the oath, was settled but was likely of origin in the century before: *Ye shall swear that well and truly ye shall serve the king's people as one of the serjeants at the law. And ye shall truly counsel them that ye shall be retained with, after your cunning. And ye shall not defer, tract or delay their causes willingly for covetise of money or other thing that may turn you to profit. And ye shall give attendance accordingly. As God helps your and his saints.*

Why this ancient and continuing emphasis on service by lawyers? It is that because the legal profession was and is a form of monopoly. The societal scheme dictates that those within its privileged borders do their utmost for those who come to them for assistance. There are no others available, i.e. permitted to do the same things. It seems fair to assume that the failure to so serve clients could result in the loss of the monopoly leaving no option but perhaps giving rise to the 'State-oriented delivery of Legal Services'.

Beyond many Masters

Perhaps to a greater extent than other professionally trained persons, the lawyer has a number of masters. They include the state, the court, the client, the profession and colleagues (Bar/Council). Some observers would add the lawyer him/herself, with their own moral standards of practice conduct and principles. When a lawyer is dealing with the law on behalf of someone or something, there may be a collision with opposing requirements for the observance of duties to two or more of these masters. By way of simple example: in preparing argument for presentation to the court, a precedent is found which is directly against the client's position. The lawyer's duty is to do the best for the client. An opposing colleague's position could be benefited by a disclosure of the adverse precedent and hurt by its non-disclosure. Also, the lawyer will usually have a sense of what, according to the lawyer's personal standards, is right and fair.

The Codes of Ethics and Conduct

Since at least 1920 lawyers in Canada have had the advantage of written direction in the ***dilemma of conflicting duties.*** In that year the Canadian Bar Association adopted certain Canons of Ethics. By way of expansion and refinement, the Association in 1974, and thorough revision in 1987, promulgated its widely used Code of Professional Conduct. The bar societies of some Canadian jurisdictions have adopted the 1974 or the 1987 Code, with or without their own additional professional conduct rules.

Further, provincial and territorial governing legal bodies have adopted legislation controlling the conduct of their members. After a long history of assisting others in knowing and applying the law on their behalf, now Canadian lawyers have had codes of professional legal conduct laws of a type prescribed for them.

In Canada today a practicing lawyer's status as a professional person hinges on obedience to one or more of those codes and relevant law society legislation and rulings. Some of this guidance found its way into writings, such as that of Chief Justice George Sharswood's essay on professional ethics. Other helpful indications on how to conduct oneself professionally in particular situations were handed down from one generation of lawyers to another through word of mouth.

However, the written Canons and the later codes and legislation have given to lawyers a direction as to the professional conduct expected of them by their peers, both generally and in some cases with particularity. A particular point concerning the written codes should be emphasized here. It is this. While the codes do not cover every fact situation which may arise in the course of the legal day, at least a suggested thrust of conduct is often discernible from their precepts for application to the matter at hand.

Are the codes merely exhortations to members of the legal profession to adopt certain standards of professional conduct? Or are they binding upon lawyers, so that ***a breach will result in sanctions being imposed?*** Probably, both questions should be answered affirmatively. The codes do indeed urge lawyers to good standards of professional conduct. Canadian law societies have alluded in the codes themselves to forms of conduct, variously described as "professional misconduct", "conduct unbecoming" and the like, which by legislation carry sanctions such as reprimand, suspension or disbarment. ***Courts too discipline lawyers for breaches of codes,*** and tend to take into consideration such breaches when, for example, dealing with a civil claim for negligence. Accordingly, while framing many of the required standards of conduct as duties or as rules with guiding principles that "should" be obeyed, the practical effect is that the profession's Canadian codes appear to accomplish the imperative without in many cases prescribing the standards of conduct in that manner.

The Lawyer's Professional Duties

In order that the matter of a lawyer's duties as a professional legal person be put in proper perspective, the obvious question must be asked: duties to whom or to what? In answer, it will be recalled that a lawyer serves several masters—the state, the court, the client, the profession and colleagues, even her/himself. One must look at all of these relationships when considering what duties the lawyer faces in any given situation. In this connection the word "duty" is often used with no indication as to the kind or scope of duty intended. Therefore, unless otherwise indicated, it will be assumed that a "duty" not otherwise delineated is to be considered as a requirement of loyalty, or of obedience, or of adherence to a system, a principle or a course of conduct, depending upon the context.

1. Professional duties to THE STATE

When discussing a lawyer's duty to the State, the term "State" is used in its broader sense of including the entity, its systems and its people. Indeed, in its Preface the Code should leave little doubt that the highest duty of loyalty is owed to what is called ***the protection of the public interest.*** That is an undefined term but perhaps not inaccurately may be taken to include the State and its systems, as well as its people. New Brunswick's Professional Conduct Handbook states in Part A, Rule 1: "A lawyer's paramount duty is to serve the cause of justice." It would be assumed that "the cause of justice" would be as espoused and encouraged by the jurisdiction or State in which the Rule operates.

While not stressing the paramount duty, British Columbia's **Canons** of Legal Ethics indicates: "A lawyer owes a duty to the State, to maintain its integrity and its law. A lawyer should not aid, counsel, or assist any person to act in any way contrary to the law." Not as directly expressed is the lawyer's duty to the people of the State, often referred to in the codes as "the public" or "the general public". With some exceptions the codes are silent on duty to the general public but with this underlying caveat: what the lawyer does should never bring harm to that public. In addition and again implied indirectly, there is the duty of showing to the public that the lawyer upholds the administration of justice. Other exceptions to the codes' silence respecting the general public include making oneself available to provide legal services to the public and looking out for the rights of unrepresented third parties.

2. Professional duties to THE COURTS

The lawyer is on reasonably solid ground when considering duties to the court. History plays a part in this. For nearly 800 years attorneys and solicitors in England have been regarded as officers of the courts in which they served and as such subject to its direction. Barristers on the other hand have not been regarded so.

In Canada the residence in the lawyer of both solicitor and barrister powers and duties are considered officers of the court and thereby made a partner in its process. The Canada Bar Association Code indicates that the lawyer's duties to the court include the duties of "candour, fairness, courtesy and respect." In a fairly long list of do'es and don'ts, the Code advises the lawyers:

(i) Not to "abuse the process of the tribunal by instituting or prosecuting proceedings that are clearly motivated by malice on the part of the client and are brought solely for the purpose of injuring another party".

(ii) The lawyer must not "knowingly assist or permit the client to do anything that the lawyer considers to be dishonest or dishonorable".

(iii) The lawyer must not "knowingly attempt to deceive a tribunal or influence the course of justice by offering false evidence", and so on.

(iv) The lawyer is exhorted to maintain towards the judges of the courts a courteous and respectful attitude and insist on similar conduct on the part of the client.

(v) The reason behind the duty to respect the court and to maintain proper decorum toward it at all times is stated to be "for the purpose of enhancing public confidence in the administration of justice".

(vi) The description as officer of the court binds the lawyer even more closely to the court and its system, and provides the basis for a substantial number of the conflicting claims of duties owed to the court and those owed to others.

It is apparent that various duties to the court are closely linked to an overall duty of loyalty to the system of the administration of justice. The court is the beneficiary of this possibly paramount state duty.

3. Professional duties to THE CLIENT

Duties to a client yet more complex because of the close human interaction that takes place in the lawyer-client relationship. Most codes acknowledge, directly or indirectly, that such duties include honesty, integrity, trustworthiness, respect, loyalty, compassion and competence synthesized into integrity, competence and quality of service. Farther, on in the Code indications are given as to what a client should be entitled when being represented by the lawyer as advocate. Fees are dealt with as well as withdrawal of legal services from a client. Many of the provincial codes follow similar lines of thought as those found in the model Canadian Bar Association Code.

(vii) It is of interest to note that in at least one other code it is indicated the actions of a lawyer in fulfilling duties to a client must be tempered by the lawyer's duty to the courts and the administration of justice.

(viii) Mutual trust is emphasized.

(ix) Avoidance of any misrepresentation with respect to the level of competence of the lawyer or the efficiency of the lawyer's services.

4. Professional duties to THE PROFESSION

The duties that a lawyer owes to the profession have similar objectives as those owed to the state and its public. The lawyer should assist in maintaining the integrity of the profession and should participate in its activities.

(x) This includes a duty to assist in preventing the unauthorized practice of law.

(xi) To abstain from involvement with interests outside the profession in which the lawyer's conduct might bring the profession into disrepute, especially, in relation to the latter, one is led to conclude that, as in the court relationship, the lawyer is to uphold the integrity of the profession in order that the confidence of the public may be maintained therein.

5. Professional duties to THE COLLEAGUES

The lawyer's conduct toward other lawyers should be characterized by courtesy and good faith. This is on the basis that "Fair and courteous dealing on the part of each lawyer engaged in a matter will contribute materially" to the end of serving the public interest effectively and expeditiously good practice between lawyers is eschewed.

(xi) Breach of such undertakings constitutes professional misconduct

(xii) To prohibit competition for clients amongst lawyers. Gentle conduct amongst lawyers.

6. Professional duties to ONESELF

Can one say that the lawyer indeed owes duties to him/herself when acting in a professional capacity? Along a spectrum one sees the lawyer, professionally engaged, attempting to fulfill duties to the State, court, client, profession and colleagues.

(xiii) The lawyers need to postulate that though professional, the lawyer must bring personal standards and values into any situation in which the lawyer is professionally engaged.

(xiv) If this is not done, the lawyer may compromise her/his own perhaps higher standards in adhering unswervingly to other standards not of the lawyer's own making, since it is under the pressure of sanctions that the latter may be being observed.

Indeed, this may be a variation of the "moral schizophrenia" of which Raymond Belliotti speaks when the lawyer is endeavouring to rationalize sets of duties under which the lawyer is practicing and which appear to conflict with the lawyer's own values.

(xv) To ignore recognition of one's own standards when dealing professionally may result in a somewhat slavish adherence to the letter, rather than to the intent, of the duties placed upon the lawyer through codes of conduct and legislation.

(xvi) To maintain minimum standards.

Conflicts of Duties: HOW RESOLVED?

There appears to be four basic steps in attempting to resolve a problem involving professional legal conduct. The *first* step is to ascertain whether there may be a professional duty or duties owed. The *second* is to determine to whom or to what the duty or duties may be owed, i.e. to what constituencies. The *third* is to ask whether there is in fact a conflict between or amongst the duties owed and the *final fourth* and critical step is to conclude on some basis which duty must give way to the other assuming there is a conflict. The majority of professional legal conduct problems appear receptive to the approach suggested above. Confidentiality toward a client versus candour to the court; loyalty to one's corporate client versus the best interests of the general public; advancing a client's position versus accommodating a colleague's missed filing date despite of many of the conflicts that needs clarification in the manner outlined.

It is out of this cauldron of competing claims for the lawyer's adherence to duties imposed that the codes of professional legal conduct and concomitant legislation have evolved. For the greater part they are true to the Aristotelian precept that "The whole account of matters of conduct must be given in outline and not precisely." Nonetheless, while not having all of the answers to particular problems faced by lawyers, the codes in many instances do indicate courses of conduct which with careful thought may point the way to a resolution. While codes of conduct prescribed for lawyers do not cover every situation which may arise in day-to-day functioning. When used in such a manner, the codes become a valuable tool to the conscientious lawyer.

A. LAWYER'S CONDUCT

Lawyers are a part and parcel of judicial system. Lawyer is an authorised, qualified, allowed professional expert to take up the cause of his/her client to the court of Law with an intention to bring justice to him.

Sporadic codes advise the lawyer not to "abuse the process of the tribunal by instituting or prosecuting proceedings that are clearly motivated by malice on the part of the client and are brought solely for the purpose of injuring another party".

Every nation is equipped with its Penal Code and Criminal Procedure Code along with many subsidiary Acts, Rules and Regulations with legislative sanction and any violation by any citizen, whosoever he/she may be, can be dealt with accordingly. Yet, there are a number of situations which are not covered by any prescribed law. The litigant, for whom the entire infrastructure of judiciary exists, has become an outsider as the entire arena of court and judicial control has been captured by Bar Associations. A number of touts remain unchecked by the office bearers of the Bar Association, who wear lawyer's aprons and roam around court premises posing themselves as lawyers. There is no process with the Bar associations to keep a check on fake lawyers. Therefore, touts can be seen even in the apex court premises. Why all the registered lawyers with Bar Association are not compulsorily asked to display their identity on their person? If they are bound to wear a black cover by virtue of law why can't there be a badge displayed with registration number? There are few instances where the Bar Associations take interest to resolve a dispute with a client and always or when a client is mal-treated by a lawyer after taking full payment.

An advocate is an appointed person by the litigants and at any moment the client can remove a lawyer and appoint another law-expert to take his services. But as soon as a lawyer is appointed, he is not supposed to exploit the already troubled litigant in any unethical ways. There is no remedy of such a situation with Bar Association who is more dependants on his collegue for a vote during election than to depend who seldom knocks their door.

The right of the litigant is superior over the right of lawyer on the premises of the court and the entire judicial system. A client is the cause of business to lawyers as well as a judicial officer. A litigant is the backbone of entire judiciary. Because people ought to suffer either by lawlessness and criminality in society and lastly get exploited by lawyers or long proceedings of the court.

There are many bad situations when the litigant who does not engage a lawyer for many reasons is mal-treated by other lawyers, staff of the court and even ignored by the judges. No matter how far the litigant is academically qualified and pleads his case a sense, the court hears him/her half-heartedly and wants to get rid of him/her as soon as possible. They feel that he does not know the law and the procedures and he is bound to waste court's time and may not maintain courts decorum.

All such apprehensions of the court may not be true to certain extent but what a client will do when he has no money and the Legal Aid Cell has refused to help him in any way? In such case, there must be a 'Department' in the Legal Aid Services that must help such unfortunate clients in drafting, conveyancing, fetching documents and taking photocopy of required citations from the library and presenting his/her case before the court, contrary to the present sorry states of 'petitioner-in-person'. He deserves every facility like a lawyer and should have a right to enter the court room and be allowed to occupy a chair in first or second row in the court which has been reserved for lawyers themselves.

It is nowhere provided in the Constitution of India that the administration and management of court premises will be given to the Bar Association, which is in practice today. The entire Court building and its management in these days have been handed over to the Bar Association. For example, the entire building of High Court in Delhi is in total control of Bar Association. So much so, the lawyers have discriminated certain public properties as exclusively 'FOR LAWYERS ONLY'. The clients are not supposed to enter these marked public places. The court libraries within the court premises are not available to petitioner in person and no one, except lawyers is allowed to enter these public properties. This situation is no less than similar to British Raj when the country was a slave and slaves and dogs were not permitted to even walk on footpaths. They were forced to walk on roads across the fast and heavy traffic. Moreover, the service windows for many services are thronged by the munshis of lawyers or lawyers and petitioner-in-person has to face lot of inconvenience and humiliation to apply, submit or receive a document.

Worst is the situation in Delhi High Court where you are not allowed inside the court building. If you want to inspect your case file or you want to ask certain queries regarding your case, you will have to complete complex formalities. Here, entry is highly restricted to litigants (even those in-person) while it is just free if you wear a black coat and do not display your identity. Touts do that. The Lawyers have no bar from moving across any gate and their mobiles are allowed inside the court room also. But for a client they cannot enter the court room with a mobile and their mobiles are confiscated, if found in their possession in switch-off form. Clients in court premises are totally at the mercy of their lawyers. There is no separate counter for petitioner-in-person. In lower courts, venders have been allowed by the Bar inside and near the court rooms. Lots of venders keep roaming through the lawyer's chambers throughout the day and in the evening many chambers can be seen with booze parties. These chambers are sold, illegally constructed and illegally transferred after the lawyer dies or leaves practice.

Once you sign the power of attorney to engage a lawyer, you are totally in his hands. Lawyers become the master of your life and your case. They will never tell you about the stage of your case, asking money every time and do not attend dates and extort and harass clients in many ways is a very common practice in courts. If you want to change a lawyer against the wish of the present lawyer, it is impossible. The Bar Association is evasive to help you to fetch a 'no objection' from any member lawyer. So you are trapped. There is no bar that your lawyer may not be contacted by the opposite party and you may loose your case. It has come to our notice that some of the lawyer refuses to sign visitors pass and the client cannot enter the court room to see the proceedings of his own case. No provision of law permits lawyers for such callous conduct with clients, is very much prevailing in almost all the courts of the country. Clients need protection by law and their rights need to be defined. For remedy to this malpractice every court must be provided with an administrative block (building) having two distinct departments. **One** shall be the Judicial Block and **another** will be Administrative Block.

The **Judicial Block** shall work under 'Judicial Commission'. This building shall have restricted entry. Here, the judicial registrar and other administrative officers will sit to regulate judicial work, that includes allocation of cases, inter-court reshuffling and shifting, constituting Benches, fixing the dates and all such works and make different arrangements and management inside the court rooms.

There will be a Commissioner to receive the complaints against judicial staff and even misconduct of a judicial officer. He will entertain/hear complaints even against technically wrong orders. He will hear a complaint against a judge who passes almost final order without framing issues. If he finds the complaint genuine, he will be empowered to take action and issue memo on the delinquent officer or pass orders justifying his action. He will accept all complaints of different nature including bribe/negligence of duty or other corrupt practices inside/around the courtroom. He will be empowered to collect and act upon a complaint against a lawyer and can notify the Bar Association to take action against the delinquent lawyer. He may also receive a copy of judgment where an appeal against a technically unsound decision, is allowed and enter that into the personal file of the errant judicial officer for the considerations of his promotion. This block shall also have a separate department for filing and processing and other relevant activities along with filing.

The **Administrative Block** shall look after all the affairs pertaining to the maintenance of premises under its control. It will have sub-departments for building development and maintenance, allotment of lawyer's chambers and their maintenance, streets and venues, shopping, typing, stamps-paper vending, stationary vending, canteens, attestation, parking and everything that pertains to maintaining the entire campus. A separate department shall look after the maintenance of all court rooms with best possible facilities of staff, electronic equipments; IT links, sitting arrangements of judicial officers, his ministerial staff, lawyers and litigants.

Such twin arrangement is possible in courts at small places like Solan in Himachal Pradesh where the total number of judicial officers is not more than four. The administrative block with all essential features mentioned above is possible to maintain. If not much classified, it may have essential number of cabins or small rooms to classify different activities in different cabins/rooms in one separate premise. It is highly objectionable from the side of litigants that the entire control of court campus at ransom of lawyers and rules made there under are insufficient and only of domestic in nature without having any universal law and any defined policy.

B. THE PROVISIONS OF CODE OF CONDUCT FOR LAWYERS

Different provisions of code of lawyer's conduct are as follows:

Section-1: Misusing membership for personal gains.

Explanation: Many members are not acquainted with law of the land. They have limited and stereotype work of processing various documents like attestation, presentation, etc. and that need not to study and practice law in court premises. Many such fake people are frequent in court and are using court atmosphere to their personal advantage. It has been also a frequent practice that such people wear white dress if not black coat inside the court premises and even inside the court room without fear. To overcome such malice every lawyer needs to display his/her registration number and name engraved on a finely designed metal badge affixed on her/his apron.

Penalty: Advocates without this badge cannot appear in court and cannot present papers before the Oath Commissioner and Registrar, etc.

Section-2: Lawyers with criminal record.

Explanation: Lawyers engage in illegal activities or having court cases against them shall have to declare to the Bar Association. In court during their appearance through an affidavit and that shall be placed on record of the case file. Lawyers who have been prosecuted through Penal Code of the country shall lose their right to practice in any court until Bar Association permits such lawyer on temporary basis for a period of maximum five years to establish a good conduct in this period.

Penalty: On getting no satisfactory report of the delinquent the license may be suspended until the case is over.

Section-3: Lawyers not properly qualified.

Explanation: Every practicing lawyer need to display their degree in their chamber which may be embossed on a specially designed metallic badge having embossed along with his/her registration number to testify that he is a qualified registered lawyer.

Penalty: Lawyer having not displayed his badge on his/her person shall not qualify to be present in the court and plead the case. In absence of badge required the Bar Association may issue such defaulter lawyer a letter of condonation for court purpose. All the logics for condonation shall have their predetermined definitions to limitise the options.

Section-4: Filing with Power Of Attorney (Vakalatnama).

(a) The text of POA form shall be drafted afresh under this section by the Bar Association keeping various provisions of this section and other such by laws, whatever applicable.

(b) The lawyer shall have moral and legal binding to attend the dates and remain cooperative to the client, with a pledge to attend the case with insurgency and care in the interest of the litigant.

(c) A copy of such POA shall be handed over to the litigant as a receipt and terms and conditions for the contract taken up mentioning payment and mode of payment as decided mutually in the POA form.

Explanation: At present the litigants have no proof what payment has been given to the lawyer and the lawyer have freehand to exploit the litigant. By having a copy of the contract and deposition of the POA in a court, everything shall be on record and the lawyers shall not dare deviate from what they have signed. Any off-the-record arrangement between the parties (lawyer and the client) shall be put on record of Bar Association for future, if reported to in case of any breach.

Penalty: Without an approved Format signed by both the parties, no case can be filed.

Section-5: Payments to the Advocate.

(a) Every lawyer shall charge his fee as per his/her level of expertise (Category viz. A, B, C and D) decided by the Bar as per

- (i) academic qualification
- (ii) years of practice
- (iii) level of practice
- (iv) number of cases done
- (v) nature of cases
- (vi) success rate in cases
- (vii) overall reputation

(b) It is mandatory for a lawyer to enter (i) the term of contract, (ii) payment decided and its mode, (iii) photocopy of the current and postdated cheques to give to the client.

(c) Every lawyer will have to display his service charges in his/her chamber as per his category.

(d) Fee has to be categorically specified for different works like for consultation, inspecting case file and giving his/her opinion, drafting and conveyencing the documents and charges for every services he/she promises to render during a particular case.

Explanation: Every Lawyer will have a binding to file his IT return on the basis of payments received.

Penalty: Breach will result suspension of license until explanation is accepted and bar on the accused is not lifted by the Judicial Commission.

Section-6: Seeking adjournments.

(a) Adjournments shall be granted as per provisions of the Second Schedule for adjournments.

(b) Adjournment asked orally by either of the parties shall be granted and mentioned in the order sheet as to why an adjournment is granted.

(c) Adjournment asked by a lawyer shall follow a written request from the lawyer countersigned by the client is mandatory.

Explanation: Adjournments for the convenience of lawyers is a worst lag in the entire judicial proceeding. In trial courts lawyers send their Munshi to seek adjournment most on the pretext that the advocate is busy in other court. Such a lame excuse by the lawyers is a usual practice. A lawyer should engage more juniors if he/she is overloaded. No lawyer can be allowed to seek adjournment for the reason that he/she is so busy to postpone his presence for next days which is not less than six months delaying justice to the client.

Penalty: A lawyer will be fined Rs. 2000/- for seeking adjournments for lame excuses like his overloaded by his own work.

Section-7: Premises of court and encroachment.

(a) It is only the area under the occupancy of lawyers in the form of approved constructed chambers in different Blocks in the building.

(b) Rest of the open space inside the court boundary wall shall be in control of a specially powered authority, may be named as 'Court Development and Works Department' (CDWD) under the control of Registrar or an equivalent officer.

(c) Within the scheduled shopping complex inside the court boundary, every court complex shall have (i) a typing block having all facilities for preparing documentation and attestation, (ii) cafeteria and (iii) library for all.

(d) Allotments to kiosks, maintenance, quality control, pricing of goods sold in these mini shops shall be in the control of court authorities and not in the control of Bar Association.

(e) Litigants shall have equal rights on services such as parking and canteen charges.

Explanation: Article-21 of Constitution of India mentions sparing space and ministerial services for the lawyers near the court premises but it does not speak of having handing-over the entire area under the sole control of the Bar Associations. The situation in civil courts and trial court is horrifying. The entire court premise is mostly found occupied in very absurd and dissolute manner. Congestion by visiting litigants every day reflects the amount of business inside court boundaries. This attracts venders, touts and un-scrupulous people who have nothing to do with litigation business of the court. Office bearers of Bar Association have no written guidelines from higher authorities as to how the space around court rooms is to be utilised to maintain order, grace and convenience of the litigants.

The un-scrupulous venders, kiosk owners and all such outsiders maltreat litigants and extort them as per opportunity they get. Parking spaces have been captured and reserved for lawyers while the litigants are supposed to park in a paid space. Bar Association has a very lukewarm attitude towards the dignity and respect of litigants and even to their own clients and have very bad treatment after they get full payment from the client.

Court Development Works Department *(CDWD): It is a special body constituted by the Administrative Block of every court premises. The function is to maintain any kind of development and maintenance of building and other structures within the court premises including the maintenance of lawyer's chambers.*

Penalty: Any person found vending, encroaching, occupy, using any court premises in an unauthorised manner shall be brought to books by the court authorities and shall be presented before the Registrar who will hear the matter and can impose heavy fine or prosecute the guilty.

Section-8: Courts to interfere for violation of code of conduct.

Though the Registrar is empowered to impose fine on a defaulter if the matter is reported to him by the 'Court Development and Works Department' (CDWD) or Court authorities, yet the regular civil court may take cognizance of an offence violating any provision of this Code of Conduct if the court deem that fit to intervene in *suo motto* manner or on the complaint by the registrar or equivalent authority of the court.

Explanation: At present no such authority exists in any civil court. Though such an authority shall work with the permission of the High Court, yet it shall work independently. We can take a lesson from formation of 'Highway Authority of India' (HAOI) for the overall development of Highways. Since this authority came into being and started working independently there is substantial improvement in highways, making them passenger savvy. Before this, the highways were in the control of criminal forces supported by local politicians. Mushrooming roadside dhabas and unauthorised stopovers are still being managed by local goons who rarely bother for traveller's basic rights. The HAOI has done a lot good to passengers by starting nice cafeteria with control rates and maintaining quality. Such an authority is needed to maintain and manage court premises to make courts more conducive to the litigants. In total absence of such authority the court premises are at ransom by those who proved to be incompetent to take care of litigants in last 60 years.

Penalty: To be dealt with court authorities by imposing fine. The Registrar will proceed for regular court for prosecution as per provisions of Penal Code/Criminal Procedure Code.

Section-9: Code of conduct has legislative sanction.

Explanation: This section has Legislative sanction to impose penalty in the form of fine or prosecution as per law of the land.

Penalty: As per Law of the Land.

Section-10: Clients interest is supreme.

(a) Ignoring, not responding, avoiding, neglecting calls from the client will amount to breach of Trust.

(b) Showing disrespect, uttering objectionable words and insulting the client in presence of other persons will amount to defamation.

(c) Matter reported against the obnoxious conduct of the advocate shall be registered with authorities and the lawyer shall be issued show cause notice under this section by the Judicial Commission.

Explanation: Bar Council and Associations have provided not only the open space of the court premises but have been allowed to have reserved space inside the courtrooms. Lawyers who is an appointee by his client, has a dignity before the court and deserves to sit inside the courtroom on chairs while waiting for his turn or hearing arguments in some case, but the client who is the cause of the judiciary is made to stand up inside the courtroom and even in property suits and civil matters he is treated like an accused.

As far as the status of accused is concerned, courts have already objected on producing the accused with handcuffs, without tying him/her in chain/rope, injured, exhausted, wounded and in any kind of bad shape. An accused is innocent until he is convicted and by all means and by virtue of all the laws he deserves to be treated with dignity. In courtroom anyone except the lawyers are mal-treated by court staff and given a harsh and insulting treatment, no matter he is fighting for a public interest. While not allowing the client to sit in the courtroom the court takes this humiliation of litigant silently and lightly. Respectable appellants/petitioner who have filed against atrocity of the system or against a criminal act of authorities or a bonded criminal believing gross violation of his fundamental rights, need not to be treated like an accused. The attitude of the court is not rational to the litigants in this matter. In courts the magistrates issue directions to its staff that the accused has not to be treated with dignity and be not allowed to sit on chair is not written any where in any form. It is highly deplorable. It seems that the court take it granted that any person who has come to the shelter of the court does not deserve any respect and dignity from it except if he/she is not a lawyer.

Duties to one's client are at once fairly and easily delineated and are yet more complex because of the close human interaction that takes place in the lawyer-client relationship. Most codes acknowledge, directly or indirectly, that such duties include honesty, integrity, trustworthiness, respect, loyalty and compassion.

Penalty: If satisfied, the hearings authorities like the Registrar (Grievance), can ask to refund the fee paid to the lawyer and permit the client to change the lawyer in spite of presently fighting to fetch a 'no objection' from the lawyer.

Section-11: Penalty for not appearing in court.

Explanation: (i) For seeking adjournments on artificial grounds, (ii) not informing the client for NDH (next date of hearing) and make arrangements in time, (iii) not preparing reply and other such documents due to be submitted in the case on next date of hearing.

Penalty: (1) The very court may take cognizance for the intentional lapse by the lawyer and may fine such an advocate minimum Rs. 2,000/- for the first chance and can double the amount in every next hearing. (2) The court may also dismiss such a lawyer who is working against the interest of justice and for bringing bad name to the profession and the appellant can ask the Registrar to help the abandoned litigant for alternative arrangements and put some ab-financial penalty on the erring lawyer for his/her misbehavior.

Section-12: Penalty for not filing documents on a schedule date.

Explanation: Lawyers may be negligent towards the interest of the client and any fine imposed by the court for not filing the documents on date of hearing go from the pocket of the litigant for the mistake of his/her advocate.

Penalty: (1) While escaping from mandatory duty towards court and the client as well the court may treat that as contempt and can impose fine on the defaulter lawyer if not satisfied with the explanation or conduct of the lawyer.

(2) The court may also suspend lawyer's license and ban his or her appearance in any court for minimum one week.

Section-13: Edibles within court premises.

Explanation: Lower courts are so dirty mess of unauthorised venders selling unhygienic substandard eatables. In some courts such venders sell poor stuff and Bar Association has no notice of this. It is because of the fact that the Bar Association is fully incompetent to provide proper space to rightful restaurant or cafeteria or have vested interest in continuing such callous situation to allow very poor quality stuff available in the court premises. The Bar Association never keeps an eye on the quality of eatables and price thereby and has no mind to mend this.

Penalty: **Supervisory Committee** sets up for surprise visits that shall impose fine of minimum 2000 rupees for any small lapse. It shall have the right to lock out any such kiosk, shop, and arrest unauthorized venders to hand over to police or oust him from the premises or detain him/her for the whole day at a place.

Section-14: Unlicensed vendors inside court compound.

No unlicensed vendor shall be allowed to roam around or occupy a nuke and corner unauthorisedly anywhere.

Explanation: In a civil court, where the biggest Bar Association has a registration of more than four thousand lawyers, the premises for the lawyers is getting short day-by-day. Bar

Association has no rule on the last limits of registration of lawyers with it. It has created great chaos inside the court compound where those who have no work on a particular day want to come to the court for searching new bait.

The condition in certain civil courts in North Delhi, is so grim that even the call girls can be seen here perusing clients among litigants, and even lawyers. Police know that all but take no action.

Penalty: Fine one thousand rupees instant or one week Prosecution.

Section-15: Lawyers chambers are in court's compound and not the private property of lawyers.

(a) All the chamber must be allotted to the lawyers for a period of not more than 25 years and its possession and occupancy shall be exclusive.

(b) The chamber or seat shall never be transferred to any third party through a sale deed and a POA, which is in practice. After a person abandons practice, he/she supposed to handover the chamber to the Court authorities to which it belongs.

Supervisory Committee: A legal body constituted by Bar Association and members of court administration Block to look after performance of various services within the premises of court.

(c) No chamber shall be extended or enlarged to construct a floor on it without permission of the authorities.

(d) No one shall sale off the floor or share the chamber without the permission of the authority and without the knowledge of the authority.

(e) Floors can be constructed by the authorities and allotted to the next aspirant.

(f) No one shall be allowed to use the allotted space for making a property deal.

Explanation: It is all in practice and some of the advocates have sold off these chambers to such people who are not lawyers such as photostat vendor, attesting oath commissioner or others near the chambers.

Penalty: Cancellation of allotment of chamber and immediate eviction if the allottee does not cooperate.

Section-16: Lawyer's duty to inform the client.

It is a mandatory duty of the council to inform his/her client about developments in the court on the date of hearing by telephone as well as in writing or after a telephonic conversation by sending a copy of the orders within a week.

Explanation: All the lawyers expect the clients to contact the lawyer each and every time and they feel that it is the duty of the client to always knock at his/her door for help. Though the format of POA must include this term and the client must be sure of his interest in the hands of a lawyer whom he/she has engage to take care of his/her litigation on contractual payment basis and for that he/she has already been paid by the client. A client for taking his services due to his/her being a technical expert should keep it in mind that a lawyer is an appointed person. A lawyer must not expect the client to go to library and find out citations to strengthen his/her case and should not be insisted to provide such material. Rather, it is the legal binding on the lawyer to ask for documents and material of support to forward his/her contention to win the case which the client has to deliver.

The lawyer has to keep in mind that after he/she takes up the job the onus lies with the advocate to take the case towards success. Any failure at any stage shall be the entire responsibility of the lawyer. In case the lawyer feels that at specific times, he is not getting due cooperation from his client, it shall be one of the terms of contract, the lawyer can use, to come out of the litigation retaining all the payments he/she had received so far by giving his/her client a written notice. The Performa of notice shall be available with the vendors in court premise and on Internet and the lawyer has not to create a fresh draft for the purpose every time.

The terms of POA shall be drafted having terms of condition and one of the terms shall be how the contract-cum-

POA can be concluded in between. It shall be a balanced document covering the interest of both the parties signing the contract-cum-POA.

Penalty: On receiving a written complaint about the conduct of the engaged lawyer, the Judicial Commission (responsible to have a control on the conduct of judges and the lawyers as well) shall hear the matter by calling the lawyer only once and take a decision to suspend his/her license barring appearance in any court for a period of one month to two months or making a compromise to continue in the case.

Section-17: Payment to lawyers includes all services including travelling expenses.

Explanation: It is a general attitude of the lawyers demanding money for every work. Most of the lawyers keep extorting money even from extremely poor and exhausted clients who pay them by selling their agricultural fields and village houses. Once a fee is decided, it is the entire responsibility of the lawyer to take care of the case and make the case win by putting his best efforts and means. A client may be asked to come to him only when he is required by the court in the case or if any subsidiary documents are to be supplied by the client or when new developments are to be clubbed with the case or in any other such circumstances.

Penalty: A complaint by the client to this regard shall amount to debar such a guilty lawyer from appearing in any court for six years after paying a penalty amount to his client, which shall be double to the fee paid by the client till then or cancellation of license for practice.

Section-18: Certificate of qualification to be annexed/ mentioned along with registration number, with every case filed.

Explanation: To avoid frivolous and fake people who are operating in the guise of lawyers need to every time put their credentials in each case they file. It has to be direct and authorization by any association or agency has not to be entertained by the court. It is a common practice that evens a peon, who calls case numbers on the door of a court, is often seen putting up lawyers dress. The entire staff of the court needs to have a dress code and have to wear an identifying mark (token) to pronounce his post.

Since the lawyers are identified only by wearing black coat or apron and a lawyer's bow (band) genuine identification of every worker in the court has to be defined by using certain known dress code. The author knows people whose wives are lawyers. The husband wears white pant and white shirt, accompanies his wife to the courtroom, and if possible, argues the matter, in the guise of a lawyer. No person without proper dress code, provided badge or an issued badge by the Bar Association and a specific dress shall be allowed in the court premises. People who are fighting their case in person shall be exempted from any dress code but they will have to get a special badge (a temporary display card) be issued to display on his/her person during a visit to the court premises.

Penalty: Any person attempting to violate this section shall be prosecuted as per law for cheating the court.

Section-19: POA shall exhibit the payment lawyer receives.

Explanation: It needs to be on record what income is declared in income tax returns. Like any other profession, lawyers too need such monitoring as the chances of generating black money are fair here. There has to be a column in the Power of Attorney format, to declare what payment has been decided between the two parties as per category of the lawyer.

Penalty: Summing up all POA of the year whose one copy shall be given to the client and second copy shall be retained by the lawyer for IT purpose. Wrong declaration of income shall be subject to cheating in a much classified manner. The defaulter lawyers shall be tried for such offence under IPC provisions.

Section-20: Lawyers chambers have to be built and maintained by the CDWD in uniform manner.

Explanation: Since the property belongs to the government being a part and parcel of the court premises, it has been handed over to the Bar Association in order to give facilities to the practicing lawyer. But the very concept has been badly misused by the allottees taking this property guaranteed on their mercy. Bar Association does not have any effective monitoring body to streamline the proper use of such places given in the form of chambers. In lower courts like Tis Hazari, Delhi, the chambers have been designed in uneven manner and painted heterogeneously. Some of the chambers have been sold out to those who are not even lawyers. In apex court some of the lawyers have leased out these chambers to photostat wallahs, stationary bookshop or attestation notary, against the terms and conditions of the allotment letter. In lower courts these chambers are constructed to make multiple storey building and have been sold out or rented out to other persons. To maintain better look the structure and design has to be decided and be maintained by allotting authority, i.e. CDWD.

Penalty: Rule violation shall amount to get deprived of allotment directly evacuating the allotted premises, if proved guilty.

Section-21: Lawyers not to be allowed to sit on pavements and open space that Is not meant for such purposes.

Explanation: The Registrar or the highest Administrative Authority in the court, responsible of maintaining an order within the entire usable area of the court building shall have a monitoring body to maintain the premises as per mutually decided policy drafted for the purpose. At least three of its members will be lawyers while two members shall be from working staff/personnel other than lawyers with five members shall be from court administration in a team of ten members. Vendors of any kind shall not be permitted to occupy any place on the sides of footpaths or any other area of the court.

Parking shall be free for all the users including lawyers and for security reason an attendant shall charge only one rupee for his maintenance issuing a slip and shall deposit total of daily collection with the torn slip with the administration. No contract shall be leased out and cannot be converted a source of income for Bar Association as it is in practice now in higher courts also in Delhi.

The Court Administration shall provide small shopping center with all necessary items in shops/kiosks to cater the needs of visiting users including lawyer's daily requirement. The price of the sellable items shall be fixed by the Administration and list of all available items shall be mandatory to display even the charges of services shall be displayed on the concerned places in an eligible manner.

Penalty: Immediate heavy challan by court administration.

Section-22: The judge shall fine striking lawyers or imposed punishment accordingly.

Explanation: A strike may be legal but it is always immoral when third party suffers. Clients remain at the mercy of the court for justice if the engaged lawyers go away from their duty. It is a sort of cheating a person who has entrusted them by paying good sum to them. The client approaches an advocate through the way of litigation to get justice after suffering at the hands of his/him defendants for a long period. He pays money to the lawyer beyond his capacity. The court takes its own time to dispose of the case but the suffering client keeps waiting for justice. Strike by lawyers shatters his hope to get justice in time and it becomes a dream for him. He is lucky if he gets justice in time during his life. .

Penalty: Minimum fine Rs. 2,000/- on the lawyer on each date.

Section-23: Report of misbehaviour by the lawyer shall be handled by the Sub-Registrar of the court or a special Magistrate created for the purpose of helping the litigants to save him/her from exploitation and misbehaviour by certain lawyers.

Explanation: The court administration needs to protect litigant's interest from touts, venders, goons, impostors, police, contractors, parking mafias and all un-scrupulous persons. Any report from a victim litigant against the misconduct, misbehavior, insulting gesture, over-charging by the lawyer or any other person of his staff or the staff of the court, the court administration may direct the matter to certain punitive authority but certainly not to the Bar Association who is crippled before its voters.

Penalty: Nabbing the offender, make fine on him/her on the spot or produced before SDM for justice. If the matter is reported to the Registrar, he may suspend license of any lawyer for a certain period, if found guilty of misconduct. Bar Association not to interfere Sub-Registrar's work.

Section-24: Sub-Registrar/Administrator/Appellant court shall sit in different places other than the very court to hear complainants against misconduct of lawyers.

Explanation: In certain lower courts where the number of lawyers is more than the capacity of the court, the advocate assembles to interrupt court proceedings and create rowdy scenes in the court. During the recent strike by lawyers the striking lawyers forced to close down courts to function by doing violence and breaking furniture of court rooms. The author is the eyewitness to the kicking of closed doors of the court rooms by supporters of striking lawyers in presence of sufficient police force with them. It is mention worthy that the judges already had adjourned the cases that day and had confined themselves into their chambers, on having prior information of such violence by the striking lawyers and their supporters/subordinate during working hours. This was all covered by the TV channels that day and was shown in the evening.

Penalty: Police officers being liberal to such offenders whosoever, they may be liable to be punished along with the lawyers who are nabbed from the court premises by the courts police (to be appointed for this purpose).

Section-25: Report of taking payment off the record shall be entertained by the Sub-Registrar under Penal Code provisions of the land.

Explanation: It is common practice by the lawyers, doctors, and high profile professionals take their fee off the record. Most of the schemes to overcome such malpractice usually fail due to mutual understanding between the parties. Still, we have to find out some way to locate the flow of money into black market. This question is, however, related with two main factors. One is professional freedom as per service provided and the second is mutuality between the two. Solution to this problem may be to decide the price on the basis of (a) Qualification, (b) Year of practice in the field, (c) amount of work he/she had handled in previous years, and (d) per centage of success achieved in the cases taken up. "Categories" of lawyers may be defined and allotted to the lawyers. The monitoring authorities may decide and take into consideration the minimum fee. For each category of lawyers and the work they are doing for the client there has to be a price defined and displayed. For example, to draft a petition, the fee of lawyer of apex court has been fixed as Rs. 1,200/- only.

Penalty: It can be handled under 'Breach of Trust' if more money is demanded or proved than decided or scheduled or displayed or quoted by the professional on record, vary. It may also be handled with 'violation of code of conduct'.

Section-26: Each lawyer has to file IT return with declaration as per receipts issued to the clients.

Explanation: Such measure shall make lawyers professionally conscious about their social and legal obligations.

Penalty: Subject to Penal Code.

Section-27: Helping a colleague by gathoring outside court or inside the court is a punishable offense to fight a lawyer's case collectively.

Explanation: It is in practice in lower courts where the Bar Association is big sized and take everything granted to force a judge to change his/her decision due to unprecedented pressure by a crowd of lawyers in the courtroom for the personal cause of their colleague. It is a commonsense that the office bearers of Bar Association come forward to present themselves collectively by joining the lawyer who has tendered his/her POA in the case. All start speaking during argument or create a pressure on the judge by the largely acceding number in the courtroom unauthorisedly.

Penalty: Such unauthorized assembly in any court case shall be treated contempt of court. The court may note down the names and identity of the lawyers along with their chamber numbers on record and impose fine, instantly, up to five thousand rupees each, which shall follow by an affidavit within a week's time after the fine is deposited with the treasury.

Section-28: Influencing police by gathering in police station to shield a lawyer shall be treated as an offence. The SHO can register a FIR and take the lawyers and others accomplices to the regular court of law.

Explanation: This provision is analogue to the above Section.

Penalty: This provision is analogue to the above Section.

Section-29: Stamp tickets venders, stationery shops, bookstore, library, cafeteria and tea stall, photostat shop, typing block, attestation counters, filing counters and enquiry counter, etc. and all other services, which are used by the petitioners-in-person or needed by litigants, shall be out of control of Bar Association and the Court Administration will maintain them for litigants.

Explanation: While a strike is declared and it is in progress, the litigants are forced to suffer maximum in many ways. Lawyers who take up responsibility to give service to their paymaster become the masters of their clients ignoring the interest of middle class and poor suffering litigants. Not only that, they want to make everything standstill by sealing off all services within the court premises. Article-21 does not allow such a freehand to the authorities and the lawyers. The exact lines are as follows:

"Building and other facilities to Advocate Association: There is a Constitutional obligation on the part of the State to provide building and other facilities to Advocate Association.

The Constitutional obligation can be read into Constitutional right guaranteed under Article-21 of Constitution of India." It has been quoted in case titled ***Advocate Association Bangalore vs. Chief Minister, Government of Karnataka, AIR 1997 Knat.18 at 32.***

Giving premises to the Advocate Association does not mean even the premises to the lawyers. It is very clear that the premises and other facilities to the Advocate Association only and not to the lawyers individually. This also means that the chambers located inside the court premises are illegally been given to unauthorised person. This wrong has become a convention and the right is claimed by the lawyers for nothing by misinterpreting the provision and using force of gathering to pounce upon the public place in their personal possession. The condition is so grave that the allotted spaces is built in the form of more than one chamber and are further sold of on POA. No one has any check on it. Illegal is going on inside the court under its wrong by those who pledge to protect the law of the land to be faithful to the Constitution.

The clause clearly says 'the space and facilities to the lawyer's Association only', and not to the lawyers at personal level. However, the misuse of this right by the court authorities under the pressure of lawyers is illegal and need to be amended to clean off court premise in the interest of the suffering citizens. Lawyer's chambers (blocks) must be separated from court Premise by doors and walls as in case of Delhi high court and the apex court.

Penalty: Cancellation of allotment shall affect, if violation of Rules framed by authorities (Court Administration) takes place. The allotment lease should not extend after the allottee does not exist any more physically or die or moved out leaving the profession and vacated the chamber.

Section-30: Touts and agents for Notary, Oath Commissioner, Registrar Marriage in the court premises shall be liable to be prosecuted.

Explanation: There are fake lawyers who maintain a kiosk for working as an intermediary to get the above-mentioned services inside premises of the court. The works, which should be done directly on a window, has been made so cumbersome for nothing or can, say creating corruption by creating confusion before a client. Such touts can be nabbed in ITOs, SEM court, Export registration office at Asaf Ali road and all such small cause courts and they work there freely in the dress of a lawyer without being registered anywhere may be without a degree. It needs only a black coat, which is freely available in the open market. Why there are no scheduled procedures to make forms, attestation, court stamps and such stationery available through a government run counter in every office where such papers are required and deposited? In Motor License Department, the scene is really horrifying. It is the office in total control of touts. Windows are not marked with what for the window is. There is no printed booklet to tell the procedure. Kiosks for preparing medical certificates and snapping instant photographs have been sold out to outsiders who charge very high to complete the documents. Touts are allowed to give bundles of documents from back door and there is utter confusion due to high rush there every day.

Corrupt officers know it well that if you want to generate black money create confusion and by making procedures cumbersome and things difficult. The working of police, courts, income tax, and sale tax department are so corrupt and out of reach of common citizens that there remains no option than to kneel down before touts who are the sons of pure corruption.

It is not thinkable that the forms are not available in Registrar of all kinds of offices, ITOs, Sale tax office, copy right office, Export Import registrar office and other such departments. Rather, these are available with a chai-wallah or three wheeler wallah who parks his vehicle outside the office or any such unauthorized person. These mandatory documents are to be made available on Internet or given with nominal cost on the counter where these need to be deposited. Officers should not have share in illegal sale of such forms, as in practice today, even outside their own office by unauthorised touts.

Penalty: Working as a touts or unlicensed venders, be prosecuted for six months by the special structured courts to help the Court Administration. Officers processing documents presented by unauthorized persons shall be booked and be punished by the Supervisory Committee.

Section-31: All the registered lawyers have defined duties towards their clients, Bar Association, Courts and the Constitution of the nation.

Explanation: Most codes acknowledge, directly or indirectly, that such duties need honesty; integrity, trustworthiness; respect, loyalty; compassion and competence jointly formulate integrity and quality of service. Some of the duties became inherent as soon as one becomes a lawyer. Such duties towards the clients may be defined as following:

(a) should assist in maintaining the integrity of the profession,

(b) should have good behaviour and respectful gesture,

(c) use of proper technical language,

(d) respect to their client,

(e) maintain secrecy and confidentiality of the case matter and not to discuss with unconcerned persons in any manner,

(f) not taking any service from the client in lieu of his/her services to the client,

(g) to keep the client informing with the latest development in the case,

(h) to serve several masters—the state, the court, the client, the profession, colleagues, even her/himself with parity and balance,

(i) to remain informed very well with the jurisdiction and court procedures,

(j) to serve the cause of justice and not to encourage offenders by giving them professional support against humanity and the society as well,

(k) a lawyer owes a duty to the State, to maintain its integrity and its law. A lawyer should not aid, counsel, or assist any person to act in any way contrary to the law,

(l) should never bring harm to the public,

(m) can adopt fairness, courtesy and respect to the court,

(n) not to abuse the process of the Tribunal by instituting or prosecuting proceedings that are clearly motivated by malice on the part of the client and are brought solely for the purpose of injuring another party,

(o) must not knowingly assist or permit the client to do anything that the lawyer considers to be dishonest or dishonourable,

(p) must not knowingly attempt to deceive a tribunal or influence the course of justice by offering false evidence, and so on,

(q) a lawyer is exhorted to maintain toward the judges of the courts a courteous and respectful attitude and insists on similar conduct on the part of the client,

(r) to maintain proper decorum towards the court in all times, even if he is failing in his/her case for the purpose of enhancing public confidence in the administration of justice,

(s) to have loyalty to the system of the administration of justice,

(t) to abstain from involvement with interests outside the profession,

(u) lawyer's conduct must not bring the profession into disrepute,

(v) the lawyer is to uphold the integrity of the profession in order to maintain confidence of public,

(w) to maintain minimum standards,

(x) a lawyer has to be loyal to his client in all circumstances.

The clauses a to x are self-explanatory and have been drafted keeping what is unfortunately in practice by certain lawyers at different levels of courts.

Penalty: Reprimand, suspension of license or disbarment by the Bar Association temporarily to permanency depending upon the magnitude of breach and violation of code.

C. CODE OF JUDICIAL CONDUCT

Why necessary in third world countries? A code of conduct for judicial officers will increase work efficiency as the decisions shall be more based on facts and figures of the case and not the absolute personal freedom and personal hunch beyond the expected ethics of a judicial officer. Therefore, there has to be certain defined bindings on the judicial officers to make them accountable before the Judicial Commission. The reasons for such a code of conduct are many. There are certain facts which are normally ignored by the court, therefore, judicial officers have to be accountable for their lack of knowledge on their faulty and technically wrong decisions bringing hardship in citizen's lives and they need to be having liability for their wrong.

1. **Because** some of the existing provisions in law are not used by the courts to avoid spontaneous load by ramifying the issue of their own as suo motto inherent powers of the courts.
2. **Because** some of the existing provisions are not used as a practice due to lack of knowledge of judges.
3. **Because** the law enforcing agencies manage to have free hand to harass a person after detention is affected.
4. **Because** the law enforcing agencies feel that every detainee has to be proved to be a culprit in order to justify the detention.
5. **Because** the police must not be allowed to unauthorisedly acquire absolute authority to arrest any person of their choice in absence of timely accountability.
6. **Because** the vigilance department of law enforcing and investigating agencies rarely do justice to their work and covering up the official offence helps them protects their public image.
7. **Because** the law framed for the protection of women (dowry, rape, sexual abuse, etc.) is more being misused by women against men to exploit their one sided Rights?

8. **Because** the accused person is detained in jail for years on remand and even the bail of innocent person takes years due to defaulted procedures and wrong self styled-autocratic ways of the investigating agencies.
9. **Because** the innocent accused is not given chance to defend himself even at the time of bail also properly.
10. **Because** due to the lapses and lacunae in procedures and easy-going negligent ways of police, once trapped in police cobweb, the career and reputation of any creative innocent citizens can be ruined forever.
11. **Because** about millions of innocent accused with their family members who suffer outside jail, are detained as under-trials even for petty offences, and no rescue is allowed on the pretext of cumbersomeness and unnecessary procedures while the government remain incompetent and disinterested to handle this situation properly.
12. **Because** presently in most of the third world nations, there are no laws on prolonged or unlimited period of detention in the country, still the detainees do not know when their turn will come?
13. **Because** the justice in these countries is not time bound and the journey into darkness continues for an uncertain period.
14. **Because** many under-trials have been forced to under go immoral and inhuman submissions before jail authorities, bonded convicts or fun seekers from outside.
15. **Because** many under trials are found killed in jails in mysterious circumstances, in the name of fake encounters, in an effort to escape, or rebelling, or rioting, or due to uncontrolled infection or malnutrition conditions prevailing in jails.
16. **Because** reports are available with International Human Right Agencies, some with their Ministry of Home for the custodial deaths.

17. **Because** the innocent citizens are bound to remain totally at the mercy of the corrupt police and the over loaded courts in these unfortunate countries.
18. **Because** police and courts cannot be the masters of citizen's lives.
19. **Because** the UN Charter of Human Rights provide certain rights to the citizens of a free nation which are under threat and violated everyday by the protector agencies themselves against the various provisions of Constitutions of these nations.
20. **Because** due to advancement in science and technology, particularly in electronics, Genetics, Molecular Biology, Biometrics, etc. we have now sophisticated laboratories for verification of various materials to be treated as evidence. And some of them are just reliable but not available and appreciated by the courts yet.
21. **Because** the investigating agency takes it granted that they have to defend the FIR at all costs and the person arrested is a criminal.
22. **Because** in presence of such procedures and offending ways of police, no body is safe in these countries.
23. **Because** for police it is not at all difficult to trap any body and put behind bars for the period they want to by implicating the innocent citizens under desired Section of law without any of their risk.
24. **Because** law of the land in third world countries needs careful review in the interest of justice. It has to be citizen-oriented than to be police savvy.
25. **Because** no court of law is competent to compensate one's lost life in jails as detainee in case of acquittal.
26. **Because** life is only one.
27. **Because** the investigating and prosecuting agencies are yet not taken responsible for the failure of any case by any decided law.

28. **Because** there are no separate homes for the under-trials who cannot be placed with convicts or bonded criminals without their guilt is proved.
29. **Because** keeping the innocent under-trials with punished criminal in the similar conditions and enforcing similar work on them inside the jail is no less than punishing them for the crime they had not committed yet.
30. **Because** under-trials are not convicts.
31. **Because** there is no formula/policy to allocate the work to the judicial officer (Magistrates/Judges) in a rational and balanced manner making them overloaded beyond their carrying-capacity.
32. **Because** allocation of work to the judicial officers is at the discretion of their senior officer in any organization is undemocratic in absence of any set and open policy.
33. **Because** the allocation of work in done by the seniors to juniors and many personal bias and considerations may interfere proper, rational and justifiable distribution of work among magistrates and judges or junior workers.
34. **Because** such distribution of work in not done by any independent body in a scientific manner.
35. **Because** senior judicial person has to look after administration at the cost of their own work of Magistrate/Judges.
36. **Because** over-loaded judges may frequently adjourn most cases to get rid of piled up cases for the day.
37. **Because** there is no independent body to monitor and observe the performance of judicial officers and prepare their own report to create track record of the magistrates and judges.
38. **Because** there is no separate body to hear the grievance of litigants against the misconduct of a judges done inside the court.
39. **Because** the 'points' given to a judge on deciding the case are not awarded as per number of **witness** and

number of the issues in the case but merely given on that basis of the number of the cases decided.

40. Because there is no provision of rewarding good judges by way of out of turn promotions.

41. Because there is no noticeable 'monetary and perks benefit' to a good judge when promoted to some key post for his/her excellent work. Rather, at more responsible position he becomes more liable to work more meticulously and exhaustively.

42. Because all the posts of quasi-judicial nature such as Public prosecutor, deciding officers in CBI, Income Tax, Sales Tax, Police Department, Presidents of consumer forums, etc. who aught to hearing the aggrieved party and impart justice to them, are not covered by a 'special body' along with judicial officers making their separate Penal.

D. PROVISIONS IN JUDICIAL CODE OF CONDUCT FOR JUDICIAL OFFICERS

The work of imparting justice to the suffering litigants is really godly. Those who do it in the name of God keep themselves balanced even during over loading of work. The situation becomes conflicting when we plan to extract maximum comfort believing that we are doing a paid job. Let us find out what best bindings we can bear when imparting justice.

Section-1: To check whether the case files are given folio number of the court after receiving a document in the beginning and there after during hearing.

Explanation: In most of the lower courts the clerks ignore putting up folio number on all the received papers in a case file may be due to overwork but this gives a free passage to mutilation and tempering of stake documents. So each paper received by the court through filing at the primary and subsequent stages have to be numbered and this will be open to the litigant to know via official inspection of the file for tallying.

Penalty: Memo on record. Entry in CR.

Section-2: To ensure whether all the sheets in case-file are stamped by a seal of court.

Explanation: After ensuring folio marking by a specially recommended numbering system, ink, etc. all the folios in all case files have to be sealed to distinctly confirming that to be documents on record of the court or may be punched with pin-punch machine as done in case of passports. The judge has to take notice of such authentication while dealing with the case in court room. He is empowered to question the Registrar concerned about this job to be completed properly through a procedure.

Penalty: Memo on record and Entry in CR.

Section-3: To mark the documents in the files of litigants for the purpose of record and authenticity by the court at the time of filing what has been received and filed on the counter itself.

Explanation: Such a marking will ensure the partics for the security of documents during year's long litigation and shall rule out the possibility of bungling on any body's part. Presently, all the documents remain at the mercy of the court. It is one sided, now.

Penalty: Memo on record. Entry in CR.

Section-4: The court will ensure following sheets annexed in the beginning of the each case file. These include.

(a) Up dated index supplied by the filing litigant and counter signed by the court staff

(b) Order sheet

(c) Adjournment sheet

(d) Court processing like inspection of file, delivery of certified copies, etc.

Explanation: Each case file is not to be treated just as a file but be treated with utmost care of the staff as issues are stake materials of ones life.

Penalty: for

(a) Memo on record
(b) Entry in CR
(c) memo on record
(d) Negative remarks in CR. (Classification as per 1st schedule of penalties)

Section-5: At the first hearing the court will ensure the presence of all ministerial sheets duly signed by the staff and shall be aimed at framing the issues and the writs, etc.

Explanation: For this purpose some additional staff to be appointed in all the court that will ensure the compliance of all scheduled instructions before putting up a case-files before the court. In case of default, the court will be having a binding to take action against the employee. Minimum penalty may be a fine of minimum hundred rupees to two thousand rupees.

Penalty: Transfer at lower place with remarks in CR to demotion.

Section-6: The case shall be drafted in a manner to have a heading of issues a litigant want to rise.

Explanation: Drafting of the case shall be done in a manner that will enable the court to gather the whole case in few paragraphs. The essential part of each drafting will be

(a) List of dates
(b) Synopsis (Summary of the case)
(c) Desired issues to be decided to be annexed in the beginning.

Penalty: Deferring seniority of one year

Section-7: In the second stage of proceedings, the judge will decide maximum number of adjournments according to the number and nature of issues in each case keeping the 2nd schedule given in chapter 13 in view and it will be

entered in the adjournment sheet for future proceedings.

Explanation: This is an essential step to make justice time bound. It will help the litigants to assess the year of their decision they would be waiting for.

Penalty: In case of not abiding by written verdicts on adjournments by the present judge or the successive judges the ultimate liability shall fall with the person handling the case and so will be liable to be penalised by two month without pay leave.

Section-8: Not to treat defendants at par with the harassed or suffering litigant who sought the shelter of court to seek justice.

Explanation: Presently a litigant of either category is treated at par. A sufferer who had put the court into action does not deserve to be treated at par with the offender and law breaker. In civil cases such complainants will have the right to sit in the court while the accused shall not be allowed to sit on the chairs. Even it is recommendable from Human rights point of view that both the petitioner and the respondents should not be maltreated by the ways of a court but at least such a treatment should not be given to a person who has come to the shelter of a court in search of justice.

Penalty: Transfer at lower place with remarks in CR.

Section-9: No one will be allowed to camp near the court room or inside the court premises.

People will not be allowed inside the court building and only authorised persons (allowed by registrar) will share the government accommodation for day-to-day work.

Explanation: Encroachments of venders and shop keepers have made court an impossible place to move. All such facilities in Peoplism will be essentially provided by government regulated cafe, public convenience, stationer shop, communication facilities and frequently available consultation chambers.

Penalty: (1) Adverse remarks in CR of the concerned officers. (2) Invalidation of all permissions with three months simple imprisonment or fine of Rs. 25,000/- unit currency or all three on vendors and encroachers.

Section-10: Each judicial officer shall write his own CR and justify its entries.

Explanation: There has to be certain rules to regulate an honest effort to create ones own CR. Negative need to be recorded and opportunity of explaining the circumstances for a negative performance shall lie within this right.

Penalty: (1) Transfer of CR file to the junior Magistrate of the other State to give its report.

(2) Filing case with Vigilance Ministry.

Section-11: Discrepancy in CR and reality shall amount to disciplinary action by a specially constituted 'Judicial Promotion Commission' comprising five/three retired judges from the same or higher court.

Explanation: Any discrepancy between the facts and revelation shall amount disciplinary proceeding as the review of CRs shall be done by Judicial Promotion Commission itself, in addition to certain procedure needs to be evolved.

Penalty: Discrepancy can amount to loss of job along with police cases filed against dodging the authorities and using fallacy.

Section-12: Every judicial officer shall be subject to 'Judicial Commission' for explanation on issues that comes before it.

Explanation: Any citizen who has a grievance against the conduct of the court or its fellow staff members is free to move to the Commission. The proceedings of the Commission shall be 'Top secret' as these will be carried out in 'camera'. A separate code of penalties shall pre-exist as a universal law for this purpose. The course of 'Disciplinary Proceedings' or the 'trial' shall be quicker and to the point and shall decide within three months or before the court case under question is decided.

After the complaint is entertained, the case shall be automatically transferred to other court without a bias. The commission is bound to protect the interest of the complainant and revision/repeated complaint to this effect are bound to be entertained by the Commission in succession.

Penalty: The delinquent judicial officer shall be subject to the Judicial Commission and in case explanation not found satisfactory, second hearing will be done by appointed authority which will be empowered to pass verdict which can amount major penalty. The second schedule shall exhibit stages of stages of action taken by authorities.

Section-13: The Judicial Commission shall finalise the appointment of Judicial officers at various levels and it will have its own rules and regulation to handle, complaints, ad hoc appointments, regular appointment and other regulatory and administrative functions of judiciary.

Explanation: Such a controlling and regulatory body shall make autocracy oust from the present system where relief to poor citizens is breaking news for the Press. Accountability to the judicial officers is one of the planks of the Constitution of Peoplism.

There are defined rules for all types of appointments of judicial officer. It includes the ad hoc appointments in short term court and regular appointments of Supreme Court Judges. There shall be no promotion in case of High Court Judges to be promoted as a Judge in the Supreme Court. Besides many other rules the 'Track Record' through quality of Judgment, justification in Judgment, image of the judge outside the court and his/her CR, will be stake consideration for the a judicial officer to be appointed as a judge of the apex court. All the judgments delivered by the aspiring judicial officer shall be studied by the promotion department of the Judicial Commission which was given mark based on certain parameters decided by the Commission. It will be a kind of mechanical work as the mandatory requirement list is used to check the filed SLP.

Penalty: Violation of prescribed rules by any of the members shall amount to be handled by head of the next judicial body in the hierarchy and penalties shall be imposed as per violation including expulsion of the defaulter member. Such member may be asked to pay penalty in cash to the concerned judicial body between one lakh to five lakhs. In case of not paying the fine the defaulter member shall be handled through normal law of the land.

Section-14: To decide cases earlier than or in time shall be rewarded by marks as per prescribed formula and be entered in CR.

Explanation: This measure is essential to encourage early disposals of cases. Such a reward in present system is scarce.

Peoplism is committed to give its best to its loyal and citizen savvy effort.

Penalty: Judicial officer found lingering on the case for their own reasons to benefit the respondents or the other party shall amount to loss of job.

Section-15: Every judicial officer will give brief of his/her performance at the end of every year which shall be added to his/her CR.

Explanation: Every judicial officer shall be entitled to send his performance annually to the extraordinary performance committee which is a part of 'Judicial Promotion Commission'. There is no bar over the number of out of turn promotions and this will scrap the present faulty, politically motivated, bureaucratic and aristocratic way of promoting undeserving senior judges in absence of entire track record of judges. There are instances where judges passing order against public interest and in favour of a cabaret don, against the police, was elevated to the post of Chief Justice in a third world a country. This Chief Justice is retired in the year 2002.

Penalty: Shall amount to the penalty prescribed in Section-10 and 11 of this Act.

Section-16: No judicial officer shall be covered by any common rules and service rules of government employees.

Explanation: Judicial officers have to be kept above rest of the organs of the system. These include police, senior bureaucrats, politicians and rest of all. Their jobs are treated above all. Their pay scales and perks will be different and superior. Their service period shall be longer than common government employees so, they will be highly protected and shall enjoy most superior position in society even after retirement to work for the nation up to the age of 65 or so. Their attending public functions and mixing with common people will be highly restrictive. (Schedule III pertains to Service Rules of the Judicial Officers)

Penalty: Violation shall be punishable by forced leaves.

Section-17: The judicial commission shall formulate rules for judicial officers for all service matters which may not be copied from government employee manual but the rules will be modulated and adapted categorically with certain identities and specificities putting more serious liabilities on the judicial officers. The judicial officers will acquire a superior place in the coterie.

Explanation: Judiciary is virtually comes in picture when all law protecting and law executing agencies are exhausted. Judiciary has an ultimate role to play as far as perseverance of established law is concerned. Unlawful doings of politicians are set right by the judiciary. Legislature frames law but judiciary is the virtual guardian of law. Judiciary is superior to legislation as far as honoring the law and establishing the law of the land is concerned. The judiciary, therefore, needs not to be influenced by legislatives who are basically motivated as ever. Theoretically, legislature looks to be placed superior to judiciary but the truth is that the position of judiciary is not at the mercy of collaboration or unscrupulous vote bank or any such crutches. It is supreme authority of a nation. Rest is the same as given above in Section-16.

Penalty: Permanent Withdrawal of license from the Bar Council.

Section-18: To keep judiciary independent from outside influences, there will be an independent body to make various governing bodies.

Explanation: The hierarchy of governing bodies and their authority will be as follows:

1. President of the country
2. Chief Justice
3. Judicial Commission
4. Judicial Promotion Commission
5. Judicial Penal
6. Jury in the Apex Court
7. High Court
8. Lower courts
   (a) Trial courts
   (b) Tribunals
   (c) Subsidiary small cause courts/Cells
9. 'People's Forum'
10. Civitals and DAC units.

Composition of these bodies has already been given in another work titled 'Alternative Democracy *syn.* Peoplism' by the author.

Penalty: Any violation in maintenance of these bodies shall be dealt with Severity and shall be dealt with special staff of the Chief Justice. Finding out the nature of violation and imposing penalties as per various sections of this ACT accordingly.

Section-19: President of the country will be the chair person of the Judicial Commission.

Explanation: It amounts to judicial inheritance. It is empowered to hear for or against the Chief Justice in special circumstances and try defaulter judges beyond High Courts and levy appropriate defined penalties in the guilty judges. The President shall be the latent head of Judicial Commission.

Penalty: The President can remove or retain the delinquent or reduce his tenure maximum for five years.

Section-20: Judicial officers shall ensure authorities that they have a commitment to make 'Justice Time Bound'.

Explanation: In Peoplism time bound justice is mandatory. Rules have been framed to make it effective.

Penalty: Period snatched by prolonging litigation shall be deducted from the service period left or analogue to Section-14 of this Act or be asked to compensate the sufferer.

Section-21: All judicial officers shall not discourage hearing of litigant in person and shall provide a 'lawyer on roll for the purpose' to draft his case in technical terms before it is placed before the court in the case observe things without coherence.

Explanation:

(a) All judicial officers will ensure that no secondary treatment will be given to a litigant who is appearing in person and

(b) Shall ask the sufferer if he needs any legal help at any stage

(c) If the litigant is below the poverty line he is provided with a lawyer from the side of court without he/she asks for that.

Penalty: Demotion.

Section-22: A judicial officer shall allow old and ailing men and ladies and children (of sufferer side), petitioner in person to occupy chair in the court.

Explanation: Respect is to be given to witness, old and ailing, old women, kids below ten years and such juvenile and fragile persons who need attention.

Penalty: Analogue to Section-8 of this Act.

Section-23: All the existing rules and protocols shall remain in force until there is a need to make any changes in them.

Explanation: All protocols and rules to maintain dignity of the post and a gap with the litigants and lawyers need to be maintained to pass unbiased uninfluenced decisions in the interest of Justice.

Penalty: Defying protocols defined for the judicial officers in different cadres shall amount to penalty analogue to Section-8 of this Act.

Section-24: The court-master/reader shall note date of adjournment/next date of hearing in adjournment sheet in the case file. The litigant or its representative can be asked for his signature against the entry.

Explanation: It has been in the notice that for getting a date declared by the court master on the date of deferring due to unavoidable reasons, he/she expects favour from the client/ litigant. The litigant shall have the right to know the next date of hearing from the court after 2.00 pm by his/her personal appearance and it shall be duty of the magistrate to write N.D.H. (next date of hearing) against the cause-list present with the magistrate in his hand.

Penalty: The court master may be given a forced leave of maximum of three days without pay by the concerned Magistrate of Judge, in case of found guilty of such deliberate attempt.

Section-25: The Court/Judge who heard the case at length and concluded hearing and announced a date for orders has to pass the orders before leaving the department in case of transfer. It is a mandatory duty of the judge/Judicial officer to impart justice at the earliest in the interest of Justice.

Explanation: It is a general observation that in such case the new judge repeats the whole proceeding for his/her convenience. The senior officer shall ensure whether the judge must not have any pending work and shall relieve him/her only after having a declaration from the Judge in this regard.

Penalty: He cannot be relieved until a transferred judge hands over declaration in this regard.

Section-26: Passing technically wrong orders to please a favourite party.

Explanation: The discretion with the judicial officers is unclassified and absolute to pass any kind of orders. It is the onus of the suffering litigant to file appeal and wait for justice for about a decade in next court to get wrong orders rectified. The limit of the callousness of judicial system is so severe that no one has ever tried to define and exemplified such order which can be placed under technically wrong orders. Some examples of such technically wrong orders are as follows:

1. Court that granted stay, vacates, it without justifying with exigency for doing so without sufficient justification. (Case No. 80/03 trial court)
2. Court dismissing contempt applications which are supported by photographic evidence and police report for repeated violation of stay order and that too without give a proper justification. (Case above)
3. Court passing almost final orders in a case when the issues were not framed and ask the contemptuous defendants to file an application against the appellants under Section-340 or Cr.P.C. to harass and withdraw the case on defendants. (Case above)
4. Expunging a party of its own without the party asked to do so in a situation when evidences have been produced by the petitioner against the party. (Case above)
5. Dismissing a case on the grounds of maintenance after hearing and adjourning the case for three years. (District Consumer Forum) (Case No. 1834/99)
6. Dismissing a case in a situation when the defendant had admitted his fault. (District Consumer Forum)
7. Court admitting a case and issuing rule without granting a stay. (Case No. 2447/88 DHC)
8. Court refuses to direct the employer to issue experience certificate to a permanent employee after a continuous unblemished record of 18 years service without giving

any justification in the order why the court cannot direct so in case no. 7 above.

9. Court refuses early hearing in an admitted case when the services of the petitioner were terminated during pendency of the case *ex-parte*.
10. Court dismissing an admitted case after keeping the petitioner waiting for 18 years by ignoring merits on which the case was admitted two decade back.
11. Dismissing a number of admitted old cases amass in large number by a Double Bench of Delhi High Court without issuing fresh notice to the parties in 2005 January after the cases came on their hearing after a gap of two decades.
12. Punishing an accused of rape on the saying of a so called victim without considering the essentiality of evidence against the accused over looking the various provisions of Evidence Act, passed by the Parliament by the apex court in the year July 2007.
13. Passing orders that the court is waiting the orders from other senior court where the reliefs asked by the petitioner were different from those asked in Delhi School Tribunal to linger on the case to approach the retirement of the petitioner and help the respondents. (Case No. 34/91, Delhi School Tribunal)
14. Partly hearing the case for three years and did not note in the order sheet that the arguments are concluded.
15. Framing a case of breach of Peace in all the members of management of a Registered Resident Welfare Association on making a written complaint against some miscreant residents in the locality and harassing Octagerians office bearers treating them as bonded criminals forcing them to furnish bond and insulting by SEM, Moti Nagar in the year 2005-06.
16. The apex court allowed fast track hearing to get bail to a convict in arms Act violation his being an influential celebrity, actor Sanjay Dutt.

17. The apex court dismisses a SLP 12067/07of a teacher citizen because the High Court of Delhi kept the petition with it pending for twenty years, saying the case came to them is highly belated. While dismissing the petition the court did mention another reason to dismiss it and that is that they are with Delhi High Court who did not attend to written arguments and did not entertain Supreme Court decision violating Article-141 of the Constitution of India.
18. The apex court grants bail to another convict who was convicted for killing an innocent old person in Punjab and now a MP and an influential political personality.
19. The high court refused to go into written arguments and dismissed the case ignoring the merits of the case on personal hunch giving benefit to rich and influential respondents. The after passing order was smiling at the petitioner.
20. It is daily routine in the courts that the judicial officers misuse their unlimited discretionary power for their vested interest of many kinds as there is no accountability of such judicial officers who are very personal when passing orders.

Penalty: Judges openly misusing their authority and jeering on the innocent sufferers must be referred to Judicial Commission and be dealt with Penal Code provisions, depending upon the volume of repercussions of such orders.

The procedure to impose penalty in Peoplism will be through the perseverance of natural justice and the delinquent judicial officer shall be given at least one opportunity to send his/her explanation to the Judicial Commission before the final verdict by the Commission is passed.

The judges shall use their power of discretion under water tight conditions and the situations shall be pre-decided by the Commission as to how the benefit of doubt and discretion can be used in a situation. Otherwise, for many cases the decisions will be affected in a mathematical way.

Judicial System in PEOPLISM: Peoplists take-up updating of judiciary to be the first work to relieve the nation from gross and repeated injustice for an indefinite period in the following ways:

1. Optimum 'population-court ratio' be formulated.
2. Formulation of 'Judge and Number of issues' therein cases ratio.
3. Re-allocation of cases to more lower courts issue-wise.
4. Short term courts to hear petty cases may be in specially arranged courts at the site of detention.
5. Ad-hoc appointment of senior lawyers as judges for short term courts.
6. Judges in high court to be appointed through a written test and proper interview. It must not be based merely on the concept of public image and recommendation of Bar Council.
7. After studying track-record of decisions made by the candidate judge, how many decisions have been vacated by the higher courts, must be considered for negative marking.
8. More scientific and logical transparent methods for the appointment of judges in the high court to be evolved.
9. Such record of all judges be available to citizens on the website of the apex court.
10. Petitioner-in-person to be encouraged.
11. Copy of receipt issued by the lawyer to the client against payment to the lawyer, to be made mandatory and be annexed with vakalatnama (POA). Any evidence of discrepancy shall amount to accountability in different ways.
12. Forums, Lok Adalats, women cells or women courts and other lower hierarchy courts, etc. be treated as short term courts not to behave like a regular courts and number of adjournments must be defined in each category of cases.

13. The rules to be framed more people-based than to be judge based or lawyer savvy.
14. Lawyers be discouraged and allowed to plead in special circumstances only in these courts.
15. Decided cases be available on website.
16. Rules, methods, formats of farms and decisions in the various level courts are made computer based on websites and available to the litigants.
17. Discretionary powers of the courts be restricted and be made shortest by using the concept of DAC System.
18. Judges should not allow any 'special mention' in their chambers and be taken as an offence.
19. Service termination, prolonged detention, special Act cases and public interest matters is to be treated on priority by specially constituted courts for this purpose.
20. Lawyers on penal of legal-aid-cells and offering free service through such cells is to be awarded by ad-hoc appointment as judges in short term courts.
21. Such experience of lawyers who have been appointed as magistrates in short term courts be considered at the time of interview for being selected as regular judges or other kind of judicial officers.
22. Special appellate courts to hear grievances and complaints against judges to fix accountability to the wrongs by the judges.
23. Separate courts for Public Interest Litigations (PILs).
24. Separate courts or specific day in the week to hear petitioner-in-person.
25. Legal assistance be made ready-available on nominal fee or without any fee to the petitioners-in-person to help drafting and conveyencing.
26. Consequential punishment must be imposed on all government agencies in case of failure of a case.

27. Salaries and perks of judicial officer shall be kept at least 40 per cent higher of any government officer under the jurisdiction of that court.
28. Judicial officers shall be trained for particular subject specialization. All judges shall not sit in all courts without being expertised and properly trained for particular discipline in particular class of the court. It is like few lawyers specify themselves for Taxation, Criminal, Service matters and so on.
29. Judges to deal with criminal cases be trained and acquainted with the latest scientific tools and techniques of forensic science and also study crime psychology in the light of Human Rights.
30. Regular exams will be held for judicial officers before any promotion to the next cadre shall be formulated by the Judicial Commission.

Essential Elements of Peoplism

19

Let us examine what the Peoplism is and how it is relatively different from democracy of developing countries like India and in other parts of the world.

Democracy is the best system of governance among all available other systems. But to take democracy a system of absolute freedom, to do anything suits to individuals, is a misconception in practice. Peoplism is a unique political system of governance. It is more direct with minimum range of discretion and works within a shortest parameter of power one enjoys in democracy. It is the first system to groom nomadic democratic population and to train less disciplined masses for democracy. Peoplism keeps crazy citizens within the limits of humanity and welfare of masses. Like democracy, Peoplism does not allow any citizen to enjoy unlimited powers and liberty to encroach upon other's rights.

Peoplism talks about how various short comings of the system of democratic governance having coordination between police, judiciary and executive bureaucracy may be overcome. Let us, by experiencing historical facts and figures, make a perfect combination of all the best qualities of different systems of governance, to make this proposal most effective for all developing countries where corruption and high-handedness have crossed all limits of humanity, man has ever seen, he is said to be civilized.

In third world nations, democracy has utterly failed to hold civil rights and protect their own Constitutional guarantees. The rulers always proclaimed and repeatedly boasted of democratic liberty and fundamental rights but that proved to be a hoax as all governments overlooked Constitutional responsibilities and shed unbearable suffrage to innocent law-abiding citizens. Here, as a routine, the police easily collaborate with criminals and influential politicians, courts have gone over-loaded disposing of their work using bureaucratic tactics in the name of vast discretion and unquestionable authority. Distortion and delusion of prescribed law, rules and defined regulations, has become the way of working. Many hardworking and honest workers and farmers are committing suicide out of frustration in want of any support from their guardians. What can be the future of such nations, where people's faith is repeatedly getting eroded in police and justice delivery system? One can imagine. Despite of going under the shelter of police and finally that of judiciary, people started settling their score themselves ignoring the presence of law.

The incidents of taking law into one's hands are increasing day by day. Public is lynching criminals in courtroom itself believing that the courts nexus with police and criminals shall not do anything to punish the criminal in time and for many years, the criminal will be let free by court on bail and in this time the caught criminal will make their lives hell. Those who terrorised and exploited peaceful citizens came out of jail clean and jeering over the presence of law. Dons became political leader in these countries. Popular political parties owned them their icon and gave tickets to contest election. In absence no better alternative while compared with other contesting candidates, they won the verdict of people and thus, yesterday's criminals got protection from law at last. Sting operations proved such stories as true.

If delaying culture of court forced people to take law into their hands judicial officer remained comfortable with the pace of progress of cases, on the other hand a sufferer stayed with *status quo*. So, out of frustration there is no wonder if he goes berserk. He may retaliate and the retaliation may be violent. Violence means supporting bloodshed. So, where do the roots of bloodshed lie, is a vital question to be solved? This is a story of mistreatment of innocents and low pace of sluggish judiciary?

History is evident that no one can run the show at gun point for a long. Britishers failed after 150 years. Liberty to crime and protection of civic rights of convicts are conflicting. This allows criminals to continuously tear-off the fabric of society, especially during the pendency of criminal cases. Moreover, organized crimes finds hide out very easily which is against the concept of transparency in democracy.

Elected public representatives stay honest to their oath in an honest nation. Out of many developing countries, there are few who can claim to hold democracy. Rather, in the guise of democracy, the officials at the bureaucracy, police in the field and thirdly, judiciary are struggling hard to survive an ethical rank over the suffering ordinary citizens. The list of such developing countries is the longest that includes more than 60% nations of the world that are passing through a transitory period of economical, social and administrative change in the lure of getting hold of true democracy. Those suffering with political instability are bound to collapse. The careful and committed patriots will survive but corrupts will vanish.

It is palpable that most of developing nations are passing through an unsafe phase and are at the brink of collapse. Gone are the days of army rulers. At least two south-east nations are breathing last. These countries are on the verge of civil war because the complete system of governance has become vulnerable to paradox. Here, the government agencies have lost their credibility in a situation when citizens have been left with no other option than to ignore them and do without them. Exploited by offenders and later sucked up by the 'system' people have either started tolerating crime or raise arms themselves against crime. Even crime inflicting police is taking law in their own hands to save their dignity, life and property. Killing criminals inside the courts by suffering masses are evidence to prove incompetence of government agencies creating a dangerous situation where people have started ignoring their presence. Police is crime prone and the judicial system has gone autocratic and bureaucratic at several places. In the name of free 'discretion' and 'independence', the judiciary has become almost inaccessible to the common citizens in these poor countries. Police may face accountability to courts but the courts have no accountability for their deliberate wrong.

Democracy is the ultimate system of governance. This is a system which is supposed to run by ordinary elected people. These elected leaders are given sufficient time period to prove their worth and do good to the people. But what may be the answer of our senior political leaders to this judicial dystrophy in last six decades?

There used to be a time when crime was not as organised as it is today. Organising it includes management skills and strategies. Criminals who could study the advantages of being in active politics have made political power organised in the form of a political party. The face of such political party is lifted as per best defined parts of the Constitution of these underdeveloped poor nations. But behind such political parties the philosophy to grab power and snatch desired comforts cannot be ruled out. Asking for more perks and salaries, judicial immunity, availability of huge public funds, amusing volume of followers and supporters make politicians more greedy to manipulate more economic comforts to their advantage.

In these developing nations, a study of economic support of active politicians reveals that either they already had enough economic resources before joining politics, such as farmers, who received large amount of compensation for their taken-over lands. Those politicians are really rare today who plunged into public life being penniless for the cause only. There are examples that leading political parties in developing nations sell off zonal portfolios like membership of advisory committees, area president, secretary etc. to the aspirants for their personal pockets. Recently, one of the political parties in west Delhi, appointed area portfolios to vagabonds and offenders having ill reputation, with no following and no contribution of them to any social cause. The rumor is very surprising. The newly appointed Vice-President runs a furniture manufacturing unit in his residential house storing inflammable timber against MCD rules; general Secretary is a lady who is an unemployed free bird and the Secretary is the son of a land grabber who flourished by selling country liquor and a 'BC' (Bad Character) of the area. But the headquarter has nothing to do with public image of its office bearers. Since they are in power they can afford to inculcate criminals as per their requirement.

In this mad race, there are few, who came to lime-light because of their own quality and patriotic inclination towards the national or human cause. Now, the trend in politics is such that those planning to be in politics, boast of social work and quickly shift for power to have public funds in their control.

There are some of the fortunate nations who believe that to be people's representative is only a social service to its people and not a paid professional. Such sensible nations have yet not passed any Bill for huge salaries and perks to the branded politicians. It is more horrifying when we hear Parliament Assembly a passing Bill to grant life-long pension to only once being a public representative in a country where more than 70 per cent population sleep with half-belly. In Peoplism, such official siphoning of hard earned public funds has been classified as 'criminal'. Thus, democracy in developing and under developed nations has been reduced to 'despotism'.

If 'Justice delayed is justice denied,' is true, it needs us to peep inside the functioning of courts and find out reasons as to why there is no fair justice and why it is delayed to the extent of its futility. So, to make justice an effective tool to fight injustice in individual and collective life, a lot has to be done at every stage. Reprehension of delay and duration of pendency of cases, encourage offenders to make repeated attempts to infringe civil liberties of good citizens adding to crime to be multiplied in third-world democracies because for courts, where a criminal case is nothing but a case-file only. Relating crime with delay and its parallel brooding during pendency of the case is not mandatory by virtue of official duty of the court. Then, why it becomes a grave concern of the citizens only?

Having a crime-case pending for years means, sustaining the crime for years. Crime has to be nipped in bud only. Though every accused is not a convict rather is taken as innocent until his guilt is established. But the most dangerous side of this logic is that until a criminal is proved guilty, by the court of law, he is free to bite off the very soul of society continuing his offence in the name of pendency of his case. Burning example of stay to nude-cabarets in capital encouraged this immoral and illegal traffic for nine year. So the crime can make its roots deeper in other form during this gestation period. The result of such immoral stay was at least 15 more cabaret shops were opened and ran with every authority until the stay was vacated after nine years. So, a proper way has to be worked out of this conflict.

Ever increasing number of litigation in the apex court is the evidence of negligence, mishandling, high-handedness, lack of reading the cases file thoroughly and studying the provisions of law by certain judges in lower courts fails the purpose of judiciary. Many courts have been noticed passing technically wrong orders even at higher court level. Due to lack of legal knowledge of judicial officers the innocent litigants have to suffer through 'an appeal' and get prolonged suffrage. A number of times, litigants are propelled to plunge into more and more suffrage by such decisions. Willingly or inadvertently, the innocent sufferers have to pay by his life and liberty when courts decide to go with ulterior-personal motive in favour of a party may be on the wrong side of law. But this is also true that it is not difficult to trace cases where certain courts behaved as 'ultimate' while passing technically wrong orders.

Remedial litigation is no less than another war beyond already fought war for justice in lower courts scarifying precious years of life. Therefore, long awaited amendments in this highly paid salaried class of the judicial system can bring radical changes in the face of a helpless country. Up to date, alert, effective and quick judiciary can change the 'face and fate' of third world countries, as judiciary is still considered to be the most effective organ, we have today.

It is disputed that the third world democracies have failed to hold responsible, literate, truth loving, committed to the cause of honest politics, to bring true freedom to the country. Today, once again we have to re-establish ideology in politics by setting some good example of devotion and commitment.

These days, you are taken in political arena not because you are extraordinary for your human qualities but the first merit is what amount of followers you have. If you are an industrialist or an old nawab, you can win a party ticket, no matter if you have certain blots on you or you are an illiterate and unqualified ill reputed dare-devil person with certain court cases on you. By hook or crook, if you can win, you will be given ticket. Young nationalists must learn to save themselves from their own ruin by bringing sensible people to power and must apply their brain than to die for a particular political party.

For corrupt bureaucrats, democracy is the easiest cake walk to mould rules to their advantage. Once you acquire a position of power, the world is in your fist. Be an IAS officer or an IPS, if have tolerance to be snubbed by your superiors, you can rule the society. All those who are manipulating such conflict, are comfortable in such immature and loose-democracy prevailing in all developing countries, today. Therefore, it is convincing to quote that "democracy in the third world nations repeatedly proved nothing but a walk into darkness". We are going through the darkness in a triumphant manner but we do not know where we are leading to.

By examining, democracy is found to be the system where feelings of citizens are to be respected by executing duly prepared and approved plans; where leaders are to be elected on moral calls than on other grounds of caste or religion. But such ideals are being lost to decide a candidate. Human quality and commitment to cause have become outdated. A country, whose political leaders have a common agenda of using loop-holes of the system, is possible only in a third world country.

Illiterate person may simultaneously be uneducated also. Both these traits keep such a person away from essential information which he needs both technically and practically. Such persons when are elected to power, they are frantic and nomadic in behaviour. They are so occupied with pleasing themselves that every thing and every body stand dwarf before them. Why Polio Pulse programs are not successful in Islamic zones. People are made to believe polio a medicine to make children impotent and finally root out Muslims from the world.

Such forged superstitious rumors are rampant in any other illiterate society and politicians having poor knowledge tolerate such misconceptions and do not go to its people to clarify the stand of the government as they themselves are superstitious and unscientific in their attitude. So, an elected representative has to be sufficiently educated and a knowledgeable person so as to understand countries law, Constitutional pursuits, scientific endeavors and programs of the government for common good, so that he can show way to people and not be guided by his ignorance or by the shrewdness of over-intelligent secretaries in his ministry.

An illiterate nation is a weak nation. A survey between illiteracy and economic development revealed few facts to establish that education is directly related with development of a nation. Let us examine a comparative study of nations classified below on the basis of literacy:

Under Developed (Many African Poor Nations)

A. Population	Highest
B. Literacy	Lowest
C. Democratic values respected	15-25%

Developing Nations (Asian Nations)

A. Population	J graphic
B. Literacy	30%
C. Democratic values respected	15-25%

American Continent Nations

A. Population	S graphic
B. Literacy	50-85%
C. Democratic values respected	75-85%

Developed Nations (Gulf and Western World)

A. Population	S graphic
B. Literacy	98-100%
C. Democratic values respected	85-99%

Illiterate nations are economically backward, is a hard fact. But this situation of ignorance cannot be left to its fate. Some one, some day has to get up to serve humanity and make this earth a better place for every one. Literacy is an essential element in the life of any nation.

Coming back to the rein situation in the third world democratic nations, it is very difficult to change state of affairs in favour of literacy in absence of political will.

Almost all of the shortcomings of democracy had been worked out by the International Society for Human Resources (ISHR) organization. We propose to shift democracy to Peoplism for giving a perfect space to the citizens of Third World for their individual involvement to make this world better. There have to be few essential traits to bring the deterrent conditions up. One of these traits is accountability which is most important to sustain any system which is rudimentary to nil in present democracy. Therefore, a thorough study of reasons and their possible remedies has to be exercised to establish real democracy by using human resources in intelligent manner and for this goal if the immature democracies need to shift to Peoplism, they should understand what real democracy means. Limited democracy can train under-disciplined citizens though Peoplism only. Let us examine first, the basic feature of Peoplism and find out how it is different from democracy?

ESSENTIAL ELEMENTS OF PEOPLISM

Recommendations from unpublished work by ISHR in last ten years through various workshops and seminars named "Beyond Survival" helped us to formulate the Constitution of Peoplism. The existing Constitution has been designed in accordance of basic philosophy of Peoplism and amendments in law, rules, regulations and various Acts and Codes have to be made to change the things to suit People at large.

Salient Features of Peoplism:

1. Accountability of all government officials
2. No slums
3. No caste based reservation

4. Public servant punishment law
5. Decentralization of Industry
6. Gram Utthan Yojna priority investment
7. Uniform court Acts
8. National religion Law
9. Revised Fundamental Rights
10. Right to information
11. Right to job (work)
12. Participation of retired brains in policy making
13. 'Citizen's Forum'
14. Three tier Parliament (Third House)
15. Time Bound Justice
16. Judicial Code of Conduct for judges and lawyers
17. Police Code of Conduct
18. Heavy subsidy on education
19. Heavy subsidy on landless or small farmers
20. Dual citizenship
21. Legalized RWAs
22. DAC system
23. Civital
24. Dharmsthals
25. New representation law
26. No luxury conditions for Government
27. Limited rights to property
28. Uniform education by public sector only
29. Improved Community health services and discouraging private hospitals
30. Negligence of duty be treated as treason to the State.

Democracy had first motto to sustain voters without authorizing them to intervene. The ruled ones are treated as outsiders/third party after the government is formed. Every one has to remain at the mercy of the system (Police, Judiciary and the Executive).

All legitimate and constitutional obligations on him are merely an eye-wash when he is rendered lonely and helpless on the road in democracy. In many cases, number wins over the Rule. A Municipal Councilor easily can diverts public funds to a thickly populated illegal slum in his constituency depriving of lawful citizen's for pleasing the vote bank. There is no law to take care of lawful old, senior citizens residing in an authorized area than to feed an illegal slum in democracy. In Peoplism, people will have a right to serve as watch-dogs and have the privilege to make complaints to specially structured Citizen's Forums, the third House, in case they find officials misusing their authority. Every thing has been defined to the citizens in Peoplism and complete transparency is ensured and maintained which is battered in third world democracy. Any one working against the defined provision of law in civil proceedings will be charged for treason against the State which is not possible in democracy. Not only Justice but every execution, every proceeding has to be made time bound. Justice is the first priority to be time bound in Peoplism such provisions are not in sight in democracy.

Distinctive features of Peoplism make both systems of government different. The ills of such democracy can be fought out by adapting Peoplism. Some of the specific features are as follows:

1. All organs of the system are accountable to 'Citizens Forums' at different levels. Yes, full right to information in sole and personal cases.
2. Over-stayed under-trials will be released without any trial unconditionally.
3. Protests against any plan sanctioned by the Parliament in greater interest of more people, such as constructing a dam will be totally banned and made 'offence against State.'

The country will have uniform syllabus, books and teaching standards. Peoplism looks after essentially required features, which were over looked in democracy.

Peoplism does not suggest democracy to be scrapped totally. Rather, many of its positive proposals may be infused with present democratic set up to alter the approach of liberal democracy to harsh Peoplism. Peoplism is the harshest system for offenders. There is no mercy to determined criminals and defaulters who use resolved provisions of law for their on benefits against innocent creative citizens. In this system we recommend 'an eye for eye' beyond a gimmick of Human Right Commission to uplift criminals.

"All third world democracies can never come out of their ills and are gradually forwarding towards total collapse through a civil war, as people have already stopped believing in police, courts, officialdom the politicians. The frustration has grown to the extent that the press too is surviving offering material pertaining to entertainment without bothering for dystrophy of heritage of their nations. All third world democracies are nothing but organized hells and the offenders have knotted every thing to their advantage in high places. Better to awake in time."

Here is the comparative table between democracy and Peoplism.

Table comparing provisions in Peoplism and democracy

S.No.	Aspect	Democracy	Peoplism
1.	Fundamental rights to the bonded criminals	Sustained	Suspended
2.	Voters participate directly in the process of Justice and can keep watch on mal-functioning of an organ of the system	Voter becomes ruled and is treated as an out-sider after the Govt. is formed	People serve as watch-dogs and have the privilege to withdraw by special voting process
3.	Is any thing time bound?	Not at all. One has to remain on the mercy of Govt.	Everyaction shall be made time bound by virtue of new law
4.	Accountability	Not there	To set new law
5.	An eye for eye	Not there	With every cruelity

S.No.	Aspect	Democracy	Peoplism
6.	Transparency in working and information from Govt. agencies	Govt. still hides the truth and proceeding is kept secret	Complete transparency is ensured except defense and security matters
7.	Trial of politicians and high officials on TV Channels	Not yet	Yes
8.	Civitals	No	Yes
9.	DAC System	No	Yes
10.	Hierarchy maintained by	Not by salaries only but by power given	Authority only will be different
11.	Control on natural assets like river water, air, their pollution etc.	In control of states	In control of Center
12.	Over-staying under-trials	Rotting and dying in jails	Will be released without any trial. Shall be released unconditionally
13.	Cabaret and fashion shows	Sponsored	Totally banned
14.	Nation building programs like Construction of dams and power projects, etc.	Stopped due to politics and factional protests	Cannot stop such constructive projects once started
15.	Reservation	Caste based for unlimited period	Economic condition based, for one generation only
16.	Development of villages	Last priority	First priority
17.	Merits in jobs	Ignored by quota system reservation	On merits only
18.	Magnitude of prosecution	As per Penal Code and magnitude of offence	By Magnitude and official position
19.	Post poll alliance and manipulation	No specific rules in practice	Not permissible
20.	Appointment of High Court Judges	Political and on Bar recommendation	By a set procedure by Judicial Commission

S.No.	Aspect	Democracy	Peoplism
21.	Amendments CrPC and revision periodically	Silent and satisfied with British legacies	Updated every two years
22.	Qualification of Minister	Not necessary	Minimum graduate
23.	Think tank inviting public opinion while framing a policy	Not yet available	Commonman will an essential part in all activities and planning
24.	Assets and belongings of Govt. officials	No way to trace	Shall decalre on PAN Card
25.	Clubbing of para-military forces with police interstate shifting	Have no concept yet	Interstate transfers possible in police services
26.	Consequentail punishment	Have no concept yet	Will be a law
27.	Uniform Education	No	Shall have uniformity for poor and rich in public sector
28.	Selling alcohols	Promoted by Govt.	Will be a law of restriction
29.	Law giving protection to man against exploitation by women	No concept yet	Law shall protect man against nudity and other exploitation
30.	Negligence of duty to be a crime	No concept yet	Negligence and deliberate misuse of power shall be declared a treason
31.	RWAs be legally empowered	No concept yet	Will constitute the third house of Parliament
32.	Judicial activism	Negative	Shall encourage

The Basic Programmes in Peoplism

1. Peoplism is a combination of democratic values, with communist nationalism and honest socialists.
2. They believe in personal growth but not at the cost of the interest of society. (nation)
3. Parity and equality for all, by all a nation can manage.

4. Strong sense of 'belongingness' of every possession to the nation.
5. Over-all development of rural areas, by decentralizing industries.
6. Improvising means to all and than to hand-over ends and quality by out of turn scrapping reservation.
7. Providing means to backward people in extra ordinary manner to bring them at par within a period of seven years.
8. Not having double standards to have Article-14 as well as Article-15 (4).
9. Reservation to women as per sex-ratio in an area,
10. Centralized education, pubic health, internal security (police system).
11. Time Bound judicial system.
12. Code of conduct for cops, layers, judges imposing accountability.
13. Banning nudity, casinos, bars, pubs, liquor vendors manufacture of smoking material and accessory materials allowing any public office to the elected representative continuously in two sucessive terms. Maximum number of years a person can have in his life will be two terms only.
14. Not any office in politics to senior citizens.
15. People beyond 65 years of age shall be appointed as advisers in the government.

The Final Commitment 20

International agencies are aware of this unfortunate situation of shamble judiciary in developing nations and are trying hard to bring all the countries at par to make the situation more judicious for the uplift of entire human race. Peoplism is an effort in this direction to suggest certain safeguards from further dystrophy of democracy.

It is apparent that various duties of court are closely linked to an overall loyalty to the system of the administration. The court is the beneficiary of this possibly paramount duty to the State.

A policeman can be caught for his wrong as a politician and first rank minister or a top bureaucrat is answerable to the court of law but judiciary can fall under the accountability only forming a public institutions like 'Citizen's Forum' or an independently constituted 'Judicial Commission'. The question of accountability of judicial officers to bind them with a code of conduct may be a remedy to increase their work efficiency. By infusing other remedies to lessen their work load, judges will have more space to study the case-files and feel more confident and practically quick. Accountability is one of the greatest tools to provide orientation to the entire positive energy of a person at all ages and stages in the right direction. Therefore, having felt at the highest place in society, nothing can stop them to become over-anthusiastic. It is need of the hour to repose our lost faith in judiciary once again.

The judicial officers (judges) must keep in mind that their door is the last door and a person had already exhausted all possible channels before coming to them. If there is no timely justice to a person, who reached court after passing through a series of successive humiliation what can be more frustrating than this? The very sense of existence of courts in such a situation is reduced to mockery.

In third world democracies, the President occupies the highest and a very specific place. Even in parliamentary democracy, the President can bring drastic changes in the stained system through small ordinances. The President can call joint session of both the houses and ask for making certain laws to deal with a particular problem. He may direct parliament to discuss, draft and pass bills on the long awaited certain national problems. It needs deep solitude deliberation, a well thought-out analysis, a positive attitude and determination to over come a situation. It has been very unfortunate for the developing nations that the President had been branded with a speech-idol only. He is kept so packed with preplanned daily schedules that he is rarely left to his original intellectual and committed folds. He is made unable to be activated for his personal ambitions and his own thinking to do something for the nation. He is not allowed to think a bit independently and is always packed with un-important programmes.

There has to be a list of problems of countrymen, State wise, available with ministries and be placed before the President, so that he/she can take up certain potential issue from it to initiate some process with top bureaucrats during his tenure. For initiating any thing positive to improve the ailing organs of the system, the Hon'ble President has to be kept free from speeches and inaugurating school functions. Bureaucrats must redesign President's agenda to lessen countries problems beyond his limitations of not being any executive head of the State.

The President's personal humane inclinations can motivate the Prime Minister to get things discussed with his colleagues and proceed to make effective legislation. He must be honoured to feel very important by inviting him to initiate some thing in the interest of millions of suffering citizens which are kept in cold bags by certain bureaucrats and political parties. A special Directorate to do research and development must work for the President. It must keep the available data up-dated through particular survey on the issues where changes are inevitable and where something is really required to be done, be at his disposal.

In a country where resources are being siphoned by the system itself, keeping citizens aloof and deprived of their basic needs, it is only the President who can put a check on such malpractice. The ever-deteriorating law and order situation, ever receding faith in police and judiciary, may grow beyond a situation of control that may burst into anger of masses causing another fall of Russian Czars again.

The mother democratic nations or developed nations are so affluent economically that a large number of their problems are not in sight. It is also just not the policy of developed nations to mischievously paint developing nations approaching collapse but the truth is that the developing nations are really more corrupt. It is just not deceptive that various problems of poor or developing nations have been highlighted repeatedly by the developed nations to pose superiority over them, but they are really guilty for absence of morality and rapidly increasing population. On the more, political leaders in power are not really handling the problems well with an intension to over come them. This is most painful that the percentage of such developing nations, which are passing through a transitional stage, is the largest in the world. Such forthcoming collapsing of one democracy with a gradual pace will be enough to spark off flare in other such nations that are passing through such similar retrogressive transition.

The apex body of judiciary has a specific role to play to avert the entire ballistic situation. Though the population of these poor nations is habitual to live in hardship because they feel that things will never change and their fate is only suffrage. But such persistent hardship is not because of our poverty but because of punishable manipulation by a business tycoon or organized goons who are using all three organs of government for their ulterior motives. To some extent, we are bound to continue slavery of lawlessness and this is more or less similar to British slavery where the Raj ruled us for long by using force against our will. People who come forward to challenge the tyranny of white collared goons in the court of law are no less than martyrs in a free nation who loose their entire career or entire life fighting against injustice. They repeatedly keep making efforts to make masses aware of their physical, human and constitutional rights. The court must attend to such hilarious citizens and honour them by giving justice to their cause. On the other hand, there are people who grew prosperous clout of society by using offence, crime and gathering unlimited money power by using illegal means must be officially marked.

Not bringing justice to the aggrieved citizens in time, in other plain words is ignoring illegality of police, bureaucrats, white collared goons and criminally manipulative politicians. In such a grave situation, if judiciary is sticking to procedural preference, it will prove damaging to entire system of governance. So, the conscientiousness of judiciary has to be the highest to save the society from untimely collapse.

If bureaucrats are promoting delaying tactics for not disposing of case-files in time; police is not filing challans for years together, the courts are expected to undo their offence on suffering citizens. But this is not possible by delaying justice for many explained or unexplained reasons. Corruption and high handedness of force-users in the system need to be punished. Above all, being most powerful in its position, judiciary has to be quick beyond a number of limitations it has.

Many advantages are not vested as Fundamental Rights of all the citizens. Rather, these will be auto-conferred by grooming virtue of the takers through their consistent workmanship in their own field. Contrary to this, certain rights shall be snatched away from those who have been flouting and breaking rules and regulations. No one is excusable in the eye of law. It can be penalized by snapping certain civic rights as we snatch liberty of movement when a convict is sent to jail to serve the term.

For meeting political ends and protecting vote-banks politicians are successful in keeping development plans suspended under one or another pretext. If they fail to manipulate, they do not hesitate to use their paid followers to initiate a public agitation with a different title. Resentment to making dams by certain NGOs is sometimes politically motivated. Otherwise, no sensible person shall come in the way of national development programmes of broad significance. All arguments are just emotionally played abandoning national interest. Therefore, the political godfathers who interfere the working of government agencies need to be covered with special and strict law. People backing these provocateurs must not be let free but punished for their sullied politics.

Politics of votes must be identified and classified. Laws must be designed to such politics. Holding national development plans, provoking people for caste feuds, communal disturbances, sustaining reservation; instigating land grabbing, unauthorised construction on public land, creating slums; capturing public land and creating vote banks etc. comes under politics-of-votes. The best way to shun the politics of vote is to disrobe land grabbers 'adult franchise right' as an inborn punishment of capturing public property by using unfair and illegal means. Grabbers detachment from their right to caste vote till they vacate government land shall disqualify the grabbers, encroachers and unauthorised developers to attract attention of corporate councilors and political leaders of the area. By doing so, the public funds with area MP, MLA and Councillor shall be invested for the lawful citizens only and those who have lost their right to vote shall have to leave the grabbed land in absence of water and electricity supply without political patronage of local leaders.

In Peoplism no class is privileged through the process of reservation of any kind. Rather the entire approach will be to provide equal opportunity to all in remote places also to grow and come at par with others. To create a specially identified vote bank in these countries the citizens have been split in two classes officially. One that falls under Fundamental Rights to equality and other that has been kept deprived of normal growth, development and progress of all kinds and taken as a privileged class being defined as 'Scheduled class of have-nots'. Socialistic boasting in these worst hit democracies has been thoroughly misusing the have-nots in the name of social justice, parity and equality. The acceptance of their classification as 'dalits' is the evidence that the entire category is living at abyss of their crushed morality that is binding them with helplessness in the name of helping themselves by putting themselves at the mercy of politicians as a reserved class.

Peoplism is no less than a preparatory school for an aspirant of democracy. It is aimed at educating raw-liberals to learn how to value achievements by their predecessors and use them carefully. Achievements will be earned and shall never come to anyone as a gift for his/her being a member of a privileged class of society is in practice in India due to the evergreen policy of caste-reservation. Privileges cannot be granted as basic rights of any person. It is a general observation that in democracy those who are privileged by extra ordinary power due to quota business need not to be aware of the techniques to utilize human resources to its maximum advantage, as they never imagine its value due to its irrational harnessing the privileges on him/her without any efforts. Rather, for them, wasting hard-earned positives of the national resources including both human resources as well as material resources has no meaning for them generating an atmosphere of negligence, carelessness, highhandedness, autocratic conduct and totally a negative attitude towards a genuine situation. Police, judiciary and bureaucracy are suffering from this syndrome bringing hardship to the common man. The entire approach of liberalization and foreign investment might have boosted country's economy in terms of government report but the common man failed to see its results. Dearness is increasing day by day and for middle class families life is becoming very harsh. Essential commodities are running out of reach of common consumer. The third world countries are fighting for economic survival, unemployment, deteriorating quality of essential services even after repeated revision of freights; school education; roads; drinking water; payments to farmers for their supplied produce; unsecured property and life in want of workable police and delayed justice are frustrating citizens to commit suicide or adapt corrupt lifestyle. The government is proving incompetent to handle public sector and surrendering them to top business tycoons who are doing brisk business from suffering citizens. The government is badly failing on all fronts because organs of governance feel unchallenged and unquestionable to masses and unnecessarily have become masters of citizen's lives.

The ghost of reservation is destroying the best of the nation beyond the issue of religion, caste, sex, etc. Such politicians have no right to make such rules to affect reservation against the doctrine of 'Right to equality', especially by introducing Article-115(4) into the Constitution of India. The politicians have their vulture-eye sufficiently for long-time, on the best of us to dispose of the best of the nation through the politics of reservation, without inviting for any consensus on the issue must be fought with tooth and nail. The quality has to always prevail and be defended from being attacked by political exercise of these unfortunate under privileged poor nations.

Out of many ills of unripe democracy caste based reservation is no less than a criminal breach of trust that is sustained by elected representatives when they are entrusted to do good to them. Caste-based reservation is a social injustice to general masses against the provisions of Article-14 to 16 of the Constitution say as under:

Article-14: The State shall not deny to any person equality before the law or equal protection of the law within the territory of India. The doctrine of equality pleads further of means of livelihood, opportunity, facilities, status, promotion, education, social injustice and against any exploitation, etc.

Article-15: The State shall not discriminate against any citizen on the grounds only of religion, race, caste, sex, place of

---

Special Commission: *A temporary Commission constituted for specific purpose to formulate certain policies beyond political interference on the issues the politicians are always illogical and unfair like on reservation, salaries of people's representatives and so on.*

birth or any of them be subject to any disability, liability, restriction or condition with regard to use public places maintained wholly or partly by State funds.

Article-16: Right to equal opportunity in matters of public appointment.

Peoplism is against handing over ends to those who have not contributed to create these end products of quality but it is committed to provide all possible means to create merits. What has been earned by hard labour and conviction by an individual is a national property first and such ends must be available to those only who have become a part of those means which are aimed at creating quality national resources (materialistic and human resources) and not to those who remained outsiders while process of making was on. Such strangers to the process of development and progress have no right to be the master of these 'ends' which are the creation of those committed citizens who used available 'means' honestly with a motive to attain personal goal and create national resources of all kinds.

It is the direct abuse of authority entrusted by elected politicians. Few such representatives have made it their right to hand over the hard earned ends to these deprived classes and amended the Constitution for their personal political mileage than to do exactly any good to the nation. Had such a political approach been in the interest of the nation, it would have given all available means and facilities to villagers in remote places to bring the have-nots up *at par* academically to those who are consistently striving hard to create quality in the nation for centuries. They should have taken care of these unattended sections of society by providing them with essential means of higher education, health facilities and other basic amenities that a citizen needs to lead a dignified life. But it was not done. What has been done is to make a strategic and clever attempt at the cost of quality without having a general consensus on the issue. Unfortunately, such tactical planning is projected with claps in the name of sagacity. There can be no other definition of politics with a convincing logic to bury the interest of qualified deserving candidates under huge number of such privileged have-nots. How treacherous can be its repercussions in the coming time, no one is trying to come out of this hazardous situation at all. Nothing more unfortunate can be for such Third World nations where politicians feel comfortable to mishandle national resources in absence of a public accountability. It is really a tangle that those who want to resist this illegal and illogical policy on caste based reservation, in the House of Representatives due to the fear of loss of a big vote bank, if they open their mouth. The truth of this situation is that such loss of quality by caste-based reservation could have been compensated by expanding means of creating quality in the gone by years. But no one could afford positive thinking to create new opportunities in the gone by years for opening new Universities and more professional colleges were in tight fist of politicians of previous generation.

Do We Really Need Judicial Activism?

21

In today's world it is only judiciary which is playing a role of true guardians of helpless poor and unprivileged citizens at large.

Those, who are making hue and cry on the issue of the role of judiciary, are irresponsible, negligent, self-caring and privilege classes. They must see the issue from the angle of helpless unsupported citizen of the country who is deprived of care from all the main organs of system of governance, *viz.* the police, the bureaucrats and the lower level of courts.

Most of the National leaders of acumen and substance came from legal profession or teaching profession who due to their commitment and oriented thinking made freedom of this nation possible. Thereafter, whosoever occupied position were only the aftermath of freedom movement. In last sixty year not even a single politician came with original ideas to look into improving things around us. Some have captured power in the name of Gandhi and pre-partition Congress. Their getting ousted and frustrated and intellectually bankrupt invented new ways of assembling other deprived of and frustrated citizens on the grounds of and religion. They have no thought or ideology and any plan to fight out national problems like over-population and poverty. Favouritism, nepotism, chauvinism, caste-ism, communalism have become philosophy of today's politicians. No one pays respect to great B.R. Ambedkar who created a wonderful document for us in the form of Constitution to give a positive direction to this slave nation beyond all those ills that were hounding a very poor nation in the time of crisis. If we see the philosophies of any political party they all are more busy as to how the other parties could be pulled down by hook and crook and capture power by using all fair and unfair means. No one is serious about good to millions of have-nots, under-trials and pending-increasing litigations.

Politicians and their workers are privileged classes and they have nothing to do with the problems of common citizens. Common citizens are the victims of those who are in power. He still suffers untenable bad life at the hands of all in authority and remains thoroughly unheard. Beyond three organs of governing the society few other equally powerful sections of society need to be quoted here. These are politicians and media persons. Thus, these two classes take responsibility to debate various issue and settle them imposing their verdict on the real users. Those who never got an opportunity to enter agricultural fields and faced suffrage from the hardship of farmers are making policies for farmers; non-science graduates are running Ministry of Science, technology and environment. Those who have never come across class room teaching are running CBSE as its chairman and setting education policies and so on so forth. This can be termed as a period of 'intellectual bankruptcy' that resulted steep fall in quality. Non-academicians unqualified and ill educated rich people are opening schools. They are becoming 'Director' of these schools and remain present inside the schools during school time interfering into everything and interrupting everyone.

Politicians are a privileged class. They never use public transport and buy their grocery themselves. They have paraphernalia to solve their all problems in police or any office. Their retaliation to judiciary is uncalled for. At a number of places they badly failed to improved public administration by amending law, rules and regulations to the extent these are required and let the suffrage of common man to continue. They gave more time to their own growth than to the well being of the nation. So much so, they failed to make a law and get a FIR registered by a sufferer. And in serious case, when the court passed orders to get it registered, they term it as interfering executive. They revolt against courts painting such a noble effort as 'Judicial Activism'.

Politicians of all the parties are very unfair to the plight of common citizens. Knowing it well that there is rampant corruption in all executive forces in the country, they are consistently evading framing rules for numerous situations. In last 60 years no work has been done to explore grey areas in different departments where no rules exist there is utter chaos at the level of public dealing and taking decisions on sensitive public issues and framing rules to that effect. Respecting law and honoring rules and regulations to strictly follow them in working has never been categorically made essential by virtue of law. Over looking existing law, has never been taken as a serious crime that generated corruption in the country. If the Parliament passes a law, it has to be universal as per definition of law. But these and made flexible and there is no punishment for deliberately making law laxative, then what is the need to frame rules, regulations and laws? Let the work be done with all laxity and flexibility. And this is what happening here since independence. In such a case when the existing law is not followed or things took place illogically, if the court asks competitive authorities to frame effective law/rules; they name as "Activism".

Every one rushes to think of framing laws (rules/regulations, codes, etc.) only after a calamity or criminal advance. Out of four boasting care takers (Legislation, police, bureaucrats and media) no one ever thought to study laws on similar countries in developed nations beforehand. And in want of any law, in many situations, none of the above-mentioned care takers had ever bothered to propose a classified framework of law/rules or legislation in advance. What has ever been done by judiciary in such a situation is no less than action as the true guardian of people to direct the effective agency to take up things seriously in the interest of citizens and make rules. But none of the four agencies did any thing. Courts raised pen to give security to citizens starting from now to report to the police, safety to the complainant in the police station by displaying identity of police officer because the court felt that to do it in the interest of common unprivileged citizens. Passing any orders that acts as a law is a feature of Constitution under Article-141 which cannot nullify with passing a Bill in the Parliament.

Courts are decorated with highest qualified intelligentsia of the country. They know the law and their limitations. They are supposed to pass orders within their jurisdiction and are the first custodians what the Parliament creates for them to preserve. If any thing that seemed to be anew to the critics of judiciary, it must be in consonance of some existing Law within the jurisdiction of Constitution.

It is only the judiciary which can look into whether the police are following the lawful course of action for detaining, investigating and treating an accused within the framework of law. It is the business of judiciary to see where the prescribed rules have been followed by the executive or not; it is the jurisdiction of judiciary to see whether action of the officer is arbitrary or not and it is the work of judiciary to look into a particular election under challenge, has taken place as per law or not. It is work of the judiciary and none else even not of legislation that creates law.

More hue a cry erupts from the legislation to the fore, only when the judiciary wants to 'define' jurisdiction of MP/MLA and does not allow any influential politicians to go beyond the law. The Parliamentarians have to scrap CPC allowing judges to take decisions *suo motto* in the interest of justice and this right is being used very sparingly and rarely by the courts. 'The member of Parliament should have been more conscious to their own conduct. The politicians must see things from their own angle also. The existing judiciary in working under heavy pressure of workload. The staff in Supreme Court works so exhaustively that looks to be horrible and pitiable for the staff especially in the defect section. But the apathy of the government is so absurd that it is not giving proper staff. It is not a fair dealing, especially in the apex court. So, if the critics of judiciary take things in positivity, they must come forward to give judges more peace and space to work in more intelligent manner and for that they should have this issue of judicial activism to gain unnecessary importance but to:

1. Appoint a Commission who should invite suggestions from the citizens and the employees working in different government departments of the short comings where there is a need for framing rules/law.
2. To pass a Bill to appoint 40,000 judicial officers and bring positive changing in over-loaded judiciary so that voters can get justice during their life time.
3. To constitute 'Judicial Commission' to make judiciary a fair part of the system of governance.

If no one comes to help the poor citizens from high handedness of media, politicians, bureaucrats and of course the police, it is the judiciary only which stands in their way like a big rock to save them for their life and property and respect. Judiciary is virtually protecting people from all four pseudo-guardians in the country. Judiciary is supreme in its position and authority and no one should try to diminish it.

The incidence of 1985 is quotable here. For the first time Article-32 was invoked by our PIL before then Mr. Chief Justice Rangnath Mishra, who is honoured as the architect of PILs in this nation, the noted counsel handling this PIL, was not very sure whether it would be getting through a hearing or not? But it was the conviction of Justice Mishra who opened the door for more PILs to come for others. Will you call it activism if the court initiates any thing good within the preview of Constitution? If yes, then we need such activism. In the same manner the entire performance of Justice J.S. Verma was remarkable when he removed the interference of higher ups to hush up the facts and used its suo motto powers to amend appointment of Director of CBI and initiated various police reforms. It was not Activism. And it could be done by judiciary only which found the higher ups in politics and bureaucracy influencing the provisions of Criminal Procedure Code. Could any thing was possible in this direction by all four care takers. Certainly not! It was the power of Judiciary who could manage it otherwise; especially politicians are always happy what is going on in the country.

In Visakha case it was only judiciary where Justice Verma simply elaborated the provisions in IPC in the form of a list of rules to be followed by the employer to ensure women workers immunity from sexual harassment in the work place. If it curtailed the liberty of the doers, the Judiciary shall always be welcomed for such moves. Justice A.S. Anand's contribution to save detainees from police manipulation was a landmark decision in the direction of police reforms. For instance if we go into the details of various decisions of the apex court which provoke the affected section of society, we shall find that whatever has been taken up by the apex court was within the preview of prescribed law and nothing falls in the category of Activism of adventurism or over-reach as has been coined differently by the politicians.

Certain Section of Press has suggested to take a middle path, is not much convincing. Law is always taken as universal entity and in the way of implementing law there can be no midway. We cannot negotiate law to our terms of suitability. It is only a political game where compromises and middle ways work. There cannot be any midway between demolition and illegal grabbing of public land in the court of law. Rather such grabbing and illegal capturing of public land falls under more than one provisions of IPC. So the court has to see the situation from law view-point and not giving a mid way. No court can have a middle path. There are clear cut rules of MCD and DDA about encroachment and land use. It was done by connivance of civic authorities under political support. The court can see the matter whether law has been flouted or not. If there is a scope of passing orders against illegal activity in the society, the court has to take action within its jurisdiction. Is it activism?

Rather, already the list of illegal colonies and illegal constructions and grabbing of public property is under the perview of the court and illegal will have to go even if you amend the law and slap the decision of erstwhile parliamentarians in their face that passed Master Plan 2001. Now, the politicians intend to pass immorally and illegally two illegal actions, if they pass a new plan to protect against sealing and demolition of illegal property by their vote bank. One, they will derogate the dignity of previous parliament that passed Master Plan 2001 and secondly, they will encourage a jungle Raj over rule of law. And it should not be allowed by the courts if the courts have to function against any such threat to their existence.

Let us have consensus on few issues at the time of general election and let the people know ulterior motive behind this anti-judiciary propaganda painting it as judicial Activism. Let the judiciary not be passive. We want active judiciary. We need a clean, quick, uni-directional, transparent, just, confident, citizen's rights and Constitutional savvy judiciary for our support.

If the politicians really want to do a good job for the suffering country men, women and children, they must equip courts with sufficient staff and required means by passing a Bill to constitute the 'Judicial Commission' as early as possible.

There has been a fierce debate on judicial activism in the country recently and a situation of confrontation between politicians and the judiciary came to the fore. The Speaker of Lok Sabha (Parliament) also warned the judiciary recently, to confine to its folds, when the Chief Justice pleaded for constitutional immunity against the question of accountability of judicial wrong and doing the work of legislation in certain recent cases. The Chief justice also refuted the charges of corruption in judiciary by the Prime Minister few days back. Like many such sporadic previous events this war of words will go on until a 'code of conduct' as well as a 'Judicial Commission' does not come in existence.

No one can have objection to positive judicial activism. There will be a hue and cry over the question of unquestionable unlimited authority of judiciary on common cause affairs of imparting justice as their constitutional rights which the courts are consistently evading for their very personal reasons and it can put lots of question marks in their minds. The question of negative judicial activism is parallelly potential when judges try to frame laws and do the work of legislation of executive. They have no right to do than under any provision of constitution even under Article-142 that empowers the apex court to enlarge powers. Enlarging powers doe not mean encroaching upon others powers being attached to finality. No one can be final over Parliamentary arena. Judiciary comes under Constitution and it cannot show itself to be the supreme over People's right to frame laws through legislative process. Explaining, elaborating, defining and enlarging law is the work of judiciary and there is no question of over reaching the other fields out side judicial jurisdiction in any law. We need judiciary to be only just and do their work more carefully preserving the rule of law in the society by imposing punishment on guilty and not damaging the sufferers as being done these days by delaying justice in a bureaucratic manner or over reaching others territories.

Doing anything coming out of ones arena is over-reach. Judiciary can do a lot even within its boundaries and there is no need and expectation of it that it will ever cross dead lines. So there is no bar on positive activism and the nation shall be thankful if the judicial officer take up there work with a feeling that millions of people are waiting for justice which being delayed for amendable reasons within control of judiciary.

In a country where sufficient law is not framed and framed law is not honoured, if no one does it, they should do it. So, we certainly need active judiciary, you can name it Judicial Activism. Listing the sequence of events from the origin of an offence to the prosecution, courts have ultimate role to play, as they come in the last. If a person becomes the victim of an atrocity by a habitual offender, he bears it to his nerve, reports that to the concerned department, where bureaucratic meddling wastes his time for a long. He then approaches the police with a dream to get a hearing and quick redressal of his problem. But he simply falls prey to the bigger jaws of police. Finding no rescue, he ultimately comes under the shelter of judiciary. So the responsibility of judiciary is the ultimate and highest because they are the final in imparting legal justice to the suffering citizens of these unfortunate Third World nations.

To have a respectable and just judiciary is bliss for a fortunate nation.

Alternative Democracy syn. PEOPLISM: *It is a new proposed programme of governance which is aimed at training the masses of third world and underdeveloped countries to understand the social and national responsibilities before adopting the best system of governance, i.e. the Democracy.*

Appendix

A. THOUGHT PROVOKING SLOGANS SHOULD BLOW THE MIND

- **Courts deserve to be the highest place in society because they preserve Rule of Law.**
- Any government becomes first offender, if it fails to give its innocent suffering citizens 'Justice in Time' and push them to misery.
- **Courts have no right to be personal.**
- **Courts exist because we approach them.**
- Innocent suffering citizens are the cause of survival of judiciary.
- **Judiciary and Police cannot be the masters of citizen's lives.**
- Try judges in case of violation of Judicial Code of Conduct.
- No Society can survive and progress in peace without Rule of Law.
- Courts need to make themselves deserving to respect and honor by their conduct.
- Courts are the guardians of us all.
- Judges deserve quorum and dignity as directed by the God who created a situation for them to occupy the highest place in society.
- **Judge is a human with blood and bones who can never do a mistake.**
- Slug-judiciary is like a monster.
- Judiciary is the custodian of Constitution.

- Keeping the case pending is a tactics to help offence to continue.
- If morality is a bygone story today, there is no bar for a judge to go corrupt.
- Peoplism consists of Judicial Commission to try corrupt judges for his/her misconduct.
- No country can survive without Rule of Law.
- **Courts are custodians of Rule of Law.**
- Courts cannot work without people's faith in them.
- If the courts have to exist, it cannot without showing respect to them.
- **Indian judiciary is in pitiable condition now.**
- Judges will have independence from multiplicity of work and titles.
- Judges in Peoplism shall be accountable to people as far as merits of an order is concerned if decision is not reasoned within itself.
- **Indian judiciary cannot be deceptive to people's faith in it.**
- **There is no other alternative to seek justice than courts or bloodshed.**
- Courts have to be careful to defend themselves while deciding a contempt application.
- **Single Bench judges have more responsibility of the full Bench.**
- Finality does not elaborate to unchallenged misconduct.
- Lest people should come on roads to seek justice in courts.
- Desperate, defeated sufferers proceed to search for his own blood or the blood of unconcerned victims in a fit of frustration.
- **Courts design society.**
- Court using antithesis in their decisions is the brothers of criminals.

- It will be the most unfortunate day for any society, when people shall prefer not to approach courts for the settling of their disputes.
- There in no need to cite many examples to establish everything given in this document. Our everyday observations are the mirror to truth of our experience with police and the Judiciary.
- **Right to justice is for citizens and not of judges.**
- Judiciary cannot be allowed to encroach on citizen's right to justice the name of procedures.
- **Lords have left India in 1947.**
- Almighty Lord is only one.
- Policeman has not been given a gun and a rod to scares innocents.
- **If a code of conduct is working for teachers, why can't it be brought in existence for police, lawyers and the judges in a free democracy?**
- Indian democracy is not widely and uniformly achieved by all.
- Liberty achieved through democracy in our country, does not include powerful police, bureaucrats, politicians and judges only.

B. REFERENCES

(I) Constitution of India
(II) Indian Penal Code
(III) Criminal Procedure Code
(IV) Civil Procedure Code
(V) Constitution of Peoplism
(VI) PIL dismissed by the apex court on 5/4/2005
(VII) Newspaper cuttings from Hindustan Times, Times of India, Indian Express, and Poineer
(VIII) Seminar reports from 'International Society for Human Resources'
(IX) Constitutions of nine countries
(X) National Reporter System (Canada) From website.

Professional Conduct for Judges and Lawyers

1. See, e.g., Black's Law Dictionary (6th Ed.); Webster's Encyclopedic Dictionary Of The English Language (Canadian Edition) p. 5; W.R. Prest, The Rise of the Barristers—A Social History of the English Bar 1590-1640 (Oxford: Clarendon Press, 1986).
2. The English and Colonial Bars in the Nineteenth Century (Beckenham, Kent: Croom Helm Ltd., 1983), Introduction.
3. The Lawyers Weekly, April 20, 1990.
4. The Lawyers Weekly, April 9, 1993.
5. All Canadian codes of professional/legal conduct and supportive legislation. See this chapter, fn. 35, infra.
6. Great Treasury of Western Thought, eds. Adler and Van Doren (New York and London: R.R. Bowker Co., 1977), p. 553.
7. Paul Brand, The Origins Of The English Legal Profession (Oxford: Blackwell Publishers, 1992), p. 122.
8. David Lemmings, Gentlemen and Barristers, subtitled The Inns of Court and the English Bar 1680-1730 (Oxford: Clarendon Press, 1990), Introduction, The

Order Of Serjeants At Law (London: Seldon Society Supplementary Series, 1984), p. 15.

9. Richard L. Abel, The Legal Profession in England and Wales (Oxford: Basil Blackwell Ltd., 1988), p. 139. Brand, p. 158.
10. Lemmings, op. cit., pp. 145, 150.
11. See this text Chapter 2, "The Lawyer-Client Relationship", paras. [12] and [13], infra.
12. See this chapter, fns. 1 and 2, supra.
13. In Professional Ethics (London: Charles Knight & Co. Ltd., 1969), pp. 15-16.
14. In Gentlemen of the Law (London: Stevens and Sons Limited, 1960), p. 258.
15. Ibid.
16. Op. cit. and especially Chapter 12 thereof.
17. See W. Wesley Pue, Becoming "Ethical"; Lawyers' Professional Ethics in Early Twentieth Century Canada (1991), 20 Manitoba Law Journal 227, at p. 236.
18. Justice E.N. Hughes of the Saskatchewan Court of Queen's Bench, Seminar on Legal Ethics (Saskatchewan: Second Annual Practitioners Seminar on Criminal Law, 1976).
19. In his work, Professional Ethics (London: Charles Knight & Co. Ltd., 1969), at p. 58, F.A.R. Bennion.
20. The Canadian Bar Association, Code of Professional Conduct, August, 1987, Preface, p. vii, hereinafter referred to as the C.B.A. Code.
21. Michael Birks, Gentlemen of the Law (London: Stevens & Sons Limited, 1960), p. 145.
22. F.A.R. Bennion, Professional Ethics (London: Charles Knight & Co. Ltd., 1969), p. 108.
23. Op. cit., p. 111 et seq.
24. 2 Geo. 2, c. 23.
25. Birks, op. cit., p. 140.

26. Bennion, op. cit., p. 36 et seq.
27. See especially Chapter 2, para. [15] et seq., infra.
28. Reported by F.A.R. Bennion, op. cit., at p. 61.
29. Op. cit., p. 63.
30. Daniel Duman, The Judicial Bench In England 1727-1875 (London: Royal Historical Society, 1982), p. 5.
31. (London: Seldon Society Supplementary Series, 1984), especially at p. 25 et seq., 88.
32. See Baker, op. cit., p. 42.
33. See this chapter, para. [12] supra. A "Role Statement", adopted by Convocation of The Law Society of Upper Canada on October 27, 1994 is instructive in this connection.
34. The Canadian Bar Association, Fifth Annual Meeting, Ottawa, September 2, 1920.
35. C.B.A. Code, adopted by the Council of the Canadian Bar Association on August 25, 1974.

    This Code has now been superseded by a revised Code adopted in August, 1987 ("C.B.A. Code"). Law Society Act, R.S.N. 1990, c. L-9. Prince Edward Island: 1987 C.B.A. Code now in effect, with additions. Major legislation: Legal Profession Act, S.P.E.I. 1992, c.
36. Professional Ethics (5th Ed.) (Philadelphia, 1970), as reprinted in part in N.B.P.C.H., Introduction, p. 4.
37. See, e.g., Ont. P.C.H., Rule 13, Commentary 7, which states in part: s. 34 of Ontario's Law Society Act, R.S.O. 1990, c. L-8, a finding; The law society (in Ontario, Convocation).
38. In Enns v. Panju et al., [1978] 5 W.W.R. 244, the British Columbia Supreme Court. Enerchem Shipmanagement Inc. v. Ship Coastal Canada and Greater Sarnia Investment Corp. et al. (1988), 83 N.R. 256 (F.C.A.), Law Society of Manitoba v. Savino (1983), 23 Man.R.(2d) 293 (C.A.), discussed in Chapter 4, paras. [4] and [19], infra, and especially the remarks of Monnin, C.J.M., at p. 300;

Molson Companies Ltd. et al. v. Amstel Brewery Canada Ltd. (1988), 21 F.T.R. 96 (T.D.).

39. C.B.A. Code, c. I, Rule and Commentary 3. See also N.B.P.C.H., Part A; Professional Code, R.S.Q. 1977, c. C-26; B.C.P.C.H., c. 1, Canon 1.
40. C.B.A. Code, Preface, pp. vii-viii.
41. B.C.P.C.H., c. 1, Canon 1(1).
42. The Roscoe Pound-American Trial Lawyers (Introduction, p. iii).
43. See, e.g., p. viii of the Preface to the C.B.A. Code which states in part: Qué. C.e.a., Division II, "General Duties And Responsibility To The Public".
44. C.B.A. Code, c. XIII, Rule and Commentaries. Ont. P.C.H., Foreword; Yuk. C.P.C., Preamble. Mark M. Orkin, Q.C. (Toronto: Cartwright & Sons Ltd., 1957) at p. 50.
45. C.B.A. Code, c. XIV, Rule (and Commentary 6). See also Ont. P.C.H., Rule 12; Commentary 5.
46. C.B.A. Code, c. XIX, Commentary 8. See also N.B.P.C.H., Part C, Rule 8; Ont. P.C.H., Rule 5, Commentary 14; B.C.P.C.H., Appendix 3, s. 8.
47. See, e.g., Abel-Smith and Stevens, Lawyers And The Courts (London: Heinemann Educational Books Ltd., 1967), p. 19.
48. See Michael Birks, Gentlemen of the Law (London: Stevens and Sons Limited, 1960), pp. 6-7; 106 et seq.
49. See, e.g., N.B.P.C.H., Introduction, which also describes the lawyer as a minister of justice; Sask. C.P.C., Preface, p. v.
50. C.B.A. Code, c. IX, Commentary 1. See also N.S.L.E.P.C.H., c. 14; N.B.P.C.H., Part B; Qué. C.e.a., s. 2.06; Ont. P.C.H., Rule 10; Man. C.P.C., c. 9; Sask. C.P.C., c. IX; Alta. C.P.C., c. 10; B.C.P.C.H., c. 1, Canon 2(1); c. 8; Yuk. C.P.C., Part Three.
51. C.B.A. Code, c. IX, Commentary 2.

52. B.C.P.C.H., c. 1, Canon 2(1).
53. N.B.P.C.H., Part B, Rule 3. Other Canadian legal conduct codes similarly provide: see, e.g., C.B.A. Code, c. XIII, Commentaries 1 and 3; Ont. P.C.H., Rule 11, Commentaries 1 and 2.
54. Indeed, the 1974 or the 1987 C.B.A. Code has been adopted or used as a model for the codes in a number of provinces and territories. See this chapter, fn. 35, supra, for the present usage of the two versions.
55. N.B.P.C.H., Part C, Rule 1. to the state expressed in this code in Part A, Rule 1.
56. See N.S.L.E.P.C.H., c. 7, Rules (e), (f); N.B.P.C.H., Part C, Rule 10; Ont. P.C.H., Rule 16, Commentary 2(c); Man. C.P.C., c. 6, Rule (d); c. 19, Commentary 6; Sask. C.P.C., c. VI, Rule (c); c. XIX, Commentary 6; Alta. C.P.C., c. 1, Rule 6; Commentary 6; c. 9, Rule 9; Commentary 9.1; B.C.P.C.H., c. 7, generally; c. 12, Rule 8(c).
57. See, e.g., Ont. P.C.H., Rule 4, Commentary 1, Qué. C.e.a., s. 3.01.03 speaks to the establishment of "mutual trust".
58. See, e.g., Yuk. C.P.C., Part One, Rule 1.
59. C.B.A. Code, c. XV, Rule. See also, e.g., N.S.L.E.P.C.H., c. 18; Qué. C.e.a., Division IV; Ont. P.C.H., Rule 13.
60. C.B.A. Code, c. XVII, Rule. See also, e.g., N.S.L.E.P.C.H., c. 19; Ont. P.C.H., Rule 19.
61. See, e.g., C.B.A. Code, c. VII, Rule; Commentary 6; c. XIX, Commentary 1; N.B.P.C.H., Part F, Rule 12; Ont. P.C.H., Rule 17; Commentary 3.
62. See especially this text, Chapter 12, "The Lawyer And The Law Society".
63. C.B.A. Code, c. XVI, Rule and Commentary 1. See also N.S.L.E.P.C.H., c. 13; N.B.P.C.H., Part D, Rule 4; Qué. C.e.a., s. 4.03.03; Ont. P.C.H., Rule 14; Commentary 1; Man. C.P.C., c. 16; Sask. C.P.C., c. XVI; Alta. C.P.C., c.

4; B.C.P.C.H., c. 1, Canon 4; c. 11; Yuk. C.P.C., Part Two.

64. C.B.A. Code, c. XVI, Commentary 4. See also Ont. P.C.H., Rule 14, Commentary 4; Man. C.P.C., c. 16, Commentary 4; Sask. C.P.C., c. XVI, Commentary 4; Alta. C.P.C., c. 4, Rule 3; Commentary 3; B.C.P.C.H., c. 1, Canon 4(3); Yuk. C.P.C., Part Two, Rule 5.

65. See, e.g., B.C.P.C.H., c. 11, Rule 7 ; N.S.L.E.P.C.H., c. 13, Commentaries 13.6-13.9; N.B.P.C.H., Part D, Rule 5; Ont. P.C.H., Rule 14, Commentary 6; Man. C.P.C., c. 16, Commentary 7; Sask. C.P.C., c. XVI, Commentary 10; Alta. C.P.C., c. 4, Rule 10; Commentary 10; Yuk. C.P.C., Part Two, Rule 3. See also this text, Chapter 9, "The Lawyer And Colleagues", para. [37] et seq., infra.

66. N.B.P.C.H., Part D, Rule 5.

67. See, e.g., Yuk. C.P.C., Part Two, Rule 7: C.B.A. Code, c. XVI, Commentary 11.

68. See, e.g., David Lemmings, Gentlemen and Barristers, subtitled The Inns of Court and the English Bar 1680-1730 (Oxford: Clarendon Press, 1990).

69. See B.C.P.C.H., c. 1, Canon 5, which has a particularly instructive approach in this matter. It reads in part.

70. Raymond A. Belliotti, Values in the Courtroom: Two Kinds of Judicial Systems, in Westminster Institute Rev., Vol. 1, No. 3 (London, Ontario: October, 1981), p. 4.

71. The Works of Aristotle (Oxford University Press), Vol. IX, section 1104, line 2.

72. At para. [27], pra.

C. BASICS OF JUDICIAL SYSTEM IN ANCIENT LITERATURE

1. प्रकितिकोपाहः सरवाकोपेम्यो गरियानः।

Prakritikopah sarvakopemyo gariyanh.

The greatest annoyance of all natural calamities is the mass frustration and people's resentment. (*Chanakyasootram*)

2. दन्डनितिमधितिअठन प्रजा सः रक्षित।

Dandnitimdhitiathan praja sah rakshit.

Judicious penalization of offenders protects the kingdom. (*Chanakyasootram*)

3. दन्डो हि विज्ञाने प्रानियते।

Dando hi vigyane praniyate.

Punishment must be imposed with great care. (*Chanakyasootram*)

4. नास्तयाग्ने दौर्म्बल्यम।

Nastyagne daumbarlayam.

Never underestimate any one. A tiny flame burns the entire forest. Helpless people can also take revenge. (*Chanakyasootram*)

5. दन्डे प्रतीयते वृतिः।

Dande pratiayate vritih.

In absence of proper punishment to the guilty, common people face crisis of survival, that results into revolt against the rule. (*Chanakyasootram*)

6. नार्थिश्ववज्ञा कार्याः।

Naarthishwavagyaa karyaah.

Never humiliate a person who is praying for justice. (*Chanakyasootram*)

7. अविनितस्वमिभादस्वामिलाभः श्रेयान।

Avinitaswamibhadswamilabh shreyaan.

It is better not to appoint any person than to choose an undeserving candidate in the interest of a nation. It is rather better to form a board deserving people to make decisions. (*Chanakyasootram*)

8. दन्डपारुष्यात सर्वजनद्धेष्यो भावति।

Dandparushyaat sarvajandweshyo Bhawati.

If the judge is personally biased and he delivers justice with a biased mind, he falls from his esteemed position and ultimately faces wrath of people at last. (*Chanakyasootram*)

9. अमित्रो दन्डनित्यामायत्तः।

Amitro dandnityamaayatah.

The gravity of retaliation of your dependents depends on your harshness or leniency. So keep your judicial system right. (*Chanakyasootram*)

10. दन्डाभावे मंत्रीवर्गाभावः।

Dandabhave mantrivargabhawh.

The courts (king) face neglect of his subordinates if it fails to maintain decorum and respect to litigants. (*Chanakyasootram*)

11. दन्डः सम्पदा योजयति।

Dandhah sampada yojayati.

It is only justice to people that makes a nation powerful. If 'right to justice' is captured by few, the state will collapse. (*Chanakyasootram*)

12. दन्डनीतिभधितिष्ठन प्रजाः।

Dandneetibhadhitishthan prajah.

Holding justice supreme by the judges make them supreme than ensure people security and their faith in judiciary. (*Chanakyasootram*)

13. दन्डनित्यामयतमात्मतरक्षणाम ।

Dandhnityamayatmaatmatrakshanaam.

We can defend ourselves only by keeping our judicial system intact. (*Chanakyasootram*)

14. नास्ति भिरोकार्यचिन्ता ।

Naasti bhirokaryachintaa.

Flatterers and duty less people do not mind to ignore their duty to the society and they somehow find out many ways to escape. (*Chanakyasootram*)

15. नियोगार्थग्राहोपायो राग्यम नित्त्यापरिक्षणं ।

Niyogaarthgrahopayo ragyam nityaaparikshanam.

प्रतिपत्रीप्रदान च तथाः कर्मविप्रायायः । ।

Pratipatripradaan ch tathah karmviprayayah.

It is the duty of the king to keep in touch with all his subordinates and dependents and keep them changing their places. He should not allow any person to a stay at a place for long time. (*Chanakyasootram*)

16. मुर्हियागिनो बध्या वासुध्या महिपते ।

Muhiryagino badhyaa vasudhaya mahipate.

सकृतकिमपिदिताम स्नाणवस्त्ररम मन्चेदुतपायः । ।

Sakritkimpiditam snannvastram munchedutpaya.

The ruler should remain in consistent touch with his subordinates and cross examine their work. He should believe that the whole water does not be squeezed in one go. (*Chanakyasootram*)

17. योयेनप्रतिबद्धः स्यात्सः तिनेदाईव्याई ।

Yoyenpratibaddhh syatsaha tinedaayeevyaayee.

सविश्वात्सो नियोक्तावायः प्रणेषु च धनेषु च ।।

Savishwaatso niyoktavaayah praneshu ch dhaneshu ch.

Only allied entities must be allowed to be together. Those understand this rule of nature can protect and rear their dependents. (*Chanakyasootram*)

18. प्राकृतिः स्वामिनामत्यक्ता समृद्धियापि न जिवाति ।

Prakritih swaminaamtyaktaa samriddhiapi na jeivaati.

अपिधन्वन्तरिवैधः किम कारोति गतौसि ।।

Apidhanvantarivaidha kim karoti gataushi.

A king without its subjects cannot live long. No one can cure a dead. (*Chanakyasootram*)

19. महात्मास्पदेनीचाः कादापि न कर्तव्यः ।

Mahaatamaaspadeneechah kadaapi na kartavyah.

No abject undeserving person be appointed at the place of responsibility. (*Chanakyasootram*)

20. प्रेहि प्रेहि पथिमिः पुर्व्येमृयात्ता न पूर्वेपितृपर्योयूः ।

Prehi prehi pathimih puvyermriyaatta na purvepitripareyooh.

O man! Go, go and go on traditional tried pathways followed by our predecessors. (*Rigveda-10/14/07*)

21. अस्सानागौहामनन्नगोहामलिंगौहमाभंगार ।

Assaanagauhaamanangauhmalin-gauhmabhangar. (Rigveda-12/14/07)

प्राशान्तोहामन्तोहमतान्तोंह चिरान्तानां ।।

Prashaantoahamanatoahmatantoaham chirantanam.

One must always keep thinking that I am alone, without a body, sexless, versatile and mostly calm, unlimited, bearing and continuous. (*Rigveda-11/14/07*)

22. अधिकारे यादन्रितग यच्छ राजसु पैशुनं ।

Adhikare yadnritam yachchh rajasu paishunam.

गुरूश्चैलीक करानामतुल्यतद बाह्मणहत्या या । ।

Gurushchaileek karaanaamtulyatad brihmanhtyaa ya.

Giving wrong decision after getting empowered to give justice; speaking a lie in the court and deceiving the teachers are these three greatest sins like killing the God. (*Anushashanparva-22/29*)

23. न च शत्रु खगेयो दरबालोअपिबलियासा ।

Na ch shatru khageyo darbaaloapi-baliyaasaa.

अल्पोअपि हि दहात्यागनिर्विशाम्ल्पहिनास्तिचा । ।

Alpoapi hi dahaatyagnivirshaamlp-hinaastichaa.

Powerful enemy should never ignore a weak enemy means taking him small because a tiny spark can burn the entire jungle. For example traces of poison can kill. (*Shantiparva-58/17*)

24. कालातिकिन्नमादेते भक्तावितान्योभारतः ।

Kaalaatikinnamadete bhaktavitanyobhartah.

भटुकुष्यन्ति याद भृत्याः स्सौरनाथसुमाहन स्मृताः ।।

Bhatukushyanti yad bhrityah ssauranath-sumahan smritah.

Extreme delay in meals and salary dependants get frustrated that joint resentment can bring different types of disasters.

25. नपारिक्ष्यामहिपाल सचिवं कुर्तुर्मदित ।

Napariksbyamahipal sachivam kurtumardit.

अकुलीना नरार्कीनो न राजा सुखमेदयाते ।।

Akuleenaa narakirno na rajaa sukhmedyate.

Arranging the means for livelihood for poor, orphaned, very old and widows their blessings and good wishes are showered by them everyday. (*Shantiparva-118/14*)

26. असतपापिष्टसचिवो वध्योलिकास्यर्धमः ।

Asatpaapishthsachivo vadhyolikasyadharmah.

सदैव परिव्यस्न क्षिपामेव अवसिद्धति ।।

Sadaiv parivayasn kshipamev avasiddhati.

Those torture innocents and human rights, his/her own country with the help of callous associates becomes the target of all sufferers and vanish son with all of them from the scene. (*Shantiparva-112/4*)

27. विभाज्यदन्डः कर्तव्यो धर्मेन्न न यादिृछाया।

Vibhajyadandah kartavyo dharmenn na yadrichhaya.

दुष्टनाम निगृहो दन्डो हिरण्यम् बाध्यताः किया।।

Dushtnam nigriho dando hiranyam badhyatah kiya.

Punishment should be inflicted after careful consideration only. No autocracy be used in doing so. To crub crime is the main theme of punishment. (*Shantiparva-122/40*)

28. नदान्दक्षत्रियोभाति नदान्दो भुमिमश्चनुते।

Nadandkshatriyobhati nadando bhumimshchnute.

नदान्दस्यप्रजा राज्ञसुखम विन्दान्ति भारत।।

Nadandasyapraja ragyasukham vindanti bharat.

The king, who does not use its powers to make justice/decide punishment to the guilty such kings (Judges), will fail to sustain for a long in India. (*Shantiparva-14/14*)

29. दान्देनापिनतशत्रुमे यो राजा न नियाच्छति।

Dandenapinatshatrume yo raja na niyachchhati.

स मृत्युमुप गृहति गर्भामिश्वत्री यथा।।

Sa mritayumup grihati garbhamshwatari yatha.

The king (ruler) who does not kill (punish) a caught hold enemy (offender) he behaves in a self-destructive manner, in the same way as a mule gets pregnant to die untimely death. (*Shantiparva-140/30*)

30. न राज्यं प्राप्तिमित्येव वर्तितव्यम सम्पतम।

Na rajyam praptimityev vartitvyam sampatam.

श्रीयंहि विनयो हन्तिजरा रूपमिवोक्तामम।।

Shriyamhi vinayo hantijara rupamivoktamm.

'Now I have got power and can do any thing', philosophy destroys a peson in the same manner as age destroys youth. (*Shantiparva-140/30 Mahabharatm*)

31. नगरे प्रतिरुद्ध सन्वहिरद्धारे बुमुक्षितः।

Nagare pratirudhad sanvahirdhware bumukshitah.

अभित्राणभुयसः पश्येद यः साक्ष्यामंनृत वदेत।।

Abhitranbhuyasah pashyed yeh sakshyamanrit vadet.

He, who gives false and unjust decision, he always remains a surrounded by his own fear and hatred every time. (*Mahabharatm*)

32. अविद्यः पुरूष शौच्याः शौचियं मैथुनमप्रजं।

Avidyah purush shauchyah shauchiyam maithunamprajam.

निराहारा प्रजाः शौच्याः शौच्यं राष्ट्रम राजकम।।

Nirahara prajah shauchyah shauchyam rashtram rajkam.

For an Illiterate, incompetent, sex indulged, starving and anarchic (without a law or a ruler) country, one must feel sorry. (*Mahabharatm*)

33. स राजा पुरषो दन्ड सनेवा शसिता च सः।

Sa raja pursho dand saneva shasita ch sah.

चर्तुणमिश्रमासम च धर्मस्य प्रतिभू स्मृतः।।

Chaturannmishramasam ch dharmasya pratibhoo smritah.

The King (Government) is known by the quality of justice that speaks by itself. The rule of law is workable in all places and in all circumstances. (*Manusmiriti through Satyarth Prakash*)

34. सोआसहायेन मूढेन लाब्धेनाकृतबुद्धिना।

Soashayen moodhena labdhenakritbuddhina.

न शक्यो न्यायेतो नेतुम सक्तेन विषयेसु च।।

Na shakyo nyayeto netum sakten vishayesu ch.

He, who is not indulged in self-realisation, not well read, ill educated, helping offenders by his ways cannot be fit to be a judge. (*Manusmiriti through Satyarth Prakash*)

35. अध्यक्षानन्विविधानकुर्यात तत्र तत्र विपश्चितः।

Adhyakshanvinvidhankuryat tatra tatra vipshichatah.

तेअस्य सर्वाण्येवेक्षरन्नृणाम कार्याणि कुर्वताम।।

Teasaya sarvannyeveksharan-nrinnaam karyani kurvatam.

Highly qualified people may be appointed in judiciary and administration. Their duties and jurisdictions be defined and their accountability be open. They have to be respected for their performance and punished for lapses. (*Manusmiriti through Satyarth Prakash*)

36. शरिराकर्ष्णा क्षियंते राष्ट्रकृष्णात।

Sharirakashanaranna kshiyante rashtrakrishnat.

राष्ट्रास्य सन्ग्रहे नित्यम विधान्मिदभाचरेत।।

Rashtrasya sangrahe nityam vidhanmidbhaacharet.

As the soul also dies after the body dies in the same way as the kingdom also dies if its people are weakened by maltreated by the administration. (*Manusmiriti through Satyarth Prakash*)

37. बहुत्वं परिगृहणियत्साक्षीद्वेधे नराधिपः।

Bahutvam parigrihniyatsakshidwedhe naradhipah.

समेशु तु गुरनेत्तकृष्तान गुनिद्धधे द्विजोत्तमान।।

Sameshu tu gurnettkrishtan gunidhedhe dwijottaman.

Both side witnesses and evidences have to be examined with conviction and decided rules in presence of other citations from learned people in the past and then the justice must be delivered. (*Manusmiriti through Satyarth Prakash*)

38. समक्षदर्शनात्साक्ष्यं श्रावणाचैव सिद्ययसि।

Samakshdarshanatsakshayam shravanachaiv sidhyasi.

तत्र सत्यम ब्रवन्साक्षी धर्मार्थाम्याम न हियते।।

Tatra satyam bravansakshee dharmarthamayam na hiyate.

There must be at least two witnesses, one who are eye witnesses and another who have heard the utterance during a dispute.

A witness must speak to truth to avoid punishment by the court. (*King*)

39. ब्रह्मानास्य चातुःषष्टि पूर्णां वापि शातं भवेत।

Brahmanasya chatuhshti poornam vapi shatam bhavet.

द्विगुणा व चर्तुषष्टिस्तद्योष गुणविद्वि सः।।

Dwiguna va chaturshatistadyosha gunvidvi sah.

The knowledgeable person must be punished in multiple way because he did the offence knowingly. (*Chanakyasootram*)

40. तिक्षाणदण्डः सर्वेरूद्वनीयो भवति।

Tikshandandah sarverudweniyo bhawati.

Punishing severely for small mistake is bad in law and brings resentment in the citizens that can come out in the form of revolt. (*Chanakyasootram*)

41. अजयतंत्रायान्तम नितिशास्त्रम।

Ajaytantrayantam nitishastram.

A nation can remain an orderly nation till it is capable to defend its policies. (*Chanakyasootram*)

42. नास्त्यनन्तरायः कालविक्षेपे।

Nastyanantrayah kalvikshepe.

Pending justice and lapsing time proves ineffectiveness and meaninglessness of justice delivery system. (*Chanakyasootram*)

Other Books on System of Governance by the Author

1. *Alternative System to democracy: Peoplism* (In press)
2. *To be or Not to be, a Nice Cop*
3. *Beyond Criminal Procedure Code*
4. *Claws of flaws of Law*
5. *Code of Judicial Conduct in Peoplism*
6. *An Innocent Absconder*
7. *Beyond Survival*
8. *The Dream Nation*
9. *Wishing you! A nation*
10. *Significant Desires*
11. *The Missing Justice*
12. *Smelting Democracy*
13. *Collapse of a Giant*
14. *Flaws of CPC-CrPC-IPC*
15. *Wanting Law*
16. *On the Edge of 'White Terrorism'*
17. *An Unfortunate Trial of An Under-trial*
18. *What is Expected of NHRC?*
19. *Corrupts of Education and Religion*
20. *Varied Breaking Points of a Common Indian*
21. *Delayed-Justice is the Lost-Justice*
22. *My Country, a Land of Amenable Absurdities*
23. *Consequential Punishment*